Thinking about the Presidency

Thinking about the Presidency

The Primacy of Power

William G. Howell

With David Milton Brent
and with a new preface by the author

PRINCETON UNIVERSITY PRESS
PRINCETON AND OXFORD

Published by Princeton University Press, 41 William Street, Princeton, New Jersey 08540
In the United Kingdom: Princeton University Press, 6 Oxford Street, Woodstock,
Oxfordshire OX20 1TW

press.princeton.edu

Second printing, and first paperback printing, with a new preface by the author, 2015

Paperback ISBN 978-0-691-16568-4

The Library of Congress has cataloged the cloth edition of this book as follows

Howell, William G.
Thinking about the presidency : the primacy of power / William G. Howell
with David Milton Brent.
pages cm
Includes bibliographical references and index.
ISBN 978-0-691-15534-0 (hardcover : alk. paper) 1. Presidents—United States.
2. Executive power—United States. 3. United States—Politics and government.
I. Brent, David Milton. II. Title.
JK516.H675 2013
352.230973—dc23   2012042074

British Library Cataloging-in-Publication Data is available

This book has been composed in Palatino

Printed on acid-free paper. ∞

Printed in the United States of America

3 5 7 9 10 8 6 4 2

For Esther, my sister

Contents

Preface to the Paperback Edition

As they are with every presidential election, the stakes of 2016 are prodigious. The United States faces extraordinary challenges both at home and abroad, and the two major parties offer radically different plans for the nation's future. Where we wage war next, what tax rates we pay, whether we make any serious headway on the issue of climate change, and so much more besides, likely depends on whether we elect a Republican or Democrat to the White House.

In the next presidential election, however, one thing does not hang in the balance. Whomever assumes office in January 2017 will not disavow the extraordinary powers intermittently seized and nurtured by Obama in the last seven years—nor those by Bush before him, Clinton one step further removed, or any of the long string of power-seeking presidents who have occupied the White House during the modern era. Regardless of her—or perhaps his—affiliation, the next president will continue to pursue the expansion of presidential power. She (or he) will have no choice.

In the larger project of building presidential power, the dominant trends have been ones of consistency rather than disjuncture. All presidents, no matter their partisan differences, their personal backgrounds, their leadership styles, or their rhetorical flourishes, want all the power they can acquire. While members of Congress regularly relinquish their own powers, and while judges do their best to avoid purely political fights between the various branches of government, presidents stand apart in our politics by guarding all the power they have acquired thus far while canvassing the landscape for opportunities to seize still more.

Why do presidents behave this way? And why don't they heed those who would counsel self-restraint? This short book—a long essay, really—offers one explanation.

Presidents care so much about power not because of who they are, but because of where they sit. The reasons why presidents are so preoccupied with power are institutional rather than personal in nature. If we are to make sense of this relationship, then we must think institutionally about the American presidency. We must investigate the expectations to which they are held, the system of government in which they operate, the incentives that govern their actions, and the constraints that they invariably confront. The point here is decidedly not to advance any normative objective, an option about which I'll have more to say shortly. Rather, it is to get clear about how our presidents can be expected to behave, whether or not we like their method or aims.

Vested with so few enumerated powers within the Constitution but expected to deliver the nation from every conceivable threat, presidents are put in an impossible position. Their only hope—however tenuous—is to build their power; to read Article II powers in the most expansive way possible; to gladly invite every speck of authority that Congress willingly delegates, and then fight fiercely against any subsequent thought of retraction; and to strike out on their own, erecting new methods of writing and implementing public policy in ways that marginalize their political opponents.

Presidents care about power for the instrumental benefit it delivers rather than any intrinsic value it confers. For presidents, power has a purpose. In fact, it has multiple purposes. With power, presidents can take steps toward sating the public's appetite for leadership. With power, presidents can advance policies designed to address the trenchant social problems that Congress either ignores or trips over itself trying to solve. And ultimately, with power, presidents can build a legacy.

In the absence of power, presidents can expect all sorts of opprobrium from allies and opponents alike. Lacking power, presidents must watch with dismay as Congress lays waste to their policy agenda. And lacking power, presidents can be reasonably assured that history will forget them.

OBAMA'S CONTRIBUTIONS TO A MORE POWERFUL PRESIDENCY

Seeing one of their own assume the presidency in 2009, constitutional law scholars and liberal Whigs anticipated that Barak Obama would restore some semblance of balance to our national politics. And for some time, he gave them reason for optimism. His rhetoric, at least, was a good deal more inclusive than his predecessor's. Gone were the repeated invocations of the "unitary executive," so prominently displayed in the legal record of the Bush White House; as was the bluster and triumphalism that, for liberals at least, seemed to define Bush's public posture.

Obama also went out of his way, at least during the start of his time in office, to reach out to Republicans, to enlist their support, and to appear generally conciliatory. However scripted or insincere they may have been, his efforts to appeal to his putative opponents had been evident since his debut on the national stage, when he reminded the Democrats assembled for their 2004 national convention of their basic commonalities with Republicans. Four years later, upon accepting the party's nomination, he reemphasized the point. "Democrats, as well as Republicans, will need to cast off the worn out ideas of the past," he proclaimed.[1] Come his election, the rush to reconciliation persisted. With both parties recognizing the need for some kind of government intervention in the wake of the economic crash, the president told Republicans to expect a plan with copious tax cuts—their policy tool of choice. The final package, however, did not satisfy Republicans, and they voted unanimously against it.

And so a pattern developed, wherein overtures toward reconciliation, often initiated by the president, yielded nothing in return. The olive branches were gradually abandoned. "I'm an eternal optimist," the president told a reporter about his gestures toward the Republicans. "That doesn't mean I'm a sap."[2]

The fallout from the repeated inter-branch negotiations over the debt ceiling may have finally convinced Obama to renounce his conciliatory ways for something more hard-headed. At that point in the summer of 2011, when the nation nearly defaulted on its loans and saw its credit rating downgraded, Americans regarded the president as a reduced figure, left to shuffle in the shadows. That kind of perception could not be countenanced. In the aftermath of this near meltdown, Obama renounced his former ways and declared his intent to act when and where Congress would not. Rather than temper the use of presidential power, Obama would extend it. And rather than functioning as an afterthought, opportunities to act independently stood at the very center of the president's attention. He made no qualms about saying so publicly, as he put it, "I have a pen and I have a phone," and he had every intention of using them both. (The debt ceiling battles are discussed at length in chapter 6.)

Like Bush, Obama guarded executive privileges over vast stores of information. Indeed, Obama oversaw the development of the single most ambitious domestic surveillance efforts ever conducted, the details of which we are only beginning to learn. The revelations are numerous in scope and still forthcoming. Among the most notable is the PRISM program, through which the National Security Agency maintains a clandestine link into the internal operations of top American-based technology companies, such as Google and Microsoft. According to another program, Boundless Informant, over three billion pieces of intelligence were picked up on American citizens in one month alone. Yet another program, which operated until 2011, focused on "metadata" of Americans' Internet habits. This program did not focus on the content of messages, but captured in bulk information about the emails Americans were sending and receiving, and where exactly in the country they were using the Internet.[3]

On matters of national security, Obama has nearly always gone it alone. Almost exclusively through unilateral directives, Obama fought terror in Pakistan, combated Iranian efforts to acquire a nuclear weapon, and ordered the escalation—and then de-escalation—of wars in Iraq and Afghanistan. On the world stage, he was alone from the moment his presidency began—quite literally, as his predecessor had instructed that only President Obama be privy to the most classified information. Forget Congress; not even his top advisers were allowed in on the innermost secrets of America's national security strategy.[4] Shortly before assuming office, Obama met with President Bush, who encouraged him to continue two particular programs. The first was the attempt to derail Iran's bid for a nuclear weapon, and the second was reliance on drone attacks in Pakistan. On both fronts, Obama heeded his predecessor's advice, as he solicited minimal to no congressional input or involvement.[5]

In 2010, the number of attacks in Pakistan reached an all-time high.[6] That same year, it was revealed that Obama had continued Bush's "Stuxnet" program, a cyberweapon targeted at Iran's nuclear program. Obama himself was informed each time the weapon had struck.[7] According to those who participated in the deliberations about Stuxnet, the president was well aware that it represented an unprecedented extension of the American security apparatus. Given the national security interests at stake, however, he felt he had no choice but to pursue this new form of unilateral warfare. The president's cyber attacks on Iran are but the tip of the iceberg; according to some leaked documents, Obama has directed the executive branch to begin planning other potential cyber attacks.[8]

Obama's management of the Iraq and Afghanistan wars was similarly based around executive action. Less than six weeks after he took office, the president announced that all troops would be out of Iraq by the end of 2011. At the time, over 100,000 were stationed there. A slightly more complicated plan for Afghanistan was implemented, as Obama sharply increased the number of troops while simultaneously planning to withdraw them in the future. As of this writing, around 30,000 American military personnel remain in Afghanistan. Obama's decision-making means that Congress tends to play only an advisory role, complaining and cheering about various decisions, but not directly informing those decisions themselves. The president is firmly in the driver's seat.

To be sure, in the late summer of 2013, Obama gave a nod toward constitutional requirements for congressional approval when it came to intervening militarily in Syria. Rather than rush headlong into a fight against the Bashar al-Assad regime, which had just used chemical weapons against insurgents within the country, Obama sought Congress's prior approval for military action. It seemed, if only for a moment, that traditional understandings of the constitutional war powers were making inroads back into the White House. Perhaps they were. But they certainly did not linger. Less than a year later, with the former al-Qaeda affiliate known as the Islamic State of Iraq and Syria (ISIS) laying waste to large portions of the northern and central provinces of the country, Obama ignored these procedural niceties and ordered a sustained barrage of strikes. "I consulted Congress on the decisions I made today, and will continue to do so going forward," Obama said.[9] Notice the language here. He consulted Congress on the decisions "he had made." Its members were but bystanders to presidential action.

Obama continues to rely upon executive agreements, which do not formally require Senate ratification, in lieu of treaties, which do. Today, most agreements reached between the United States and other nations fall under this former category. While not as far-reaching as treaties, executive agreements nonetheless reflect substantive policy decisions on a broad range of areas, from defense to narcotics to telecommunications. Since

2000, the number of treaties has flat-lined while the number of executive agreements has exploded. Whether the president is launching attacks at adversaries or forging agreements with allies, he is crafting the decisions within the confines of his own branch of government.

Where legislative action is either unlikely or impossible, Obama has passed executive orders to expedite his policy agenda. In a domain where presidents historically have exercised little independent authority, Obama issued orders in 2014 that increased the minimum wage for companies contracting with the federal government. His frustration with congressional inaction was plainly evident when announcing his decision, which increased pay from $7.25 to $10.10 an hour. "While Congress decides what it's going to do—and I hope this year, and I'm going to work this year, and urge that this year they actually pass a law—today I'm going to do what I can to help raise working Americans' wages."[10] Sometimes, the president has had a sense of humor about the situation. "Let's pass some bills," he recently told Congress. "It's lonely, me just doing stuff."[11]

In the summer of 2014, he announced a slew of immigration reforms that most certainly would not withstand legislative scrutiny. Indeed, the very fact that Congress refused to enact immigration reform through the traditional lawmaking process served as the president's primary justification for doing so alone. From congressional intransigence, Obama had inferred that "since they don't expect to pass a bill I can sign, I should go ahead and act on my own to solve the problem."[12] As a result, various policies one might expect to fall under Congress's purview—such as granting work permits to undocumented immigrants and changing deportation rules—were instead claimed as the president's territory.

Obama has been equally energetic when pushing purely domestic policy. Without any statutory authority to do so, Obama has extended deadlines and reshaped central provisions of the Affordable Care Act, his single most important (and controversial) domestic legislative achievement. In total, the president issued 24 executive orders to revise components of the ACA. When the rollout of the website hit the skids (more on this below), the president single-handedly delayed the deadline by six weeks. Similarly, when concerns arose about the law's looming deadline for large employers to offer healthcare to their employees, the president delayed the deadline by a full year.

Leveraging the 1970 Clean Air Act, Obama advanced sweeping environmental regulations. To the considerable consternation of Republicans within Congress, Senator Mitch McConnell from Kentucky, Obama took on the coal industry, shutting down existing coal-fired power plants and suspending the opening of new ones. He created the first national policy on global climate change. He issued rules intended to reduce industrial emissions of hazardous pollutants and the production of carbon dioxide from cars and factories. After resurrecting it in the aftermath of the great recession, something discussed at greater length in chapter 2, Obama required the auto industry to comply with new fuel economy standards and required them to invest in hybrid and electric vehicles. The list of environmental rules goes on and on.

Obama also exploited his discretionary authority as chief litigator, as represented in his Solicitor General, to advance his policy objectives. Wary of the federally enacted Defense of Marriage Act, Obama refused to defend it in court. Eric Holder, Obama's Attorney General, sent a letter to Congress explaining the decision. The president had decided on his accord that a standing law, passed by Congress and signed less than twenty years prior, was in violation of the Constitution, and thus should not and would not be enforced. Once again, rather than soliciting prior input, Obama merely informed Congress about a decision he had already made.

Singularly and collectively, these actions have given Republicans fits. "It is a transparent attempt to shirk the department's duty to defend the laws passed by Congress," said Republican Congressman Lamar Smith, after the DOMA decision was announced.[13] Republican Senator Ted Cruz described the Obama presidency as "imperial."[14] Others warned that Obama was ignoring the Constitution and endangering the republican system.[15] The term "dictator" floated about.

Unable to undo the president's policy directives by rhetoric alone, House Republicans in the summer of 2014 opted to sue him. A vote in the House authorized Speaker John Boehner to pursue legal action against the president over the implementation of ACA on the grounds that his actions had been "inconsistent" with the Constitution. In a letter to his colleagues meant to explain the proposed lawsuit, Boehner lambasted Obama for "circumvent[ing] the Congress through executive action, creating his own laws and excusing himself from executing statutes he is sworn to uphold."[16] Constitutional law experts expressed ample skepticism about the case's legal merits.[17] Even fellow Republicans doubted the legal case would succeed. But to confront an ever-expanding executive, Congress had to try *something*. "We won't know until we try," said congressman Diaz-Balart.[18]

There is, of course, some irony in the fact that members of Congress are now looking to the courts—the "least dangerous" branch, and one that historically has been reticent to intervene in purely "political questions"—to do what their own branch of government so colossally has failed to accomplish. Moreover, those bringing the case plainly do so not out of strict obeisance to the Constitution, but because they oppose the ends to which Obama's power is being put. Wrapping partisan objections in constitutional language is not new, of course. As Bertrand de Jouvenel remarked over a half century ago, this in response to the barrage of legal criticisms levied against president Truman, "A curious coincidence, is it not, that everyone who condemned the decision also considered that it exceeded the competence of the President, whereas nobody who approved it took this view of the constitution?"[19] In our politics, now as then, debates about who should wield public authority really function as proxy battles over what is to be done with that authority.

Regardless of how the Republicans' case shapes up, there is merit to their complaints about the president. Obama has ignored certain laws. He has interpreted others in ways that conform to his, rather than Congress's, core convictions. He has worked around Congress, not merely executing the law but also creating it. He has stretched the meaning of the "take care" clause and the commander in chief designation well beyond the Framers' intent.

The thing is, nearly every president before him did so too. If logical consistency means anything to Republicans today, they will put Bush's policies in their sights as well. Likewise, those Democrats who sit so quietly now, but who just a few years earlier were spitting invective at the gross abuse of the Constitution under Republican rule, need to join in the chorus of calls for a judicial corrective to the contemporary state of executive politics. Of course, neither will. And presidents, in the main, will be the better for it.

Innovations

In many ways, we have seen, Obama picked up where Bush left off. His policy objectives differed dramatically from his predecessor's. But their efforts to build, protect, and expand executive power were much the same. To the ongoing project of presidential expansion, nonetheless, Obama proffered innovations of his own. One of the most important hid in plain sight: the president's efforts to rewrite major education policy through waivers.

Obligations over education policy are enshrined in state constitutions, not the federal constitution. Some of the most striking policy developments of the last half-century, however, have come at the behest of the national government. Tracing back to the original Elementary and Secondary Education Act (ESEA) of 1965 and following on with the creation of a federal Department of Education under the Carter Administration, the federal government generally, and the American president in particular, has sought to influence the ways in which children learn around the country.

Such developments came to a head under the George W. Bush Administration. Indeed, arguably the single most important domestic policy achievement of the Bush presidency was the 2002 enactment of No Child Left Behind (NCLB). With this law, the federal government helped propagate new systems of accountability, ones that set clear benchmarks for student learning and consequences for schools and districts that failed to meet them.

Though initially endorsed by Democrats and Republicans alike for its focus on student outcomes and the attention it brought to achievement differences between white and non-white students, NCLB today raises hackles. Too many districts and schools have failed to meet standards that are simply impossible to achieve. Moreover, a preoccupation with standardized testing, advocates of school choice on the Right and union backers on the Left insist, have corroded our schools and made the teaching profession less attractive.

What has Congress done to fix the law? Nothing. At least nothing of real consequence. In 2007, NCLB was first up for reauthorization. Seven years later, it remains so. And in the interim, Congress has not taken any significant steps to fix the most glaring faults of this legislation.

Rather than continue to wait for Congress to fix NCLB, Obama began in 2012 to offer waivers to individual states. Though NCLB remained on the books, Obama told states that they were free to ignore its most onerous provisions. Under NCLB, schools that failed to make what came to be known as "Adequate Yearly Progress" targets faced a series of escalating, costly sanctions, which ranged from being required to provide tutoring and school choice to undergoing restructuring. Each year, these targets would rise until the 2013–2014 school year when states were expected to reach 100 percent proficiency. Of course, none have. Rather than face the consequences of this (universal) failure, states had the opportunity to opt out of this provision of the law, while still receiving the financial support it provided.

There was, however, a hitch. And when thinking about presidential power, this is where things got interesting. To receive a waiver, Obama required states to take up alternative education policies endorsed by his administration—policies, you will note, that differ from the contents of NCLB and that most likely would not traverse the long legislative process in Congress.

Under the waiver system, states were required to intervene in at least 15 percent of their Title 1 schools, which served mostly low-income students. The Obama administration did allow states to design their own performance measures and ranking systems to evaluate schools. But in exchange for such flexibility, the administration also required states to design and implement teacher and principal evaluation systems that meaningfully differentiated performances and used student growth data as a contributing factor. The new systems, which had to be piloted in districts during the 2013–14 school year, were meant to be used in personnel decisions. States also were required to adopt and implement college- and career-ready standards in reading, language arts, and math.[20]

These policies, it bears emphasizing, are quite controversial. Teachers unions, the single most influential interest group in education, have long opposed them. State legislatures have adopted them, for the most part, only sporadically; and then, in only piecemeal fashion. Congress has not so much as debated them in any serious fashion. With Obama's waiver program, however, these policies were nearly universally adopted. As of August 2014, 45 states and the District of Columbia had submitted requests for waivers. Of these states, all but two (Iowa and Wyoming) had their plans approved.

As a general matter, legislation has always trumped unilateral and administrative directives emanating from the president. Executive orders and the like, as a result, have traditionally had to operate in the gaps between legislative pronouncements. But this is no longer so. Through waivers, Obama effectively remade federal law, at once dismantling his predecessor's signature policy achievement and codifying in law his own education policy. Rather than working around statutory law, then, the president refashioned it entirely on his own. And so doing, he established an important precedent for subsequent presidents to do likewise.[21] Stay tuned.

Retrenchment?

Of course, not all the trend lines point upwards. Much, in fact, has been made of two that have declined rather sharply under the Obama administration. Obama has not issued anywhere near as many signing statements as his immediate predecessor. And you have to go back roughly twenty years to find a president who issued executive orders at a comparable rate to Obama.

These observations are often invoked by liberals trying either to defend the president against charges of imperialism or to bait the president into acting more aggressively on behalf of their shared agenda. And the observations, as far as they go, accurately describe the president's actions. The relevant question is not whether Obama has issued fewer signing statements and executive orders. He has. The relevant question is what we should make of such facts.

Let's consider them each in turn. For a variety of reasons, the drop in signing statements says very little about Obama's interest in power. For reasons discussed at length in chapter 2, the influence gleaned from signing statements remains very much a work in a progress; now, more aspirational than material. Moreover, there is no evidence that Obama's decision to issue fewer signing statements signals a general intention to follow the strict will of Congress when interpreting and executing the law. Indeed, the whole point of the House Republicans' court case against Obama is premised on the notion that the president decidedly is not abiding by the letter of the law.

Executive orders, however, are another story. Whereas signing statements constitute mere recommendations to bureaucrats and judges about how to interpret the law, executive orders have legal and policy standing in their own right. An executive order, like any unilateral directive, retains the weight of law until and unless another branch of government, be it Congress or the judiciary, amends or overturns it. The drop in executive orders, therefore, would appear more consequential—particularly if it signaled a willingness of Obama to renounce formal powers. Rather plainly, though, it does not.

Why not? The first answer concerns the unilateral actions that we are counting. It is true that Obama has issued fewer executive orders than Bush. It also is true, though, that he has issued far more memoranda. Recent research by the presidency scholar John Woolley suggests that Obama is substituting memoranda for executive orders. And good substitutes they are, as both instruments allow presidents to advance substantive policy aims in a wide range of domestic and foreign policy domains.[22] So doing, he is following a long tradition of presidents who shuffle policy initiatives across different kinds of unilateral directives, who rename and rebrand policy directives over the course of their time in office, and who invent altogether new ones in a continual effort to elude congressional reporting requirements and public scrutiny. Moreover, many of the most controversial unilateral actions that the president has taken—particularly with regards to the implementation of the Affordable Care Act—have not the assumed the form of any well-established policy directive. The president simply issued the orders and his subordinates obeyed.

A deeper lesson also bears remembering. The regularity with which a president exercises any particular policy option does not provide an unadulterated view of the influence he wields over policy matters or the interest he has in acquiring power. Just because a president issues more or fewer executive orders does not mean that he exercises any more or less influence over policy or that he cares any more or less about power. In the nation's history, Franklin Roosevelt issued more vetoes than any other president. If you wanted to point to this fact as further evidence of Roosevelt's obvious historical importance, though, you would have to upgrade your assessment of Grover Cleveland (remember him?), who issued the second most vetoes overall; and who, on an annual basis, issued more vetoes than even Roosevelt.

When he assumed office, Obama would have loved to issue a batch of directives implementing his policy agenda in total, all at once. Obviously, he did not. He could not. Other political actors—in Congress, the judiciary, the bureaucracy, and the larger polity—stood in his way. There is no great mystery about this. The opportunities that presidents have to exercise influence and to acquire new sources of authority are circumscribed. And knowing that they will be overturned in the second instance, presidents usually will not act in the first. Inaction, though, need not betray indifference. Typically, instead, it reveals a president aware of his lot—the limited opportunities he has to promote his policies, the careful orchestrations needed to build his power, and the many political opponents who devote their days to obstructing him.

A great deal of political science scrutinizes the institutional conditions under which presidents can influence the content of public policies. And none of this scholarship—at least none that is credible—suggests that presidents will act at every turn, that their optimal strategy is to govern full throttle by issuing more and more orders and handing down more and more directives.

What may look like impuissance instead reflects the strategic choices of a calculating president. Presidents, all presidents, survey the political landscape for opportunities to press out on the boundaries of their power. Presidents want a great deal more power than they have. Desire, however, does not always translate into empowerment. And though they want power, they are careful not to appear rapacious. For reason discussed at greater length in chapter 7, presidents often demur, tip their hat to congressional prerogatives, and offer a nod to the Constitution. Doing so is good politics. But when they do so, we should not take them at their word. Clear-eyed assessments of the institutional environment in which politicians work provide a great deal more information about their true incentives than do their own self-serving testimonials.

That Obama issued fewer signing statements or executive orders than Bush is no indicator of retrenchment. And it certainly is no harbinger of a kinder, gentler presidency; an executive, meek and mild, who will strictly obey the limits on his power demarcated by constitutional law scholars and libertarians. No sir. Obama's presidency is very much a product and piece of the modern era, in which public expectations of the presidency compel presidents to do far more, and claim far more, than their constitutional authority permits.

LIMITATIONS AND SETBACKS

None of this is meant to suggest that Obama had his way at every turn with Congress, the judiciary, or the American public. That Obama sought to expand his power does not at all mean that he acquired nearly the influence, nor tallied nearly the wins, he would have liked. To the contrary, he was scandalized by the killing of J. Christopher Stevens, the U.S. ambassador to Libya in September 2012. He has experienced numerous legislative failures, as in his efforts to push gun reform legislation in the aftermath of the tragedy at Sandy Hook Elementary School in December 2012. He has endured reversals of fortune, as the political gains associated with the Arab Spring devolved into Civil War in Syria, continued fighting and slaughter in the Gaza Strip, and political unrest in Egypt and Libya. And leaks, particularly those orchestrated by Edward Snowden and Julian Assange, besotted his presidency.

At home, nothing in Obama's second term in office did more to hurt his presidency than the rollout of the health insurance exchanges in the fall of 2013. The problems began with the website, healthcare.gov, through which Americans were expected to purchase health insurance. Simply put, the website was not ready for public use when it launched on October 1—and especially not ready to be used by the 20 million people who navigated toward it. In pre-testing only days before it went live, the website crashed; on the day it went live, placeholder text was still visible. The website crashed repeatedly in its first month. Of course, websites crash constantly, even those sponsored by the federal government. But the Affordable Care Act mandated that Americans sign up. The failed website was thus more than a failed website. It was a hindrance to complying with the law for well-meaning Americans.

And problems were not limited to the website. While promoting the legislation, Obama had repeatedly promised Americans that, if the bill passed, they would not lose their healthcare. "If you like your [health-care plan], you can keep it," he said in some form or another many, many times.[23] Literally, the president was correct. The law itself did not remove Americans from their healthcare plans. However, providers of healthcare plans responded to the ACA by significantly overhauling their coverage and dropping some customers from their rolls. Obama's principled promises had, in practice, turned hollow. Republican and Democratic lawmakers were furious, with one Democratic aide rather poetically telling a reporter that "the White House shit the bed."[24] The public was even angrier. After all, they had been told that, if they lacked healthcare, they would be required to purchase it—but the website that was meant to sell it to them did not work. They were told that, if they had healthcare, they would be allowed to keep it. This was effectively false; and again, if they were dropped from their coverage and then tried to repurchase it, they encountered a broken website. In the month following the rollout of ACA, a paltry 32 percent of Americans approved of Obama's handling of health-care, a new low. Obama's approval ratings also cratered to the lowest levels of his presidency.

What should we take away from this? And what should the next president learn from this? At the most basic level, Obama's failure was not one of policy choice, overreach, or, as his critics liked to say, of ignoring the will of the American people. Rather, the most fundamental reason this series of events damaged his presidency so much was that it exposed his lack of mastery over a policy domain that he himself had vested political capital. Of course, governing snafus are part of any presidency. One measure of a president is how he reacts to the failures of the government that he is thought to lead. Is the president in front of the crisis, projecting control and taking active steps to abate it, or is he behind the crisis, appearing either unwilling or incapable of keeping up.

The damage wrought to Obama's presidency, then, had less to do with the events themselves and more to do with his appearing distant and reactive. Rather than exhibiting control, exuding command, he spent most days chasing a scandal that was eluding him, trying to catch up to headlines documenting setbacks for which his administration lacked answers. Each day that the website remained inoperative, Obama's policy ambitions unraveled a bit further, and the carefully constructed narrative that he had built, as all presidents must, of competence, problem-solving, action-oriented, accountability, and common-sense governance lost its grip on the American public. Unable to project the semblance of command, Obama's efforts to exert actual command came off as desperate and grasping.

The president's problems, as such, were two-fold. Materially, he failed to exercise sufficient power over the actual design or implementation of the ACA's rollout. And symbolically, he failed to project the image of one who is in control, one who commands mastery, one who is powerful. The website failure, as such, revealed, just as it exacerbated, the very paradoxes that encourage presidents to seek and guard power in the first place. We demand presidents to do far more than their formal powers will permit; we refuse to discount our evaluations of their performance according to those powers that are to be found in the Constitution; and we reward presidents primarily on the basis of the magnitude of their policy accomplishments rather than their efficacy.

FALLOUT, WORSE AND BETTER

You may or may not like what Obama has done during his time in office. You may or may not like the ways in which policies are generally made today, the tendencies of presidents to lurch toward opportunities to exercise influence. And you may become especially perturbed about the purposes to which such power is put, the kinds of policies that presidents seek to promote and defend with the powers they accrue. To such outrage, I offer no balm. This is not a book that seeks to laud or condemn Obama, or any his predecessors for that matter. Rather, it is a book that attempts to make sense of him and them—and to do so in institutional terms.

That presidents seek power at nearly every turn, and that the American public places such a premium on presidential action, does not imply, much less guarantee, that the public welfare is enhanced as a result. To the contrary, presidents often face extraordinary incentives to act when non-action, or at least delayed action, might be in the nation's best interests. A just and efficacious resolution to some crises may require modesty on the president's part. The material interests of the public and the safeguarding of cherished values may require deliberation, caution, and care on the president's part. None too often, perhaps, it may be best for the president to demur, to stand aside, and to let others bask in the limelight.

There can arise great distortions and greater costs, then, when presidents behave as presidents must if they are to thrive politically. In their attempts to command a political environment that is stacked against them, presidents may confuse boastfulness for genuine leadership. In the rush to act, presidents may push policies that are ineffective or downright noxious. In seizing power at nearly every turn, presidents may exacerbate deep and growing imbalances to our system of separated powers. And in justifying such seizures with arguments that are dubious on both empirical and principled grounds, presidents may simultaneously erode the public's trust in government and the constitutional foundations on which it was built. (But see chapter 2, where I have more to say about the Founders' expectations about presidential ambitions, virtue, and self-restraint).

Of course, the incentives that encourage presidents to seek power may have positive externalities as well. As Congress delves ever deeper into the layers of dysfunction, and as the two major parties demonstrate their ever more refined skills at sniping and grandstanding, a more powerful president may step into the breach and productively offer policy solutions to vexing social problems. In thinking about trenchant social problems like climate change, the mass emigration of Latin American children to the United States, a convoluted tax policy, and latent terrorist threats, it is difficult even to conceive of Congress, much less the courts, yielding a productive pathway forward. Within our existing political system, the president may offer the only viable hope for solving social problems. As such, a presidency that is expanding in power may redound to the public's welfare.

Both the benefits and costs of presidential action were recently on full display, as we have seen, in the realm of education policy. Incapable of addressing the faults of NCLB, Congress effectively opted out of the task of reforming federal education law. One can take issue with the specific policies that the president adopted. And many have. But nearly everyone recognizes the need for some kind of reprieve from the utterly unrealistic expectation under NCLB that all children would be reading at grade-level by 2014. Congress could have offered it, but chose not to. Indeed, Congress remains to this day perfectly within its legal rights to reauthorize the law and do away with all the waivers that Obama has seen fit to distribute. But still, it chooses not to. Instead, it was the president who stepped in and offered a solution to a burgeoning crisis. In so doing, though, Obama paved the way for future presidents to dismantle other laws not to their liking, and thereby upend conventional understandings of the chief executive's obligation to "take care that the laws are faithfully executed."

How do these various costs and benefits shake out? I, for one, have thoughts about the matter. Such thoughts, though, are for another book. Debates about the desirability of a more powerful president exceed the scope of this book. For now, I leave the matter at this: that presidents have political reasons to guard, nurture, and seize power, does not mean that the public is better for it—at least not always.

As students of the institutional presidency, our first and primary job does not involve passing judgment on the things that presidents do. Our purpose does not lie in praising presidents when they act in ways we like, and condemning them when they degrade some constituency, value, or objective that we hold dear. Rather, our job is to clarify why presidents behave as they do, whether we like what they do or not. Our purpose is to illuminate the ways in which presidents draw upon those political resources made available to them in order to respond to those political incentives set before them.

This book does not ask you to applaud presidents as they seek and defend power. Unapologetically, it asks that you see this preoccupation for what it is: an effort to overcome constitutional deficits in their ongoing struggle to meet pervasive demands for leadership. As long as presidents have institutional incentives to build power, then build power they will.

William Howell
August, 2014

Notes

1 "Barack Obama's Acceptance Speech." August 28, 2008. Published by CQ Transcriptions.

2 Alter, Jonathan. *The Promise: President Obama, Year One.* (New York: Simon and Schuster, 2010) p. 129.

3 For more on these programs, see: "NSA Slides Explain The Prism Data Collection Program. *The Washington Post*, 10 July 2013; Greenwald, Glenn and Spencer Ackerman. "NSA Collected US Email Records in Bulk for More Than Two Years Under Obama." *The Guardian*, 27 June 2013; Greenwald, Glenn and Ewen MacAskill. "Boundless Informant: The NSA's Secret Tool to Track Global Surveillance Data." *The Guardian*, 11 June 2013.

4 Woodward, Bob. *Obama's Wars.* (New York: Simon and Schuster, 2010) pp. 1–2.

5 Sanger, David. *Confront and Conceal: Obama's Secret Wars and Surprising Use of American Power.* (New York: Random House, 2012) p. XII.

6 Roggio, Bill. "Charting the Data for U.S. Airstrikes in Pakistan." The Long War Journal. Accessed August 21, 2014 via http://www.longwarjournal.org/pakistan-strikes.php.

7 Sanger. p. XII.

8 Greenwald, Glenn and Ewen MacAskill. "Obama Orders U.S. To Draw Up Overseas Target List for Cyber Attacks." *The Guardian*, 7 June 2013.

9 "Statement by the President." 7 August 2014. Accessed August 21, 2014 via http://www.whitehouse.gov/the-press-office/2014/08/07/statement-president.

10 Parsons, Christi. "Obama Raises Minimum Wage for Federal Contractors." *The Los Angeles Times*, 12 February 2014.

11 McManus, Doyle. "Obama Tests the Bounds of Lame Duckery." *The Los Angeles Times*, 16 August 2014.

12 Nakamura, David. "Obama Readies Executive Action on Immigration." *The Washington Post*, 1 August 2014.

13 Savage, Charlie and Sheryl Stolberg. "In Shift, U.S. Says Marriage Act Blocks Gay Rights." *The New York Times*, 23 February 2011.

14 Cruz, Ted. "The Imperial Presidency of Barack Obama." *The Wall Street Journal*, 28 January 2014.

15 Amira, Dan. "Obama Has Issued Fewer Executive Orders Than Any President In Over 100 Years." *New York Magazine*. Accessed August 21, 2014 via http://nymag.com/daily/intelligencer/2013/01/obama-executive-orders-guns.html.

16 Boehner, John. "Memo to House Colleagues on the Separation of Powers." Accessed August 21, 2014 via http://www.speaker.gov/general/memo-house-colleagues-separation-powers.

17 Gerstein, Josh. "5 Questions About John Boehner's Lawsuit Against Barack Obama." *Politico*, 16 July 2014.

18   Rogers, Alex. "House Grants Authority to Sue Obama." *Time*, 30 July 2014.

19   Bertrand de Jouvenel, 1957. *Sovereignty: An Inquiry into the Political Good.* (Chicago, IL: University of Chicago Press) p. 4.

20   At the time, most states (44 and the District of Columbia) already met this requirement through participation in the Common Core State Standards initiative, but states that did not want to use the Common Core could also receive a waiver if their university system endorsed the states' standards.

21   Indeed, had he won the 2012 election, Mitt Romney might have issued all sorts of waivers to the Affordable Care Act, a law that he steadfastly opposed as a presidential candidate (even though as governor he had seen the enactment of the ACA's state template), and that he probably could not have overturned legislatively. To justify such issuing such waivers, Romney would need only point out that he was doing to Obama's domestic policy achievement what Obama had done to Bush's.

22   According to Phillip Cooper, memoranda are but "executive orders by another name." For a longer description of both policy instruments, see chapters 2 and 4 of his 2002 book, *By Order of the President* (Lawrence, KS: University Press of Kansas).

23   Gore, D'Angelo. "Fact Check: If You Like Your Healthcare, You Can Keep It." *USA Today*, 11 November 2013.

24   Parnes, Amie. "WH-DSCC Powwow." *The Hill*, 5 January 2013.

Preface

Whereas David Mayhew famously argued that members of Congress care first and foremost about their electoral fortunes, in this short book, we argue that presidents care about power: about acquiring it, protecting it, and expanding it. While individual presidents obviously hold many other concerns dear (an interest in shaping policy, building a legacy, strengthening their party, among other things), the primacy of power considerations sets presidents apart from all other political actors. The search for and defense of power, in one way or another, informs nearly everything the president says and does. Power is the president's North Star.

The men and (someday) women who eventually become president may not come into this world with an appetite for power. An interest in power may not even inform their original decisions to seek the office. Rather, the need to acquire, protect, and expand power is built into the office of the presidency itself, and it quickly takes hold of whoever temporarily bears the title of chief executive. This concern for power descends on and then seizes even the most reluctant modern presidents, those whose modest ambition is merely to serve the public interest. For what the public expects of the president, as we shall soon see, is not modesty at all. It is nothing short of mastery.

Presidential candidates who foreswear the use of certain power instruments during a campaign—compare, for instance, Senator Barack Obama's principled arguments for the sparing use of signing statements and President Barack Obama's regular and controversial employment of them—quickly learn to appreciate their merits once in office. And those who continue to resist the imperatives of power—James Buchanan, William Taft, or Herbert Hoover—are predictably repudiated by their contemporaries and largely forgotten by subsequent generations.

We do not rule out the possibility that some presidents may enjoy power for power's sake. As the political scientist Robert Spitzer aptly notes, power can act as a "narcotic" for those who sit in the Oval Office. But the main reason presidents care so much about power has less to do with their addiction to grandiosity and far more to do with their constitutional inability to address the extraordinary expectations put before them. The mismatch between public expectations of the president and the formal constitutional powers he is granted yield a nagging preoccupation with power. At every turn, presidents must guard what power they have been given and invent what power they can in order to satisfy a public longing for leadership.

Presidents' interest in power, then, is primarily instrumental in nature. Most presidents most of the time want power for what power can give them: a way of placating today's public and tomorrow's historians who stand in judgment of them. Presidents need not have spent a lifetime nurturing a taste for power in order to fixate, at nearly every turn, on power once in office.

That presidents want power is one thing. That presidents should have it is quite another. Since the nation's founding, arguments favoring and opposing a strong executive branch have been a mainstay of America's philosophical and political tradition. As the book unfolds, we will introduce some notable figures—ranging from Woodrow Wilson to Ron Paul—who have come down on one side or the other of this normative divide. But while we harbor our own opinions about this issue, the argument we lay out here should not be read as either an attack or defense of a bold, empowered presidency. That is a discussion for another book. Here, instead, we make the case that an abiding preoccupation with power helps explain a great deal of what presidents actually do, regardless of whether the public interest, the constitution, or our national polity is made better for it.

Along the same lines, the argument we present here does not advocate for any specific normative object of presidential power, even though normative content is the president's stock in trade. By their very nature, government policies and actions are laden with normative considerations—a fact that goes some distance toward explaining why imprecations of presidential overreach and the perceived abuses of executive authority nearly always come first, and certainly always ring loudest, from members of the opposition party. Liberals could not stand the idea of a powerful president as long as George Bush remained in office. Their concerns promptly lifted, however, the moment that Obama took office; and now conservatives are having their turn at deprecating the privacy intrusions and regulatory extensions that they associate with a strong presidency. Partisans will always judge presidential power on the ends toward which it is aimed. Once again, though, this book eschews these normative debates about the particular uses to which presidents invest their authority.

Here, we focus strictly on the positive claim that presidents, for better or worse, seek power. With this claim, our hands are full enough. To make this argument, we need to clearly define what we mean by power. We need to trace the origins—both intellectual and historical—of presidents' preoccupation with power. We need to explore how this motivation affects the actual behaviors of men in office. We need to consider the consequences for those presidents who, upon occasion, do not embrace power—who dissemble when action is called for, who delegate when decisions must be made, who retreat in the face of calamity. And we need to identify the origin of those forces—be they appeals to conscience, political tradition, legal doctrine, or the adjoining branches of government—that stymie presidents' ambitions.

Explaining presidents by reference to a single motivation comes at some cost. Inevitably, the nuance and character of individual administrations is lost. By design, continuities across presidential administrations overshadow differences. And one risks devolving into caricature, both of the men who serve as president and of the diverse obligations that come before them.

But there are benefits to this approach as well. By recognizing the character and potency of power considerations, we can make sense of presidential actions that otherwise appear irrational. Fixing our eyes on the fundamentals of the American presidency, we can guard against distraction—and with so much being said about presidents during the twenty-four-hour news cycle, distractions run wild. By seeing presidential motivations for what they really are rather than for what we would have them be, we may distinguish partisan pleas for executive forbearance from attempts at genuine reform aimed at achieving balance across the various branches of government.

This book, we hope, will reach two communities. The first and more familiar (at least to us) consists of scholars of the American presidency, with whom we share an allegiance. We have long thought that our field would benefit, as the literatures on Congress and the courts already have, from a clear and simple articulation of what presidents want. Such distillations provide common points of departure that, when successful, can help to organize and integrate scholarship with wildly different methodological orientations. Progress, though, does not hinge on either acquiescence or consensus. There are plenty of things about Congress that cannot be readily explained by reference to its members' concerns about reelection. Likewise, scholars are bound to disagree about the relative importance of power considerations to presidents. Yet by scrutinizing the explanatory powers of these singular motivations, scholars foster a common conversation that, at its best, productively moves a subfield forward.

We also hope this book reaches a second, larger audience: an American public struggling to make sense of all the political machinations in Washington. Public debate about presidents, we have long thought, resembles the endless jawing about college and professional sports. Analysts devote countless hours of radio and television airtime and inches of column space bellyaching about the relevance of each and every dimension of players' and coaches' lives for the outcome of an upcoming game. They worry about how recent charges of a linebacker's infidelity will affect a quarterback's confidence to stay in the pocket; how a recent spat between coach and player bodes for a team's morale; how wind currents and religious convictions and familial strife will bear on the outcome of a game. From this rich stew are born analysts' endless predictions, nearly all of which are distractions.

Forecasting events in the future and making sense of those in the past, in most cases, comes down to a handful of foundational dimensions of the game being played. The outcome of most baseball games, particularly come playoff time, ultimately hinges on good pitching. In football, it's about matchups at key positions and sound coaching. In any given game, of course, other factors may come into play. But the amount of attention devoted to these factors grossly exceeds their general importance. Most of what is offered up as analysis is really just prattle.

So it is with presidents. On news shows and talk radio programs, in opinion magazines and the ever-expanding blogosphere, presidents' lives are dissected again and again. Washington insiders opine about all matter of things—presidents' families, moral sensibilities, emotive qualities, leadership styles, personal relationships with individual legislators, speaking skills—as if every piece of minutia offered unique insights into presidents' actual behavior in office. But they do not—at least not reliably, and certainly not about the things that matter most: the decisions presidents actually make about the content and implementation of public policy. In actuality, presidents work in a highly institutionalized setting, face a common set of expectations, and confront a reasonably well-defined set of political allies and opponents. Hence, when acting in their official capacity, presidents' actions are a great deal more predictable than our talking heads would have us believe. If we want to understand actual presidential behavior, we would do well to simply ignore the preponderance of what political analysts say: like sportscasters, these analysts are more interested in entertaining their audience than in offering meaningful insights into actual outcomes.

What should we monitor when making sense of presidential politics? Like in the sporting world, we should look toward fundamentals. This book makes the case that a sustained interest in power should count among them.

Acknowledgments

In all manner of ways, friends, colleagues, and students have shaped the arguments in this book. Chuck Myers, who kindly invited me to participate in Princeton University Press's "Thinking about . . . ." series, has provided all the support an author could hope for. Absent his encouragement, this book would not exist. David Brent started out as a student in my undergraduate seminar on the presidency, then became my research assistant, and now, for his imaginative intellect and fantastic writing skills, quite appropriately appears on the cover page of this book. Significant portions of this book originated from conversations with my friend and mentor, Terry Moe. For helpful feedback on early drafts of this manuscript, I thank Jeffrey Cohen, George Edwards, Dan Galvin, Doug Kriner, Ben Lynerd, Paul Peterson, Stephane Wolton, and three anonymous reviewers. Hannah Cook, Colleen Dolan, Alfredo Gonzalez, and Ethan Porter provided excellent research assistance. Last, I dedicate this book to my sister, Esther, who faces life's challenges with a fierce determination worthy of any president's admiration.

William G. Howell
Chicago, IL

Thinking about the Presidency

CHAPTER 1

On Being President

What do we expect of our president? The answer is at once obvious and unbelievable: everything.

We want our president to stimulate our national economy while protecting our local ones—and we roundly condemn him when either shows signs of weakness. We call on the president to simultaneously liberate the creative imaginations of private industry and regulate corruption within. We call on the president, as the main steward of the nation's welfare, to resuscitate our housing and car industries while reducing the national debt. We bank on the president, as commander in chief, to wage our wars abroad while remaining attentive to all emergent foreign policy challenges beyond today's battlefields. We look to the president, as the nation's figurehead, to be among the first on the scene at disasters, to offer solace to the grieving, to assign meaning to lives lost and ruined. All this we expect presidents can do. All this we insist they must do.

From the very beginning, the nation's presidents have fielded a long litany of policy challenges. In his brief "First Annual Message to Congress" (now more popularly called the State of the Union address), George Washington talked about security, foreign affairs, immigration, innovation, infrastructure, education, and the standardization of weights, measures, and currency. With the possible exception of the last item, all the issues that Washington prioritized have remained on the president's agenda.

In the modern era, however, the items on this list of issue areas have proliferated; hence, it is the modern American presidency to which the arguments of this book speak most directly. Today, presidents must offer policy solutions on trade, health care, the environment, research and development, government transparency and efficiency, energy, and taxation. They must clean our air and water, protect our borders, build our infrastructure, promote the health of our elderly, improve the literacy rates of our children, guard against everything from the effects of Midwestern droughts to the spread of nuclear weapons—all this and more. Fundamentally, presidents are charged with striking a balance between the nation's competing, often contradictory priorities: intervening abroad versus spending at home; cutting taxes versus protecting social programs; keeping Americans secure versus keeping Americans free.

There is hardly any domain of public life, and only a few of private life, where the president can comfortably defer to the judgments of others, where he (before long, she) can respond to some plea for assistance with something akin to "I hear you, but I can't help you," where he can insist that action on the matter is above his pay grade. It is difficult even to conceive of an aspect of public life wherein the president is given a pass—where he can either hesitate before acting or forego action altogether without incurring the media and public's wrath. Harry Truman's desk placard that read "the buck stops here" was not a point of vanity. It was a gross understatement. All bucks circulating in politics stop with the president. And they do so whether the president likes it or not.

Just ask Mike Kelleher, President Obama's director of presidential correspondence, about how much Americans expect from the president. One hundred thousand e-mails, ten thousand paper letters, three thousand phone calls, and one thousand faxes arrive at his office every day. And nearly all of these communiqués include pleas for presidential leadership of one form or another. The president receives petitions from the elderly to deliver their retirement benefits, appeals from business owners to stem their operating costs, and requests from activists of all stripes to attend to the environment, nuclear proliferation, and foreign affairs. Though more mundane, other requests reveal the extent to which American citizens feel perfectly entitled to burden the president with personal tasks and obligations. They offer recommendations on which books he ought to read; their children pepper him with questions and advice of their own; distressed Americans seek solutions to their emotional, psychological, and medical issues; and the moral police deliver benedictions to ban certain video games.

The list of obligations put before the president continually evolves, and nearly always in expansionary ways. Presidents now offer leadership in policy domains for which the federal government lacks any constitutional responsibility. Consider, by way of example, recent presidential efforts to reform public education. The 2002 No Child Left Behind (NCLB) Act is widely touted as George W. Bush's signature domestic policy achievement. And with good reason. NCLB is credited (or blamed, depending on one's view of the matter) with introducing and fortifying accountability provisions in all public schools, which universally include rigorous standardized testing provisions. Not to be outdone, Barack Obama devoted considerable efforts through his "Race to the Top" initiative to reform school governance. Through competitive grants, the president cooked up yet another mechanism by which the federal government might further intrude into state and local education policy—in this instance, by advancing merit pay for teachers, charter schools, the development of data systems capable of tracking student performance over time, and the establishment of clear standards for progress. Moreover, in the last year Obama has unilaterally offered waivers for the most onerous provisions of NCLB to those states who adopt the president's preferred education policies. That public education formally falls within the province of state (and by extension local) governments did not dissuade either Bush or Obama from taking up the mantle of education reform, searching for (and often inventing) new ways to make their mark.

Yet no matter how much the president says about any particular policy issue, it is never enough to satiate the public's thirst for presidential leadership. Recall, by way of example, President Obama's 2011 State of the Union address. Even before the big day, the requests poured in from all corners of political life. As the *New York Times* chronicled, "Interest groups have buried the White House with a barrage of unsolicited advice about what they want him to say." The wish list included stricter gun control laws, curbs on the bullying of gay American children, protections for existing welfare programs, and cuts to those very same programs.

Eventually, of course, the president had to decide for himself what to say. And though his speech ran the better part of an hour, the chattering classes still saw fit to castigate the president for neglecting their pet causes. Many criticized Obama for not focusing enough attention on the deficit. Though Obama did propose measures to tackle the problem, he supposedly neither offered an adequate number of solutions nor displayed sufficient leadership to ensure their passage. Other observers, meanwhile, criticized the president's lack of specificity, while still others charged that the president devoted *too much* time to the deficit, and not nearly enough to the related issue of jobs. Some pundits even lamented the president's oversight of certain aspects of education, a topic that he indisputably discussed at length.

With all the demands competing for his attention, it is no surprise that the president cannot hope to get by with a light, easy work schedule. Every minute of a president's day is scheduled, usually months and sometimes even years in advance. On July 1, 1955, to select an entirely arbitrary day, President Eisenhower went home to his farm in Gettysburg, PA. His time at home included two and a half hours set aside for entertaining colleagues from the White House and the cabinet and their spouses. Earlier that morning, the president's day began in Washington with breakfast with a senator, followed by ten other appointments that included discussions on world disarmament and minimum wages, a cabinet meeting, and a meet-and-greet with forty-three boy scouts. Reflecting on this mad-dash daily schedule, Eisenhower wrote to a confidant, "These days go by at their accustomed pace, leaving little time for the more pleasurable pursuits of life . . . by the time I get to the office I am in the midst of politics, economics, education, foreign trade, and cotton and tobacco surpluses."

Fast-forward fifty years, and we discover a president's official schedule that is even more serried. On July 1, 2005, to pick yet another date at random, President George W. Bush held his customary intelligence briefing, received an award from the National Society of the Sons of the American Revolution, oversaw a bilateral meeting with the prime minister of Kuwait, spoke at length with Supreme Court Justice Sandra Day O'Connor and two senators, publicly announced O'Connor's resignation, visited with and subsequently presented Purple Hearts to some soldiers injured in Iraq and Afghanistan, and finally retreated to Camp David.

Presidents must attend not merely to the multitude of issues waiting on their desks, but those popping up around the country and world. Hence, in 2010 alone, President Obama took 65 domestic trips out of Washington. His predecessors also showed the same zeal for domestic travel, holding an average of 649 public events outside the DC area per presidential term between 1989 and 2005. Internationally, Obama took 16 trips to 25 countries in his first two years as president, while previous presidents between

1989 and 2005 made dozens of trips abroad each term. Both Clinton and George W. Bush tallied an impressive 75 international trips in their respective presidencies.

When presidents travel domestically, they do not just attend town hall meetings or give policy speeches; when overseas, they do not merely attend diplomatic meetings. Presidents also make commencement speeches, attend ceremonies to commemorate the birthdays of prominent historical figures, and appear at disaster sites. They visit American troops, offer remarks at nongovernmental conferences, and commemorate historical events like the D-Day invasion.

How much of the president's travel is attributable to expectations? Just contrast the political fallout from George W. Bush's Hurricane Katrina flyover in 2005 (a political catastrophe that we discuss at length in chapter 6) with the warm reception of his Thanksgiving visit to American troops in Afghanistan in 2003. Perennially, the president is expected to be at the right place at the right time, no matter the distance required for travel or the competing obligations vying for his attention.

So great are the public's expectations of the president, in fact, that most Americans see their entire government in the presidency. They invest in the president their highest aspirations not just for the federal government, but for the general polity, for their communities and families, and for their own private lives. Constantly, Americans berate their presidents to say more, to do more, to be more. While occasionally paying homage to limited government and constitutionalism (topics that we discuss in greater length in chapter 5), Americans, in general—and especially when it matters most—beseech their presidents to take charge and lead.

The extraordinary demands placed on presidents have not eluded scholars. Richard Neustadt identifies no less than five sources of demands for presidential aid and service: executive officialdom, Congress, his partisans, citizens at large, and from abroad. To succeed, presidents must find ways of placating all of these interested parties, no matter how unreasonable their individual demands, or how inconsistent their collective claims.

By Clinton Rossiter's account, presidents are men of many "hats," a familiar but strained metaphor given that presidents cannot ever return any of their responsibilities to the rack. By constitutional mandate, Rossiter recognizes, presidents serve as chief of state, chief executive, commander in chief, chief diplomat, and chief legislator. But their responsibilities do not end there. Presidents also serve as chief of party, voice of the people, protector of the peace, manager of prosperity, and world leader. The burden of these ten functions, Rossiter insists, is nothing short of "staggering," even "monstrous."

Neustadt and Rossiter offered these reflections in the mid-twentieth century, decades before Arthur Schlesinger decried the emergence of an "imperial presidency"; before George W. Bush initiated and then Barack Obama continued a largely clandestine war on terror; and before Charlie Savage sounded the alarm bells over the president's presumptive "takeover" of the national security apparatus. If the scope of presidential functions was monstrous before, in the last half-century it has grown exponentially more fearsome.

Because of the tremendous growth in responsibilities and expectations put before them, contemporary presidents must demonstrate fluency in policy domains that utterly eluded the attention of presidents who held office just a generation or two ago. Today, if any branch of government is involved in a policy domain, then so is the president.

AN IMPERATIVE TO ACT

In every policy domain, presidents must not only demonstrate involvement, they must act—and they must do so for all to see, visibly, forthrightly, and expediently. Deliberation must not substitute for action. Presidents are free to think and talk, but they absolutely must do.

To reap the praise of today's public and tomorrow's historians, the two audiences who matter most to presidents, executive actions must have three qualities. First, they must be open for all to see. The public naturally distrusts the president who works behind the scenes, who recoils from public view in order to cavort with advisors and plot a way forward. The public demands a commander in chief, not a manager in chief. And those presidents who are perceived, fairly or not, to assume the latter mantle— think Jimmy Carter or Dwight Eisenhower—cannot expect to keep company with the greats.

The president's actions also must be decisive and, whenever possible, swift. The less light that shines between an observed challenge and the president's response, the better. Equivocation, particularly in the face of crisis, will never do. Even when justified, delay reliably invites criticisms (recall the browbeating Barack Obama received in the summer and early fall of 2009, when he and his advisors contemplated the merits of expanding the U.S. military presence in Afghanistan). And nothing more reliably induces snickering from the opposing camp than appearing caught off guard (recall the mockery to which George W. Bush was subject when, on September 11, 2001, he did not spring to his feet and start issuing orders after an aide whispered in his ear that the nation was under attack). While they need not meet challenges instantaneously, presidents must convey to the public from the get-go that they have a plan ready to be set into motion.

Finally, presidential actions must be demonstrative. Facing extraordinary problems, presidents must gather their resolve and press onward. The words "but for" must not enter their vocabulary, as the excuses that follow, no matter how authentic, almost never resonate. Presidents must eschew a defensive posture. They must never concede the peoples' fate to anything except their own making. Even amidst military catastrophe and economic ruin, presidents must insist that the nation's brightest days lie ahead, that the industry and imagination of the American people shall not be squandered, that the shining city upon a hill, as Ronald Reagan put it, awaits us still. Hence, in their finest moments, presidents stand tall and issue calls to arms (as George W. Bush did, through a megaphone no less, atop the rubble of twin towers), defy international convention in the service of some larger good (as Barack Obama did when ordering a surgical strike to take out Osama bin Laden without informing the Pakistani government), and insist the federal government can act, must act, in the face of utter calamity (as Franklin Roosevelt did twice, first in the aftermath of the Great Depression and then in response to the imperialistic designs of totalitarian regimes in Europe). Such presidents in such moments appear—how else to put this?—distinctly presidential.

Through their actions, in short, presidents must appear nothing less than masters of their environments. They must orchestrate not only the political universe, but the material world that surrounds them. They must appear in command. They must lean forward into the headwinds. And they must appear utterly unflappable: George Patton, John Wayne, and Tiger Woods (circa 2001!) all rolled into one.

Constitutional Limitations

Such is what we expect of our presidents. How, then, are they to meet such extraordinary demands? What formal powers do they have at their disposal? The answer, especially in the modern era, has been "not enough." To make good on the avalanche of expectations laid before them, particularly since the early twentieth century, presidents must grapple with a Constitution that does not grant them nearly enough explicit powers. As Clinton Rossiter puts it, the president's "authority over the administration is in no way equal to his responsibility for its performance."

The presidency created by the Constitution, to be sure, was a significant improvement on its predecessor under the Articles of Confederation. Between 1781 and 1789, presidents under the Articles served for just one year, were chosen by Congress, and acted as nothing more than presiding officers. The office of president of the Continental Congress was most analogous to the modern-day Speaker of the House: like the Speaker, the president of the Continental Congress refrained from participating in debate and voted last; and only then if his vote would be decisive. But unlike the Speaker, the president of the Continental Congress had no power to assign delegates to committees, to wield any kind of agenda control, or to lean on members to vote one way or another.

Under the Constitution born of the Philadelphia Convention of 1787, the president experienced a form of liberation. Formally, executive independence was secured through elections: the president was to be elected by the people (if indirectly), not by the Congress, as occurred in the First Republic. Moreover, rather than vesting veto powers in a council that was selected by the Congress as some would have preferred, veto authority rested solely with the chief executive. In addition, and not trivially for the times, Congress could not change a standing president's salary, nor could any individual serve simultaneously as president and as member of the

House or Senate. With the Constitution's ratification, the presidency had its own base of authority. At last, the American presidency had become, if not a coequal branch of government, then at least an independent one.

Additionally, and crucially, the Framers created a unitary presidency. Unlike the deliberative bodies inhabiting the legislative and judicial branches of government, the president, by design, sits alone atop his governing institution. This is not to say that he wields complete control over all goings-on within the executive branch. Far from it. Over the course of the nation's history, the president has struggled mightily to control the burgeoning administrative state, nearly always with mixed results. But a more basic point warrants recognition: the fact that the Framers created a singular presidency—rather than a plural one as some, such as James Wilson, would have preferred; and as others, such as David Orentlicher, argue for today—proved to be a great boon to those who occupied the office.

Independent and singular, what enumerated powers does the president formally wield? In comparison to the ten presidents of the First Republic, the forty-three presidents of the Second have enjoyed a veritable bounty of constitutional authority. Unilaterally, the president can issue pardons and vetoes, convene and adjourn Congress "under extraordinary circumstances," and exercise all of the attendant powers of commander in chief. Subject to congressional approval, the president can also make treaties with foreign nations and appoint federal judges and government officials. Under the Articles of Confederation, prior presidents could only dream of wielding such influence over the content of public policy and the makeup of government.

To say that the president's enumerated powers exceeded what came before, however, is not to claim that they were (or are) nearly sufficient for the challenges at hand. Several of these constitutionally acquired powers, for starters, amount to very little at all. Though presidential pardons are not subject to either congressional or judicial review, presidents historically have used them sparingly, and rarely in ways that have significant policy consequences. Meanwhile, in the contemporary era, when Congress is nearly always in session, the power to convene its members "under extraordinary circumstances" hardly exalts the president's bargaining stature. This provision may have offered meaningful leverage when

Congress met for just half of each year, as it did during the eighteenth and nineteenth centuries—when traveling from one's home district or state to the nation's capital was a treacherous affair. Today, the provision offers little.

The remaining powers explicitly conferred under the Constitution are either reactive to or shared with an adjoining branch of government. Although he is free to veto legislation, the president cannot propose it. Nor can the president directly engage in any of the daily negotiations and horse trades (offering amendments, issuing holds, and the like) occurring on Capitol Hill. Constitutionally, the president must rely on sympathetic legislators to do his bidding within the two chambers of Congress. The president, as such, resides at the tail end of the legislative process, capable of rejecting those bills he does not like (though subject to a congressional override) but lacking constitutional authority to work positively on behalf of his preferred policy agenda.

In negotiating treaties and appointing judges and bureaucrats, of course, presidents can move their preferred policy agenda forward. In both instances, though, the president's actions are formally subject to Senate approval. And if the Senate refuses to give as much—either because its members dislike his actions or they simply cannot be bothered to affirm the president's treaty or nominee—then the president must either concede defeat or, as we shall soon see, employ alternative tactics for negotiating with other states or controlling the bureaucracy.

None of this is to say that the president's veto, treaty, or appointment powers are inconsequential. On the contrary, they matter a great deal. A substantial body of scholarship convincingly documents, both empirically and theoretically, how presidents can wield these powers in order to materially affect the composition of legislation, the terms of foreign agreements, and the makeup of government. The claim here is more modest. Whatever influence the president's formal powers do confer, it is not nearly sufficient for the job at hand. Equipping a president with just his enumerated powers to meet the onslaught of public expectations is akin to sending a soldier into urban warfare with just a straw and some wadded up tissue paper. He may get by for a while. But as soon as his enemies gather and mount an offensive, his only real option is to flee or play dead.

On this point, even the Founders would have agreed. The Founders certainly did not think that they were creating a presidency capable of offering the kind of leadership demanded today. Quite the contrary, in fact. When constructing a new presidency at the Philadelphia Convention, individual delegates expressed genuine worries about the threat of executive tyranny. Antifederalists, meanwhile, remained quite convinced that the fragile system of separated powers erected by the Constitution's Framers would inevitably collapse, and from the rubble would return the very monarchy against which a revolution had just been waged. Hence, a good portion of the *Federalist Papers*, and particularly those parts authored by Alexander Hamilton, the great champion of a strong executive, was devoted to assuaging concerns that the presidency under the proposed constitution would not lapse into a monarchy. Again and again, Hamilton intoned, the Constitution delivered a president who could help overcome the deficiencies of the Article of Confederation, but decidedly not one who would assume all the powers of a despot. Indeed, his entire discussion of the executive branch in Papers No. 67 through No. 77 was framed as an effort to dispense with the "jealousies and apprehensions," which falsely imbued the presidency with "royal prerogatives" that would make even the king of Britain blush.

The Framers' predominant concerns lay in the possibility of legislative, not executive, overreach. While there was a consensus that the presidency would inject much needed "energy" into the federal government, nearly all of the delegates at Philadelphia, as well all three authors of the *Federalist Papers*—Hamilton, James Madison, and John Jay—assumed that Congress would remain the primary branch of government. Madison referred to the "general supremacy" of legislatures in Federalist No. 43 and their "impetuous vortex" of power in Federalist No. 48; Governor Edmund Randolph of Virginia insisted that it was nothing less than a "maxim" that the powers of government exercised in legislatures threaten to "swallow up the other branches"; and even John Locke, who assembled the philosophical underpinnings for much of the American system of government, called the establishment of legislative power "the first and fundamental positive law of all commonwealths." The fate of the Union crucially hinged, the Founders assumed, on goings-on within Congress. Whether the federal government would meet the first-order challenges of the day—raising taxes to pay down the debt, assembling troops needed to protect the nation's borders, and the like—would crucially depend on decisions made within the House and Senate.

But with great responsibilities, the Framers also recognized, come great risks. Indeed, it is precisely because they worried about legislative encroachments on the weaker executive branch that the Founders gave the president the veto power. And it is in no small part because they wanted to temper the influence of demagogic majorities—to "destroy the evil effects of sudden and strong excitement," as James Kent put it in his *Commentaries*—that they divided the people's branch into two chambers whose members served different, though overlapping, political jurisdictions for variable amounts of time. In this sense, the very design of the first branch of government originated in the Framers' efforts to ensure that it would not run roughshod over the other two.

What are we to make of these constitutional ruminations? One thing is plain: the disjuncture between the public's appetite for leadership and the president's constitutional capacity to deliver virtually guarantees the onset of disaffection. Swept into office on a wave of great promise and hope, the president predictably disappoints. Congresspersons, judges, and bureaucrats deliberately undercut him or simply ignore him altogether. Unforeseen events overwhelm him. And thus far we have said nothing about the many interest groups and media outlets laying still more claims on, and traps for, him. It is an impossible job, one that is sure to age, and sometimes even destroy, the hardiest of souls.

The Primacy of Power

If the most explicit powers enumerated in Article II of the Constitution do not confer what presidents need, then presidents must look elsewhere: in vaguer provisions of the Constitution; in still vaguer notions of the public good; in statutes enacted by current and past congresses; and, perhaps most strikingly, in aspects of policymaking entirely of their own making. In the chapters that follow, we bear witness to this undertaking. For now, though, a more basic point needs to be established. No matter their ideological commitments or partisan affiliations, regardless of their personal backgrounds or philosophies of governing, all presidents nearly all of the time seek to guard and expand their base of power.

Though perhaps not a single-minded pursuit, power—both its attainment and maintenance—infuses all presidential actions, whether these efforts involve bargaining with others or the acquisition of altogether new sources of influence. They are a staple of the modern American presidency and are built right into the fabric of our system of government. This is not to say, of course, that presidents only care about power. Concerns about power are not (or at least they need not be) enthralling to individual presidents, a source of intrinsic, personal gratification. Rather, concerns about power logically precede presidents' many other ulterior motivations: enacting good public policy, undoing the work of their predecessors, responding to a perceived public mandate, and securing their place in history. For in order to accomplish any of these things, presidents need power. And so it is power they seek.

A Working Definition of Presidential Power

In previous work, we, like many other scholars, have taken a rather narrow conceptual view of presidential power, one that focused exclusively on presidential efforts to alter the content of public policy. Other scholars of the presidency—such as Robert Dahl, who wrote about the capacity of one political actor to convince another to do something he otherwise would not do—have assumed a largely procedural notion of power. In this volume, we mean to invoke a much more expansive view of power than either of these formulations.

We offer here a conception of power that encompasses influence over all of the various doings of government: writing policy, designing the administrative state, interpreting and then implementing the law, or any combination thereof. By focusing on outcomes as the key determinant of power, our definition is more consonant with Richard Neustadt's view toward presidential "influence on government action." But even Neustadt's definition is too narrow for our purposes. Whereas Neustadt hones in on each president's "personal capacity to influence the conduct of men who make up the government," we allow for the possibility that presidents wield influence no matter how deficient their "personal capacity" might be; and that often, rather than relying on others to do their bidding, presidents strike out entirely on their own.

Power, thus conceived, may be in the service of any number of objectives; sometimes altering existing government practices, other times thwarting efforts by the adjoining branches of government to do so. It is most easily recognized when employed to materially alter the doings of government. And as we shall see, presidential power is nearly always harnessed in the service of changing the status quo, of reshaping and redirecting the government, and of assigning altogether new imperatives as subjects of legitimate public authority. But power matters just as much when it is deployed to protect an existing state of affairs. For reasons we discuss at greater length in the next chapter, the task of detecting and then measuring power in these two scenarios requires reference to different counterfactuals. In the former case, the relevant point of comparison is the status quo; in the latter, it is a new policy advanced by the president's political opponents. In both instances, though, the possibilities of power remain vital.

Power, too, may assume a variety of different forms. Under some circumstances, power may involve impelling—either by glint of persuasion or coercion—other political actors to do things that they otherwise would not be inclined to. Alternatively, power may involve convincing other political actors to do nothing at all, when they otherwise are predisposed to action. Once again, the relevant counterfactuals for measuring power in these two scenarios differ, but power itself is conceptually the same.

Presidential power need not involve efforts to manipulate the actions of other political actors. Instead, presidential power may involve, and frequently does involve, the exercise of direct unilateral action. Sometimes this consists of firing bureaucrats or dismantling administrative agencies with whom or which the president disagrees. Other times it involves intervening in policy domains directly; setting public policy, and then placing on others the onus of revising the new political landscape. The definition of presidential power we offer here also accommodates these types of actions, as power is to be gauged by reference to the variable outcomes it produces rather than the particular channels through which it is directed.

All of these potential sources and characterizations of presidential power, you will notice, have a common reference point: namely, government outcomes. By wielding power, presidents ensure that the federal government's behavior, and by extension the life of ordinary Americans, looks materially different than it would if only Congress and the courts were in charge. As we monitor presidents' efforts to claim and assert power, then, we must train our attention on the outcomes they produce—the ways in which government policies are written, interpreted, and implemented.

In a system of government as decentralized as our own, assessing any politician's power, including the president's, is no easy matter. Given the sheer number of actors involved in the policymaking process, it is often nearly impossible to parse the various contributions of each. Moreover, when assessing presidential power, a host of secondary considerations that too often preoccupy pundits and social scientists alike—lamentations, for instance, about the near inevitability of policy compromises, the fickleness of public opinion, and the inscrutability of government processes—easily distracts. In the next chapter, we will address the challenges of discerning power in greater detail. For now, we merely want to settle a conceptual matter: power is as power does; and presidential power, in particular, is to be measured against the outcomes it produces.

Power Considerations across the Various Branches of Government

Other political actors, to be sure, also care about power, and on occasion we see these political actors grasping for more of it. How else can we understand Chief Justice John Marshall's masterful assumption of the power of judicial review in the landmark 1803 Supreme Court case, *Marbury v. Madison*? What, if not an interest in power, explains the assembly of laws enacted in the early 1970s—which altered the budget process, prohibited the impoundment of appropriated funds, intensified oversight of the executive, and expanded the array of executive activities that would be subject to a legislative veto—that are collectively known as the "congressional resurgence"?

Similarly, we occasionally find the adjoining branches of government attempting to curb not just the policy actions of individual presidents, but the president's very claims to power. Prominent examples here include the 1973 War Powers Resolution, which sought to limit the president's military authority; *Clinton v. City of New York*, which stripped the president of his newly acquired (and congressionally delegated) line-item veto power; and the 1954 Bricker Amendment, which would have dramatically curtailed the president's ability to independently forge agreements with other nations.

Such efforts to curb presidents, it bears recalling, have generated mixed results. Though majorities, and even supermajorities, occasionally rally in order to clip the wings of a president in midflight, the sense of outrage that spurs these actions eventually, and often rather abruptly, dissipates. Since 1974, members of Congress have done precious little to ensure that presidents abide by the strict requirements of the War Powers Resolution. In the half-century since Congress failed by a single vote to pass the Bricker Amendment, presidents have relied on executive agreements with rising frequency. And though they can no longer formally strike elements of laws with which they disagree, presidents nonetheless have developed other means—for instance, signing statements, discussed at length in the subsequent chapter—by which to communicate their views about specific aspects of legislation to the bureaucrats charged with implementing them and to the judges who stand in their judgment.

Congress and the courts have the wherewithal to stall, even halt, the president's quest for power. But as soon as the attentions of these adversaries drift to other matters, and they invariably do, presidents reliably resume—if not right where they left off, then wherever their detractors put them. More to the point, we just as often witness legislators and judges disavowing what power they have, either by refusing to exercise their discretionary authority over a particular domain or by explicitly transferring it to the president. Over the years, Congress has delegated extraordinary powers over the domestic economy, the exercise of military force, the budget, state emergencies, foreign trade, and on and on. Sometimes, such delegations of power are narrowly defined and laden with various reporting requirements and the like. Just as often, though, Congress confers broad authority for the president to define and resolve some policy challenge almost entirely as he sees fit. It is unfathomable that a president would do the same.

Once such powers are granted, they are rarely retracted. Sitting on the books at any time are sweeping delegations of authority, many of which were enacted decades prior, which presidents can use to justify their policy initiatives. Consider, by way of example, the literally hundreds of emergency powers expressly granted to the president over the course of the twentieth century. These powers enabled presidents to take such extraordinary measures as enacting wage and price controls, intervening unilaterally into labor-management disputes, establishing limits on housing rents, impounding funds formally appropriated by Congress, and many, many more. Though quick to delegate these emergency powers, Congress has proved incredibly lackadaisical in formally declaring an emergency's passage. As a consequence, delegations of power during crises that had long since passed remained on the books for presidents to make of them what they willed. Indeed, it was not until the 1976 National Emergency Act that Congress got around to imposing much discipline on this state of affairs.

Just as crucially, members of Congress and the courts regularly turn a blind eye to the power-grabs of sitting presidents. Whereas power considerations only weakly motivate congressional representatives, as Terry Moe has pointed out, they utterly preoccupy presidents. It is no accident, then, that presidential power has not merely been granted. It has been taken. Successive presidents with radically different policy agendas have acted entrepreneurially to expand their influence over foreign and domestic affairs; and once acquired, these same presidents have fiercely guarded their influence against perceived judicial and legislative encroachments.

While they certainly monitor power dynamics, members of Congress and judges cannot be said to hoard their own power or throw fits any time an adjoining branch claims new power. For presidents, meanwhile, the search for power is primal. It is inconceivable that a president would delegate his own constitutional authority to execute the law to others, much as members of Congress have freely handed over extraordinary lawmaking powers to the president. And it is equally inconceivable that presidents would stand quietly by as either the judicial or legislative branches encroached on their own authority, as both have so often done when presidents have encroached on theirs.

Power and Its Constraints

Neither today's public nor tomorrow's historians—the two audiences, you will recall, that matter most to presidents—show much regard for presidents who cloak themselves in the Constitution and invite deliberation. Rather, both audiences reward the president who refuses to let the Constitution, the corpus of statutory law, or anything else disrupt the possibilities for action, for bold leadership, for a rousing insistence that he will provide the guidance and energy needed to steer the nation through its moments of peril.

Evidence abounds of presidents seeking power. Witness them relying on executive orders, executive agreements, proclamations, and national security directives in lieu of legislation and treaties; see them building and rebuilding an administrative apparatus around them; listen to them emphasizing the importance of loyalty when appointing individuals to the more distant reaches of the federal bureaucracy; look on them issuing signing statements, which allow them further opportunities to reinterpret the meaning of laws; observe them directly engaging the public; and hear them, more recently, invoking the unitary theory of the executive to justify their actions. While different presidents from different parties may advance different policy agendas, all, in one way or another, seize on opportunities to fortify their influence over the writing, interpretation, and implementation of public policy.

Logically, however, none of this implies that presidents exercise all the power that they would like. Presidents are seekers of power, not paragons of power. Ample scholarship emphasizes the historical contingencies and institutional constraints that limit a president's ability to exercise his unilateral powers, centralize authority, politicize the appointments process, issue public appeals, or refashion the political universe. Some basic facts about lawmaking further limit the president's ability to have his way: executive orders and executive agreements are not perfect substitutes for laws and treaties; signing statements do not have any legal enforceability; and the formal powers that presidents retain are entirely insufficient to meet the extraordinary expectations deposited at the White House's doorstep. Even in the policy domain where all observers concede that presidential power reaches its apex—that is, in war—presidents often must confront mobilized opposition within Congress and the courts. Presidential power is still contested, and it always shall be. Indeed, when presidential power becomes absolute, then we must stop calling it "presidential."

We will have more to say about the very real limits of presidential power in this book's final chapter, for they go some distance toward explaining why individual presidents, in their rhetoric, may preach prudence and humility; and why, in their actions, they may not lay claim to anywhere

near the power that they would like. But make no mistake: such incanta-
tions and temperance are largely the product of political strategy. They are
not disavowals of power. Given the opportunity, presidents nearly always
lay claim to new powers, just as they resist the sporadic efforts of others to limit existing ones. Power consolidation is the presidential modus
operandi.

CHAPTER 2

Bearing Witness

To find presidents seeking power, we need not look far. At nearly every turn, we see signs of presidential entrepreneurialism. In some instances, presidents create altogether new policy devices over which they exert nearly complete control. In others, they reorganize the federal bureaucracy in ways that suit their power and policy interests. And even when a policy would appear settled once and for all, presidents still look for ways to have their say over its interpretation and implementation.

The case studies that follow hardly amount to an exhaustive accounting of such activities. Presidents do a great deal more than just sign national security directives, appoint policy czars, and issue signing statements. And some presidential activities—such as, most recently, Obama's unilateral dismantling of federally enacted education policy through the granting of state waivers—represent significantly greater power grabs than those documented here. Still, in these three domains we see the sheer variety of presidential efforts to augment their power, just as we learn to appreciate the differences between a president's appetite for power and its realization.

FABRICATING A NEW POWER

On September 14, 2001, the U.S. Congress passed a joint resolution authorizing President George W. Bush to "use all necessary and appropriate force against those nations, organizations, or persons he determines planned, authorized, committed, or aided the terrorist attacks that occurred on September 11." By granting the president such broad military authority, Congress publicly declared to the world America's intention to wage all-out war on al-Qaeda and its allies. What neither the world nor Congress knew, however, was that the decision to eliminate al-Qaeda had already been made in secret by the White House ten days earlier—on September 4, one week before 9/11. Indeed, as early as June 7, the National Security Council (NSC) had presented a draft of a presidential directive to key members of the cabinet. By September, that draft had become National Security Presidential Directive (NSPD) 9, which the president was preparing to sign before the terrorist attacks; and ultimately did sign, in an amended version, in October.

At no time was Congress informed about NSPD 9. Indeed, it was not until Defense Secretary Donald Rumsfeld appeared before the 9/11 Commission in March 2004 that the directive's existence became known. And yet the objectives of NSPD 9 were startlingly similar to those laid out by the congressional resolution of September 14. According to Rumsfeld, these were: to eliminate the al-Qaeda network; to use all elements of national power to do so—diplomatic, military, economic, intelligence, information and law enforcement; and to eliminate sanctuaries for al-Qaeda and related terrorist networks—and if diplomatic efforts to do so failed, to consider additional measures. The extent to which NSPD 9 actually authorized such actions is unknown. To this day, the contents of the directive remain classified.

In this way, Congress's authorization for the "War on Terror"—widely considered to be one of the most expansive delegations of military authority to a president in U.S. history—was supplemented by a secret order from the president himself to take aggressive action against al-Qaeda. To this end, Bush relied on a tool utilized by every president since Harry Truman, the national security directive. Presidents have called these directives many things and deployed them for a variety of purposes. Ultimately, however, modern presidents have come to use classified security directives as a way of centralizing authority within the White House and insulating executive decision making from congressional and public oversight.

The Origins of National Security Directives

The rise of national security directives can be traced back to the centralization of military and foreign policy decision making in the executive branch following World War II. After the surprise attacks on Pearl Harbor, prominent members of the armed forces realized that managing military intelligence and coordinating modern global warfare required unifying the Army, Navy, and other branches of the armed forces under a single banner. Once the war ended, military personnel immediately began pushing for a national security apparatus that could effectively gather intelligence and efficiently coordinate both emergency and long-term policy decisions among various federal departments (including the State Department). After hashing out a plan that met with approval from various military and civilian department heads, President Truman sent a bill to Congress outlining the new unification structure. This bill, with some legislative tweaks, became the National Security Act of 1947.

Debate on the legislation was spirited but short, since nearly everyone in Congress agreed that the national security system needed to be centralized and streamlined. As the *New York Times* noted at the time, Democrats and Republicans did not disagree about the military's unification: "President Truman is vigorously in favor of it. So, apparently, is the leadership of both major parties." Most of the discussion in the House and Senate centered on precisely how the military should be unified, what the unified apparatus should be called, to what extent the Air Force and Marines should be included, and how much power should be accorded the head of the unified forces. In the end, the final bill was broad and sweeping, creating the structure of the modern American military and national security bureaucracy as we know it today: all armed forces were unified under a new cabinet-level office, the secretary of defense; the Central Intelligence Agency was officially established as the central body for gathering intelligence; and the National Security Council (NSC) was created as a means of coordinating decision making between various branches of government.

According to the final legislation, the NSC's function was to "advise the President with respect to the integration of domestic, foreign, and military policies relating to the national security so as to enable the military services and the other departments and agencies of the Government to cooperate more effectively in matters involving the national security." The National Security Act went on to list the staff members who would make up the council (the president, vice president, the secretaries of state and defense, and the secretaries and undersecretaries of other executive and military departments) and to enumerate the duties of the NSC. Among the clauses enumerating these duties was Section 101-d, which stated:

"The Council shall, from time to time, make such recommendations, and such other reports to the President as it deems appropriate or as the President may require." From this short phrase, the broad power of national security directives was born.

The breadth of discretion granted the president under the National Security Act did not escape all members of Congress. On the Senate floor, Edward Robertson referred to the bill as a "blank check," arguing that Congress's "traditional role as the sole legislative agency of the government" would receive "a drastic setback" were the bill to pass in its existing form. Senator Robertson suggested revising the legislation to include on the NSC "the chairmen of those congressional committees most intimately concerned with the broad aspects of national security." Representative Wayne Owens proposed that executive authority over the new Security Council be curtailed. After reading Section 101-d aloud, he suggested that the NSC be required to provide copies of all its advisory papers and reports not only to the president, but also to the Speaker of the House and the President of the Senate. Owens bemoaned the fact that "there has not been one word said about the Congress, the representatives of the people themselves, having one word to say about the plans that are being made 1 year or 2 or 3 or 4 years ahead" within the NSC, and he called his plan to include congressional leaders "a safeguard which the people need." Despite this plea, Congress summarily rejected Owens's proposed amendment.

In part, Congress members' reluctance to establish stricter oversight of the NSC and the president stemmed from a legitimate concern about the protection of highly sensitive classified information. In response to Representative Owens's suggestion that the NSC report all its research and policy memos to congressional leaders, Representative Wadsworth replied: "If you do that, then you will be reporting to the entire world." Many members expressed the hope that the NSC would provide the president with vital and timely information necessary to safeguard the nation from future attacks—which, after all, was part of his constitutional function as commander in chief. Moreover, Congress members expressed their belief that the existing system of government would adequately check the exercise of executive authority. It was Congress, after all, that still controlled the appropriations for all aspects of the security apparatus: as Senator Wayne Morse succinctly put it, "We are the ones who vote the funds."

And Representative Chester Holifield asserted a still broader belief in the values of United States and its leaders: "I, for one, have too much faith in the American people and in their devotion to democratic ways—too much trust in the President and the Members of Congress whom the people elect—to fear the establishment of dictatorship in this country."

Initially, at least, national security directives were not conceived as a pathway for circumventing existing checks on executive power. In authorizing the executive to request information and reports from his National Security Council, Congress intended merely to provide the president with the capability to "fashion a more definite, a more coordinated, a more responsible and effective military policy." Congress members imagined that NSC policy papers would aid in the president's ability to exercise his existing authority. Rather than running an improvisational war, as many thought FDR had done, future presidents were expected to deploy NSC policy papers and the other resources of the National Security Act to rationalize the process of going to war.

As with most administrative laws, however, the National Security Act had unintended effects. Though created to unify the decision-making process on foreign and military policy, the act actually exacerbated bureaucratic infighting among the federal departments. To placate the Navy, its former chief James Forrestal was named the first secretary of defense, which led the Army, Marines, and Air Force to jockey for position at the National Security Council. Meanwhile, the rift between the armed forces (now unified under Defense) and the State Department continued to grow, as each department vied for the president's attention. And amidst all this conflict, the newly created CIA attempted to carve out a place for itself as an independent agency even as it relied on preexisting intelligence institutions within the armed forces to share information. With it quickly becoming a bureaucratic fiasco, President Truman largely avoided the National Security Council in its early days. Indeed, of the council's first fifty-five meetings, the president personally presided over only eleven.

Truman still needed a way to unify national security policy and disseminate policy decisions across all executive branch departments, however. To accomplish this, he turned to National Security Council policy papers (NSCs). Arising out of the language in Section 101-d, these papers in initial drafts contained research and policy proposals prepared by various departments and agencies and sent to the president's desk. Sometimes, a specific agency such as the CIA or the State Department would draft a proposal on its own, usually because it wanted the president to entertain a certain policy. In other instances, President Truman would request that a department explore the feasibility of a specific policy directly. In either instance, the president would examine the paper's proposal and discuss its findings with his closest advisors in the White House. If he deemed the proposal to be the best course of action, the president would sign off, making it an official NSC policy paper. These papers constituted direct orders from the president to the state and military apparatus on issues of national security and foreign policy.

It was in this last step—signing off on certain policy recommendations, thereby transforming them from *reports to* the president into *orders from* the president—that national security directives really came into being. Congress clearly intended NSC papers to be research reports, prepared by various departments under the NSC, which would help the president make decisions. By signing off on them and issuing them back to the NSC departments as orders, Truman subtly turned them into a decision-making tool in and of themselves. Like an executive order, this new tool streamlined decision making and provided a clear statement of executive policy. But unlike an executive order, or any other unilateral directive available to the president, this tool was classified and therefore not subject to congressional review. Indeed, by rejecting the Owens Amendment, Congress had explicitly forsaken its own oversight over NSC reports.

It is not clear that Truman saw his appropriation of NSC papers as a run around congressional authority, and there is little in his use of these new security directives to suggest any explicit aim toward expanding presidential power. More likely, Truman was merely attempting to cut through bureaucratic infighting and set a clear policy agenda for various departments and agencies. Some of Truman's directives were specific plans of action for the CIA or the State Department. Others, such as NSC 68, laid out a general policy of Cold War containment relevant to all armed forces and foreign-service diplomats. Overall, these papers tended to remain within the confines of what the National Security Act had set out to do— streamline decision making and allow for long-range policy planning— albeit via a different avenue than Congress originally imagined. Truman was coordinating national security policy, as was his constitutional duty as commander in chief. That he did it via directives rather than reports likely seemed, at the time at least, a matter of little consequence.

Truman's successors in the oval office, however, pushed further. Subsequent presidents were more than willing to expand on the vague relationship between the president and the NSC enshrined in Section 101-d. Indeed, they fully recognized the utility of national security directives and adapted them to suit their own purposes. The centralized and classified nature of authority afforded by such directives has made them a remarkably flexible tool for carrying out executive agendas, even in the face of growing congressional opposition.

The Evolution of NSDs

Under President Eisenhower, the use of national security directives was formalized, and a framework for creating security policy was established that remains largely intact to this day. Eisenhower appointed Robert Cutler as special assistant for national security affairs, a precursor to the position of national security advisor, which currently oversees the NSC. Cutler, in turn, streamlined the process by which policy was formulated and recommendations were made. In his own words, Cutler created a "policy hill." Lower level staffers in various departments, often State or Defense, conducted research and formulated policy proposals. These proposals then worked their way up the chain of command. If consensus was reached at the departmental level, the head of the department would present its recommendations to the National Security Council. If the NSC and the president approved it, this document would then be signed by the president, directing all relevant individuals and agencies to act according to its recommendations. In this way, the president stood firmly atop the "policy hill," thereby centralizing authority over all security decisions within the White House.

Proceeding from the precedent set by Truman, the Eisenhower administration expanded the use of national security directives to overcome specific detriments to its influence. As the first Republican president since Herbert Hoover, Eisenhower inherited a massive amount of government policy not to his liking. Some of this policy was still relevant; other parts of it Eisenhower was keen to overturn or change to suit his own agenda. Eisenhower used national security directives, in no small part, to clarify the policies of his new administration. In his first NSC papers, the president laid out his approach: unless otherwise specified, all existing presidential directives would remain in place. This cemented the status of national security directives as not merely short-term initiatives applicable under a given administration, but as policies that carried over from one administration to the next. Having affirmed the power of such directives generally, however, Eisenhower deployed additional NSC papers to repeal specific Truman directives with which he disagreed. And so, for example, during his first year in office, Eisenhower signed NSC 162/2, which simultaneously repealed Truman's NSC 68 and articulated a New Look policy emphasizing the use of trade and international economic policy in the fight against the Soviets. By both cementing the precedent for using security directives as a tool of executive authority and implementing them to overturn previous administrations' policy, Eisenhower established a template for centralizing decision making within the executive branch via security directives.

Upon coming to office, President Kennedy also wanted to distinguish his policy agenda from that of his predecessor. Again, the previous eight years of opposing party rule had created a bureaucracy whose loyalty he could not trust. (Recall, for example, the dubious policy advice that Kennedy received leading up to the ill-fated Bay of Pigs disaster at the beginning of his term.) Unlike Eisenhower, however, Kennedy's solution to the problem of cutting through existing bureaucracy was to largely avoid the bureaucracy altogether. While he left in place the existing security policymaking apparatus set up by Eisenhower, Kennedy primarily relied on ad-hoc committees and small policy groups to furnish policy recommendations. This approach deemphasized the importance of the NSC, but in no way did it deemphasize the president's use of national security directives. On the contrary, Kennedy's reliance on a small but diverse cohort of trusted advisors—the so-called "best and the brightest"—merely centralized authority further within the White House.

Under Kennedy, national security directives took on a new, formal name: they were now called National Security Action Memorandums (NSAM). This established a precedent, continued by subsequent presidents, of officially renaming security directives immediately upon entering office.

Exactly why Kennedy chose to rename NSC papers NSAMs is unclear. The indeterminacy, however, may well have been the point. Perhaps no piece of evidence more clearly evinces the way presidents have used national security directives than the fact that each administration feels the need to rename the tool and then expand on its usage. In this way, presidents have long been able to gloss over not only the contents of national security directives, but also their very existence as an institutional tool for administering policy. By constantly changing their name, their function, and how they were created, presidents have been able to consistently use national security directives for new purposes without attracting unwanted attention from Congress or the public.

The Kennedy administration used its newly created NSAMs to implement a broad range of policy initiatives. In addition to authorizing covert military actions abroad, Kennedy expanded the interpretation of "national security" to encompass international economic issues. The administration used NSAMs to formulate positions on the gold policy of the U.S. Treasury, the effects of U.S. investment in Europe, and the terms of development loans for the U.S. Agency for International Development. These policy initiatives all fell loosely under the purview of the president's Article II powers. By using national security directives to authorize and coordinate such policies, however, Kennedy was able to classify his decisions as top secret. (Their contents were not made publicly available until several decades after his death.) In this way, Kennedy deployed national security directives as a way of insulating high-level decision making from congressional or public oversight—a practical necessity for some security issues, perhaps, though likely not for policies pertaining to sugar imports from Latin America, which also appeared in Kennedy's policy record. The president seemed to relish the advantage of secrecy that security directives afforded: in less than three years in office, he issued a whopping 272 NSAMs.

As presidents Johnson, Nixon, Ford, and Carter continued to use national security directives (under various names) to secretly implement an increasingly wide array of policy initiatives, critics of expanding executive authority called for greater public accountability. This tension came to a head during the Reagan and George H.W. Bush administrations. Upon entering office, Reagan immediately initiated an aggressive policy of covert action to undermine communist governments in Latin America. In particular, he allocated $19 million to the CIA to support Contra paramilitary groups rebelling against Nicaragua's Sandinista government. Congress discovered that Reagan had authorized military action without congressional authority and reacted by passing the Boland Amendment, which explicitly prohibited the executive branch from using military funds in Nicaragua. Yet despite this blatant check by the legislature, the president continued to fund covert CIA actions. Eventually, this controversy led to the Iran-Contra scandal, in which the Tower Commission found that NSC policy groups set up by President Reagan (outlined in NSDD 77) had negotiated illegal arms sales to Iran, allegedly to fund Contra activities in Nicaragua without using military funding. Despite the publicity the scandal received, Reagan escaped formal censure, and those administration members who were indicted had their cases thrown out on appeal or were pardoned by Reagan's successor, George H.W. Bush.

In the aftermath of the Iran-Contra scandal Congress created a subcommittee to investigate the scope of presidents' national security powers. The subcommittee was particularly concerned about the use of national security directives to circumvent the legislative process. A report authorized by the subcommittee found that security directives regularly embody not just specific instructions for executing policy but also "foreign and military policy making," which did "not appear to be issued under statutory authority conferred by Congress and thus do not have the force and effect of law." In the wake of this investigation, however, the Bush administration stonewalled. The NSC refused to declassify any existing security directives or make their contents available to subcommittee members. Upon being summoned to testify before a subcommittee hearing, National Security Advisor Colin Powell declined to appear, citing executive privilege.

Recent presidents Clinton, George W. Bush, and Obama have continued to implement and expand the use and scope of national security directives. Exactly how these presidents have used such directives, however, remains largely unknown. Unlike other tools presidents have for unilateral action, such as proclamations or executive orders, national security directives are not subject to the Freedom of Information Act. They are not published in the National Register, and indeed their very existence often remains unknown. Even the subsequent declassification of certain directives is entirely at the discretion of the former presidents who issued them. Often, these documents are made public by presidential libraries decades after a president has stepped down from public office. And even then, certain particularly sensitive directives are at least partially redacted. Given Congress's inability to successfully exert any pressure on presidents to release the content of national security directives, we may never know exactly how Bush and Obama have used this tool of executive authority. We may not ever learn the exact contents of NSPD 9, the presidential directive George W. Bush used to authorize America's war on al-Qaeda.

Fashioning for Oneself

Based on how national security directives have evolved over time, we can hazard a guess as to how recent presidents have used them. They are likely being used for a wide range of tasks, from asserting long-range strategic goals to authorizing immediate covert actions. And they are likely being used to articulate and implement policy across a broad spectrum of issues, from terrorism to nuclear disarmament to trade and economic policy. Note, though, that when it comes to national security directives, we are not bearing witness to the full scope of their use. To acertain how presidents and their close advisors are shaping the policies that augment their authority and determine our collective future, archival research may bear less fruit than imagination.

The rise of national security directives exemplifies the way modern presidents nurture the powers of their institution. When faced with an obstacle to their authority, presidents use whatever tools are at their disposal to circumvent that obstacle. Often, presidents expand on a preexisting power or apply a previous statute in a new way in order to realize their desired outcome. In the case of security directives, Congress initially granted to Truman a way to coordinate foreign and military policy within the growing executive branch bureaucracy. For his part, though, Truman rather promptly paved a way for future presidents to create policy across a broad spectrum of issues without bureaucratic interference or public scrutiny. And once a president creates a new tool of authority—or appropriates a previous tool in a new way—a precedent is established for subsequent presidents' adoption and adaption of this tool to suit their own purposes.

Thus each new administration builds on the power accrued by the previous administration, producing, over time, a rich, potentially controversial, but immediately unknowable body of public policy.

A Czar Is Born

When President Barack Obama took office in 2009, he assumed, even more than most presidents, the weight of enormous expectations. The country was in trouble: abroad, the military was enmeshed in two wars, and international opinion of the United States was low; at home, the economy was in the midst of one of the worst recessions in its history, with millions of Americans losing their jobs and homes. As a candidate, Obama had spent the previous two years convincing the American people that he would provide the leadership needed to extract the nation from this catastrophe. On Inauguration Day, after swearing to "faithfully execute the office of President of the United States," Obama reminded the public of his domestic policy mandate:

> The state of our economy calls for action, bold and swift. And we
> will act, not only to create new jobs, but to lay a new foundation
> for growth. We will build the roads and bridges, the electric grids
> and digital lines that feed our commerce and bind us together. We'll
> restore science to its rightful place, and wield technology's wonders
> to raise health care's quality and lower its cost. We will harness the
> sun and the winds and the soil to fuel our cars and run our facto-
> ries. And we will transform our schools and colleges and universities
> to meet the demands of a new age. All this we can do. All this we
> will do.

The months of campaigning on "hope" and "change" were over. Now it was time to realize that hope. It was time to act.

But the new president had a problem. In order to deliver on his promises, Obama had to use the institutional powers granted to his office. This meant relying on the vast, complex bureaucracy of the executive branch—nearly 2 million people—to help him "faithfully execute" his agenda. Even more worrisome than its massive size was the basic fact that the bureaucracy was not of his making; it was organized and led by preexisting officials whose interests did not necessarily match his own. Given this obstacle, how could the president hope to achieve his ambitious policy goals—goals that the public strongly expected him to fulfill?

The most obvious answer is the constitutional one: the president has the power to appoint cabinet members to oversee the various bureaucratic offices under his purview. By selecting leaders whose opinions and loyalties he trusted, Obama theoretically could ensure that the full powers of the executive branch would be directed toward addressing his stated priorities.

In practice, however, the constitutional solution is flawed for at least two reasons. The first centers on efficiency considerations. When the Founders granted the president power to appoint a cabinet, they could not have imagined that the executive would oversee such a massive bureaucracy. Through cabinet appointments alone, the president cannot possibly control the many layers of executive bureaucracy. Cabinet secretaries, for all their use to the president, are also beholden to the administrative units beneath them. They only have so many resources to reconfigure the departments they oversee. Moreover, a cabinet secretary's influence, however gleaned, is strictly limited to her own department. When working to develop alternative energy sources, for example, the secretary of energy cannot assign a task to someone in the Environmental Protection Agency without jumping multiple bureaucratic hurdles and bypassing various lines of authority. And since a president's interest in control relates to his interest in policy, the fragmented nature of the appointment system unavoidably proves wanting.

The second flaw in the president's constitutional prerogative to appoint a cabinet is the Constitution itself: specifically, the Senate's confirmation power over all cabinet appointments. As a check on executive power, the Founders granted the Senate power to oversee the appointment process, ultimately voting yea or nay on the president's proposed candidates. While Senate confirmation requires a simple majority, the votes of at least 60 senators are needed to break a filibuster and bring the candidates to an up or down vote. Even with a substantial Democratic majority, President Obama could not expect his cabinet and subcabinet nominees to breeze through the Senate. Recent confirmation battles in the Bush and Clinton administrations had made it clear that confirmation hearings would be a contentious, protracted process. So even if Obama felt confident that he could use experienced, loyal cabinet members to effectively manage the bureaucracy and achieve his ends—and to be clear, he could not—he knew that these confirmations would take months to pass through the Senate; and further, that some cabinet choices might not get confirmed at all.

Faced with lofty public expectations to achieve policy goals, an inefficient bureaucracy that did not necessary share his goals, and a constitutional solution to the bureaucratic problem that promised to be neither efficient nor politically expedient, Obama did what many presidents before him had done: he sidestepped the bureaucracy and the Senate and appointed czars.

A New Administrative Post

"Czar" is political shorthand for a special policy adviser who is appointed by the president, without congressional oversight, for the purposes of coordinating and centralizing the activities of various executive branch offices. The exact origins of the term are somewhat disputed. Colloquially, the first presidential appointee to be named "czar" was Nicholas Biddle, who took office in 1822 and oversaw the second bank of the United States; and whose powers, some charged, approached those of Russia's imperial ruler at the time. During the New Deal Era and the Second World War, the Roosevelt administration created a variety of special positions to oversee the rapid expansion of government programs. Critics of the administration began calling these Roosevelt appointments "czars": Leon Henderson, for example, who directed the new Office of Price Administration, became known as the "Czar of Prices."

The term *czar* became commonplace by the second half of the twentieth century, when the executive branch experienced its most dramatic expansion. Presidents Nixon and Reagan both touted their use of high-profile "drug czars," who were appointed unilaterally (this particular position was eventually formalized and made subject to Senate confirmation under the George H.W. Bush administration). Under the presidency of George W. Bush, the use of czars reached dramatic new heights, jumping to twenty-eight from seven under President Clinton.

Picking up where Bush left off, President Obama has continued to rely on czars, and to a greater extent than any previous president before him. In his first three years in office, Obama appointed thirty-three policy czars without any formal congressional oversight. Some of these positions oversaw broad policy arenas (healthcare czar, energy czar, Middle East czar). Others were more focused on overseeing specific issues (cybersecurity czar, domestic violence czar, Asian carp czar) or even specific legislation and policy initiatives (auto recovery czar, stimulus accountability czar, Guantanamo Bay closure czar).

Public and Congressional Reaction

Obama's propensity to appoint and rely on czars sparked a heated debate about the scope of executive power. As early as May 2009, opponents of the administration began invoking czars as an illustration of broad presidential overreach. Republican senator John McCain joked that Obama had "more czars than the Romanovs." Demonstrators at a rally in Washington protesting big government held signs that read, "Czars belong in Russia." And Karl Rove, a former advisor to President George W. Bush, expressed his concerns via Twitter: "Darned if I can figure out all the czars, except a giant expansion of presidential power." His response holds a twinge of unintended irony: Rove himself had been the Bush administration's "chief domestic policy coordinator," and his appointment was not subject to Senate approval; he had been, in other words, Bush's "domestic policy czar."

Congress, for its part, did not take kindly to Obama's avoidance of the Senate confirmation process. Indeed, many of its members viewed czar appointments as a power grab worthy of a dictator's emulation. In a speech on the Senate floor, Republican senator Lamar Alexander proclaimed the practice "undemocratic." His colleague in the House, Republican Jack Kingston, chided the Obama administration for creating a parallel government "that is outside of the Constitution and the authority of Congress." Nor did the criticism come from Republicans alone. Robert Byrd, the most senior Democrat in the Senate and a regular champion of the Constitution, was concerned enough to write an open letter to President Obama. To his mind, appointing czars was dangerous and potentially unlawful:

"They [the czars] rarely testify before congressional committees and often shield the information and decision-making process behind the assertion of executive privilege. . . . The rapid and easy accumulation of power by White House staff can threaten the constitutional system of checks and balances."

In addition to diminishing Congress, the appointment of czars, some argue, also undermines the president's own cabinet members. Putting someone else in charge of a policy area that normally falls under a specific department effectively transfers authority from the administrative state into the White House. When this happens, say critics, the hierarchies required to make bureaucracy function properly begin to crumble. When Obama appointed Carol Browner "energy and climate czar" in 2009, former energy secretary Spencer Abraham called out the president publicly for undermining his own secretary of energy, Steven Chu. "I would hope that the White House lets Dr. Chu have the authority he needs to get his job done," Abraham said. "If there is the impression, rightly or wrongly, that the authority doesn't lie in the seventh floor of the [Energy Department's headquarters] then you'll spend a lot of time with people trying to bypass the process and go around the department to where they think the authority does lie." Andrew Card, former chief of staff for President George W. Bush, summed up this criticism in a sentence: "It will I think have the tendency to cause cabinet members to feel as if they're subordinate."

For the Obama administration and its defenders, however, czars are instrumental in solving the country's myriad problems—and hence, in mitigating their own political challenges. Rather than causing disruption, czars give presidents a way to streamline and centralize the vast bureaucracy of the executive branch. As Leon Panetta, Obama's secretary of defense and a former chief of staff to President Clinton, put it: "[It is] a very complex bureaucracy . . . the simplest way to cut through it is . . . at the White House level." Former White House press secretary Robert Gibbs echoed this sentiment: "Lots of these [czars] are designed to bring many different efforts together and coordinate them in a way that is more structured and efficient than the governmental work chart might ordinarily allow."

Many of the administration's defenders also see appointing policy czars as a necessary response to the increasingly protracted Senate confirmation process for presidential appointments. These defenders point to research on the persistent gridlock of the current appointment process, which leaves important seats within the executive branch empty for long stretches of time and endangers the government's ability to function properly. Czar appointments, which avoid the confirmation process, reduce the hardships of transitions between administrations, allowing the president and his team to "hit the ground running" on policy matters of vital national importance.

More often than not, though, Obama has forgone justifications entirely, choosing to ignore the metadebate about the constitutionality or political efficacy of czar appointments. Instead, he has simply acted, repeatedly anointing czars to play crucial roles in implementing some of his most high-profile policy priorities. Nowhere was this more evident than in his administration's handling of the auto industry crisis.

The Auto Bailout

Upon entering office in 2009, Obama faced an immediate challenge: the auto industry was tanking. Of the three largest American auto companies, General Motors and Chrysler were in particularly dire straits. (Ford was also eager to find a solid line of credit, but it had money set aside to aid in its turnaround.) Not only were these companies losing revenue—thanks to the recession and rising gas prices—but they also had committed themselves to costly bargaining agreements with United Auto Workers (UAW). The agreements paid unionized workers in the auto plants a rate far above what competitors in Japan and other countries offered their workers. Employees at GM plants received particularly generous benefit packages, and both companies appeared to suffer from poor management. The companies' financial reports contained unrealistically optimistic projections of future revenue, and there was a dearth of new products in their development pipelines. In short, the major auto companies were in danger of going under, unless they could find a quick and significant influx of cash. With credit markets frozen and no private investors interested in stepping into the breach, the Big Three turned to the White House for assistance.

The prospect of a bailout of the auto industry put the new president in a bind. Many of his cabinet appointees had not cleared the Senate yet, and already he desperately needed advice on the proper course of action. The stakes, moreover, were enormous. Investing billions of dollars in giant manufacturing companies put obvious strains on the president's efforts to secure a $700 billion economic recovery bill. Polls showed that the public, already wary of the president's proposed stimulus plan, was not especially keen on the idea of a costly bill that used tax dollars to bail out giant, mismanaged corporations. And yet the consequences of doing nothing and letting the auto companies fail were equally daunting. More than 1.5 million people were employed directly by the Big Three; another 1.5 to 2 million had jobs in industries that relied on the auto manufacturers for business. A massive industry failure could potentially cost more than 3 million people their jobs, 2 million people their health care, and an additional three-quarters of a million people their retirement pensions. Inevitably, such devastating loses would ripple outward into other sectors of an already weak economy, potentially pushing a recession into a full-blown depression.

With all this in mind, Obama set out to make a firm and immediate decision regarding the auto industry crisis. During the presidential transition, President Bush and Obama's policy teams approved an initial investment of government funds into General Motors and Chrysler. Then, in office, Obama set forth on his own to create a Presidential Task Force on the Auto Industry. To help the task force coordinate its efforts and advise it on policy recommendations, the newly inaugurated president also appointed a special advisor to the Treasury Secretary tasked with managing the crisis. To fill this new "car czar" position, he appointed Steve Rattner.

Who was Rattner? He was a former financial journalist for the *New York Times*, who left the paper in 1982 to work as an investment banker for Lehman Brothers. He was an extremely successful corporate leader who rose through the ranks of Lehman, Morgan Stanley, and Lazard before making millions as the cofounder of Quadrangle Group. And he was a major contributor to the Democratic Party and backer of Obama's presidential campaign, a man who *New York Magazine* once called the "D.N.C.'s A.T.M." There was one thing, however, that Rattner was not: an expert on the auto industry. As the head of UAW, the CEO of General Motors, and many critics of the administration all complained, Rattner knew little about the specifics of the auto crisis. Indeed, Rattner himself subsequently admitted that he "came into this project with . . . less than zero knowledge of the auto industry. Nearly all I knew was what I had read in the popular press."

Though he may not have known much going in, Rattner quickly became the administration's point person on the auto crisis. Drawing on his own financial experience, he adopted a private equity approach to the problem. General Motors and Chrysler's books were a mess, but the underlying problem, Rattner thought, was one of management. An influx of capital and the right management could turn the companies around. Rattner thus became the deciding vote within the administration in favor of bailing out the auto industry—a bailout that ended up totaling over $80 billion dollars. With Chrysler, the government was able to use its own investment to entice a deal with the foreign automaker Fiat, which took control of over 20 percent of the company and placed its own leaders in top management positions. With GM, the White House played an even more significant role. The Presidential Task Force instructed the Treasury Department to become the majority investor in the auto company and to oversee its bankruptcy. Rattner was central in this process: he led negotiations between GM and UAW to create a new bargaining agreement; and he fired GM CEO Rick Wagoner, replacing him with Ed Whitacre, a former CEO of AT&T who, like Rattner, had no prior experience in the auto industry.

Rattner and the Presidential Task Force were given a tremendous amount of leeway by the president to act quickly and decisively. As a result, the entire bailout and restructuring process took a period of mere months. By the summer of 2009, Rattner's job was essentially complete. And since the bailout took place in the midst of the administration's first months in office—a time of flurried action on everything from financial stimulus to early plans for health care reform—not as much attention was focused on the auto bailouts as might have existed under other circumstances.

Many of the actions Rattner himself took as car czar were behind the scenes. When he recruited Whitacre for the CEO job, for example, Rattner did not meet with him at the White House—he took him out for a steak dinner in downtown Washington. Eventually, as more details came out about Rattner—and as Rattner later faced a probe into allegations of misconduct during his time at Quadrangle—criticisms of the administration's czar approach to the auto bailouts escalated. During the 2012 Republican primary, for instance, Mitt Romney and others argued that the Obama administration had not been transparent in its dealings with auto companies. In spite of this criticism, however, President Obama got what he wanted: the issue was taken care of expediently and, all things considered, without much public fuss. Under the guidance of the czar and Presidential Task Force, the Treasury Department was able to effectively coordinate with other agencies and departments within the executive bureaucracy to secure a complex, multibillion dollar bailout with relative ease.

While advocates and opponents of the president's czar appointments may disagree on the merits of the practice, they all agree on its outcome: the executive's increased control over public policy. Czar appointments provide the president with a way of taking control of the executive branch's bureaucracy and increasing the odds that his preferred policies will be enacted. They also insulate him from public scrutiny, allowing the White House to pursue a wider array of policy matters with relatively more discretion. If the president has a special interest in devoting resources to a specific policy agenda, he can use a czar to coordinate the various offices within the vast executive bureaucracy and bring the full powers of the executive branch to bear on the issue. Moreover, the use of a czar is particularly appealing, as it deprives the Senate of the ability to deny the president his preferred choices to lead the bureaucracy, thereby ensuring that the president will be able to fill the position with a person who shares his policy preferences and on whose loyalty he can depend. In this way, czars provide an avenue for presidents to partially avoid not one but two potential obstacles in their quest for power: the inertia of government bureaucracy and the gaze of congressional oversight.

Signing Statements: Aspirations for Power

When Congress calls the president to task for overstepping his constitutional boundaries, or when legislators attempt to curtail presidential power by passing bills that hinder his ability to act, presidents tend to respond in one of two ways. Frequently, the president simply ignores congressional calls to curb presidential power, as the Reagan administration did when Congress held hearings on the use of national security directives. At other times, however, presidents feel compelled to publicly defend the scope of their authority. These latter instances illuminate the administration's views on presidential power, making manifest the true aspirational goals of the presidency.

In April 2011, for example, Congress passed a short-term budget agreement in order to temporarily avoid a government shutdown. In a victory for Republicans, the bipartisan bill also included a special section—Section 2262—on czars. As discussed above, legislators had long opposed President Obama's use of czars to coordinate executive branch policy. In an effort to curb the practice, Section 2262 of the new budget contained language explicitly prohibiting the president from using discretionary money to fund four czar positions: the health care czar, climate change czar, urban affairs czar, and auto industry czar. Finally, it seemed, Congress was taking a stand: the executive branch could no longer avoid oversight of crucial bureaucratic appointments.

By inserting the restriction on czars into an emergency budget bill, congressional Republicans put Obama in a bind. On the one hand, his administration relied heavily on czar appointments to cut through an otherwise intransigent executive bureaucracy. By signing the legislation, Obama would set a precedent for future encroachments into executive branch hiring. On the other hand, vetoing the bill was politically untenable: aside from the small section on czars, the short-term budget was exactly what the president had been urging Congress to put on his desk for weeks. With funding about to run out at the end of the budgetary process, Obama could not afford to send the legislation back to Congress with the hope of it being rewritten. He had to take the bill as it was and either sign it or not.

Rather than bow to fate, the president managed to slip out of the knot Congress had tied around him. Obama went ahead and signed the budget bill. At the same time, however, he issued a "signing statement"—a memo from the president that offers commentary on a piece of legislation he is approving. Obama's statement on the budget asserted that, while he generally approved of the bill, he explicitly rejected Congress's limits on his authority to hire czars. As he put it:

> Section 2262 of the Act would prohibit the use of funds for several positions that involve providing advice directly to the President. The President has well-established authority to supervise and oversee

the executive branch, and to obtain advice in furtherance of this supervisory authority. The President also has the prerogative to obtain advice that will assist him in carrying out his constitutional responsibilities, and do so not only from executive branch officials and employees outside the White House, but also from advisers within it.

Legislative efforts that significantly impede the President's ability to exercise his supervisory and coordinating authorities or to obtain the views of the appropriate senior advisers violate the separation of powers by undermining the President's ability to exercise his con-stitutional responsibilities and take care that the laws be faithfully executed. Therefore, the executive branch will construe section 2262 not to abrogate these Presidential prerogatives.

Never mind the explicit and binding language of Section 2262, Obama declared. He would "construe" it in a way that directly contradicted its plain meaning, thereby leaving the president's power to appoint czars undisturbed. As one reporter summarized at the time, the administration's message to legislators was, "We know what you wanted that provision to do, but we don't think it's constitutional, so we will interpret it differently than the way you meant it."

Obama's opponents were having none of it. "The president does not have the option of choosing which laws he will follow and which laws he can ignore," said Representative Steve Scalise, the Republican who authored Section 2262. In the *Wall Street Journal,* pundit John Fund wrote that Obama, "who taught Constitutional law at the University of Chicago [and] is remembered by his students there as a fierce critic of presidents who overreached and abused their executive authority," was now "singing a different tune." Many observers called the president out by pointing to Obama's own previous stance on signing statements. As a candidate in 2008, the then-senator was asked at a campaign rally if he would "prom-ise" not to use such statements as a means of dismissing portions of legis-lation he didn't agree with. Obama responded decisively and affirmatively. He explained that when presented with a bill, an executive has only two possible courses of action: "The president can veto it or sign it." And by signing it, Senator Obama insisted, a president must accept the legislation in its entirety. As he assured the crowd, "we're not going to use signing statements as a way of doing an end run around Congress." After the czar signing statement, one liberal columnist observed, "there is simply no question that Obama is now asserting exactly the power that, when demagoguing this issue during the campaign, he insisted was illegitimate and he would not exercise."

A Slow Start

Obama's signing statement on czars attracted attention in part for the apparent hypocrisy of his position. But the practice itself was nothing new. Like most presidential tools, the use of signing statements has evolved over time. James Monroe seems to have been the first president to attach a note to a bill he was signing, and subsequent presidents sporadically did the same. Nineteenth-century presidents issued only a handful of signing statements, though some attracted a fair measure of controversy. In 1830, for instance, President Jackson signed an appropriations bill, but added a statement, taking issue with a specific provision in the legislation. The House responded by criticizing Jackson for overstepping his constitutional boundaries. In 1875, President Grant appended a statement to another appropriations bill, notifying Congress that he disagreed with the constitutionality of a specific provision, which sought to close certain diplomatic offices. However, Grant also admitted that a signing statement was an "unusual method of conveying the notice."

The practice of issuing signing statement did not take off until the middle of the twentieth century, when President Truman issued 118 such statements over the course of his presidency (just twenty years earlier, Hoover left office having issued only 12). During his three years in office, Kennedy issued another 80. Lyndon Johnson, his successor, issued more than 300. And while Nixon only penned 169 statements during his six years in office, Carter took only four years to write 247 of them.

Raw tallies, however, tell us only so much about the president's reliance on signing statements to influence public policy. The contents of most signing statements during this period had little bearing on how judges or bureaucrats would ultimately interpret statutory meanings. Most administrations through Carter, after all, used signing statements for rhetorical purposes—as President Clinton subsequently did in 1997, when he celebrated the signing of an omnibus appropriations bill. "This bill is good for America," Clinton wrote in a statement, "and I am pleased that my Administration could fashion it with the Congress on a bipartisan basis." Not exactly the stuff of controversy.

With Reagan, A Shift

Beginning with the Reagan administration, however, presidents began regularly using signing statements to challenge one or more legislative provisions. In 1984, to consider an early example, Reagan signed a bill on competitive contracting but issued an accompanying statement that directed executive agencies not to follow a specific statutory provision because, in his view, it was unconstitutional. A contractor who would have been helped by the provision sued the government, and a federal judge ruled in March 1985 that the executive branch had to follow all provisions of the bill the president had signed into law. Still, the administration persisted in its claims. Attorney General Ed Meese responded to the ruling by defending the president's right, under Article II's "take care" clause, to independently interpret both the Constitution and relevant statute, and to act accordingly. Despite the court's ruling, therefore, the executive branch would continue to treat the offending provision in the contracting legislation as unconstitutional. The judiciary's response to such a bold act of defiance was swift and decisive. In a highly critical opinion, a federal appeals court upheld the lower court's decision and insisted that the executive branch abide all provisions of all legislation. In addition, the House Judiciary committee threatened to cut funding to the Justice Department unless the administration backed down. Faced with attacks from all sides, the Attorney General finally relented. Though battered, however, the administration was not broken. Indeed, the whole incident served as a harbinger of many more changes in signing statements to come.

Meese's defense of the 1984 signing statement on contracting illustrates the Reagan administration's larger effort to expand presidential power. As Meese would later recall, the president and his advisers saw the legislative field as a battlefield, in which the executive branch had to vie with Congress and the courts for control. "We were up against the 'establishment,' " said Meese, including "a Congress whose senior members ranged from skeptical to overtly hostile" and judges who were part of "the problem." In this fight, the president was faced with "a major threat" to his constitutional authority: namely, "legislative opportunism that arose out of the Watergate controversy during the early 1970s." The administration felt that "Congress had used this episode to expand its power in various ways vis-à-vis the executive branch"—a perceived imbalance which the branch as a whole, and particularly Meese's Justice Department, sought to correct.

Though Meese's attempt to defend the contracting statement ultimately failed, his stance inspired others to push forward. In August 1985, the attorney general received a memo from two young Justice Department officials, Steven Calabresi and John Harrison. In it, the lawyers argued that signing statements could be used to expand the president's influence over judicial rulings. They pointed out that "activist judges" frequently referred to a bill's legislative history, including transcripts of congressional debates that took place while the legislation was being written, in order to justify their preferred interpretation of a given statute. Given this reality, Calabresi and Harrison argued, the president should use signing statements to ensure that his opinions received fair representation in a legislative history. Others soon joined Calabresi and Harrison's advocacy for an expanded use of signing statements. Future Supreme Court justice Samuel Alito Jr., then in the Office of the Legal Counsel (OLC), argued that the "primary" objective moving forward should be to "ensure that Presidential signing statements assume their rightful place in the interpretation of legislation."

Buoyed by these arguments, Meese wrote to the West Publishing Company, which put out the *U.S. Code Congressional and Administration News*, and convinced them to publish signing statements in their records alongside bills' legislative histories, thereby cementing the statements' legitimacy. In addition, the attorney general asked the head of the OLC, Ralph Tarr, to formally stipulate how signing statements might be used to advance presidential interests. Tarr responded with a seven-page report in which he argued that signing statements are "presently underutilized and could become far more important as a tool of Presidential management of the agencies." Tarr argued on behalf of an even more robust policy of signing statements than the one offered by Calabresi and Harrison. Rather than just inserting the president into discussions concerning judicial interpretation, Tarr viewed signing statements as a way of controlling the executive bureaucracy. "The president can direct agencies to ignore unconstitutional provisions or to read provisions in a way that eliminates constitutional or policy problems." In this manner, Reagan's legal team viewed signing statements as a way for their boss to have the final word in a law's legislative history, thereby influencing how other political actors would subsequently interpret and implement its central provisions.

Gathering Momentum

The Reagan administration's embrace of signing statements catalyzed still more executive activity. Over the eight years of his presidency, Reagan issued 86 provisions that raised objections to statutory provisions, accounting for 34 percent of the nearly 250 statements he issued in total. In just four years in office, George H.W. Bush issued nearly as many signing statements as Reagan: 228, of which almost half raised some sort of legal objection. Clinton continued the practice, penning a record 381 signing statements over two terms, 70 of which expressed some form of objection.

Critics in Congress and the press periodically decried what they viewed as a growing incursion of presidential authority into the legislative and judicial realms. But it was not until the George W. Bush administration that simmering objections boiled over into a lengthy public debate about the legality of signing statements. With aplomb, Bush took the practice of issuing signing statement to new heights. Though he issued only 161 signing statements over the course of eight years, nearly 80 percent of these statements raised substantial objection to legislative provision. Boldly, Bush used those statements to challenge nearly 1,200 specific provisions in laws that he signed, more than twice as many statutory objections as all previous presidents combined. And whereas previous administrations usually based objections to a given provision's legal merits on specific constitutional argument, Bush and his legal advisers were not shy about advancing broad constitutional claims to presidential authority.

In March 2006, for example, the president signed a bill reauthorizing the Patriot Act. Since its enactment in 2001, the law had come under significant criticism for its perceived abuses of American civil liberties. Rather than simply renew the act verbatim, then, Congress added new oversight restrictions, including mandates that the Justice Department report regularly on its activities to specified committees. Eager to move forward, Bush signed the bill into law. When doing so, however, he issued a statement that underscored his intention to ignore these new restrictions:

> The executive branch shall construe the provisions of H.R. 3199 that call for furnishing information to entities outside the executive branch . . . in a manner consistent with the President's constitutional authority to supervise the unitary executive branch and to withhold information the disclosure of which could impair foreign relations, national security, the deliberative processes of the Executive, or the performance of the Executive's constitutional duties.

This language was typical of the Bush administration's signing statements. In his first term alone, Bush invoked broad powers associated with the "unitary executive" no fewer than eighty-two times in order to rebuff even the slightest legislative incursions on executive authority. His arguments were not couched in legal specifics—the above statement, for instance, does not attack the offending provisions based on a prior Supreme Court decision. Nor did the signing statements raise legitimate questions as to the possible meaning of a legislative statute—the administration was clearly choosing to "construe" the Patriot Act provisions to mean the exact opposite of what they were intended to mean. Rather, as Obama would later do in his statement on czars, President Bush repeatedly asserted his dual prerogatives of deciding when Congress was infringing on his constitutional authority and then declaring that such infringements were null and void.

Bush's signing statement on the Patriot Act spurred significant outrage. Democratic members of Congress roundly decried the president's blatant refusal to abide the basic rules of the legislative process. "It is not for George W. Bush to disregard the Constitution and decide that he is above the law," warned Senate minority leader Harry Reid. From Senator Russ Feingold's vantage point, the White House had "assigned itself the sole responsibility for deciding which laws it will comply with, and in the process has taken upon itself the powers of all three branches of government." Even some moderate Republicans, such as Senator Arlen Specter, chided the president. Congress's authority to legislate "doesn't amount to anything if the president can say, 'My constitutional authority supersedes the statute,'" Specter complained. Meanwhile, observers and critics began compiling research detailing the full extent of Bush's use of signing statements. In the *Boston Globe,* staff reporter Charlie Savage began writing regular pieces on the administration's signing statements policies—reporting for which he received a Pulitzer Prize. Other news organizations followed his lead: all told, more than 150 newspaper columnists and editorial boards across the country joined together to call for an "end to signing statements."

In response to this groundswell, the American Bar Association (ABA) assembled a task force to investigate the constitutional arguments for and against signing statements. The bipartisan task force came back with a strongly worded recommendation arguing that the ABA should oppose any presidential signing statements that explicitly aimed to ignore or misconstrue certain portions of the bill being signed into law. Such signing statements, the task force insisted, undermined the very fabric of America's legal system: "If our constitutional system of separation of powers is to operate as the Framers intended, the President must accept the limitations imposed on his office by the Constitution itself. The use of presidential signing statements to have the last word as to which laws will be enforced and which will not is inconsistent with those limitations and poses a serious threat to the rule of law." Going further, the task force addressed the argument, first made by Ed Meese and then repeated by Bush's legal team, that the president held a prerogative under Article II's "take care" clause to execute only those portions of a law that he believed to be constitutional. "The president's constitutional duty is to enforce laws he has signed into being, unless and until they are held unconstitutional by the Supreme Court," wrote the ABA authors. "The Constitution is not what the president says it is."

Scholars soon joined the fracas. Phillip Cooper, one of the first academics to research signing statements in earnest, compared their use to a "substantive line item veto statement"—a power that the Supreme Court had deemed unconstitutional during the Clinton administration. "Clearly, presidential signing statements have come to be a potent, and a potentially very dangerous, tool of presidential direct action," Cooper concluded. In her 2008 book, *Bad for Democracy: How the Presidency Undermines the Power of the People,* professor Dana Nelson categorized signing statements as one of the "power tools"—along with executive orders and national security directives—that "allow the president to enact both foreign and domestic policy directly, without aid, interference, or consent from the legislative branch." Professor James Pfiffner summarized the critical consensus: "The Bush administration used [signing statements] with the clear purpose of expanding executive power at the expense of Congress and the courts and to accomplish goals it could not achieve through the legislative process."

Restoring Some Perspective

For all the controversy generated by Bush's signing statements, their contributions to presidential power are less certain. Although presidents plainly would like signing statements to retain the weight of law, much like executive orders or proclamations, they plainly do not. And though presidents would gladly equate the contents of signing statements with a supercharged legislative veto—one that allowed presidents not merely to strike, but to rewrite, the contents of laws—they simply have not acquired any such legal status.

We still lack any compelling evidence that signing statements have systematically altered judicial interpretations of congressional statutes. In a report prepared by the Government Accountability Office (GAO), nonpartisan researchers concluded that federal courts "infrequently cite or refer to presidential signing statements in their published opinions, and these signing statements appear to have little impact on judicial decisionmaking." Though Calabresi and Harrison's initial Justice Department memo may have jump-started a signing statement revolution, it does not seem to have achieved their intended aim, which was to offer the president a way to influence court decisions.

The truth is that signing statements inhabit a legal terrain somewhere in between its proponents' and critics' boldest claims. On the one hand, signing statements, in and of themselves, are constitutionally sound. Although nothing in the Constitution empowers the president to attach his opinion to a bill he signs, neither does anything in the document explicitly bar him from doing so. The president is, in essence, free to say whatever he wants about a piece of legislation. Moreover, that he does so openly and transparently, rather than via private communications with bureaucrats and judges, may be in the public's best interests. As Glenn Greenwald, a pundit who frequently advocates for curtailing presidential authority, put it: "It's vastly preferable for a President to openly declare his intent to violate the law than to do so secretly." There is, moreover, a clear and important difference between publicly objecting to a statutory provision and actually violating that provision through one's actions. If any member of the executive branch, including the president, does act in a way contrary to a specific statute of a law on record, then that action is itself illegal. But the legality of the action and the signing statement are unrelated. Again, Greenwald: "If an action taken by a President in fact contravenes legal or constitutional provisions, that illegality is not augmented or assuaged merely by the issuance of a signing statement."

On the other hand, the broadest interpretations of signing statements present problems of their own. Though signing statements are constitutional, they do not obviously hold any legal weight—or at least the courts have not confirmed as much. Signing statements are not direct orders issued to members of the executive branch, such as executive orders, memoranda, and national security directives. Nor have they secured uniform acceptance as part of the legislative material on which judges and justices render their decisions. Signing statements are legal, but they are not law. They merely articulate the president's views about the correct interpretation, constitutionality, or preferred policy implications of a given statute. It is up to judges and bureaucrats to decide what stock, if any, to place in these opinions.

It remains an open question whether signing statements will eventually achieve the aspirations set by Meese, Calabresi, and others. For now, they remain a work in progress, a potential source of presidential influence, to be sure, but one that has not yet delivered nearly the influence that presidents would like. But for our purpose the importance of signing statements lies less in what they are than in what they signify, particularly about the president's relation to power. By boldly reinterpreting statutes and asserting broad claims about the president's prerogatives in overseeing the executive branch, signing statements reveal presidents' appetite for power, both in shaping the individual policies to which they are attached and in strengthening the president's position in the legislative process.

Signing statements themselves are not a "power tool" used to interpret or execute a policy agenda, but they do elucidate the far-reaching influence presidents imagine for themselves.

How Do We Know Presidents Are Exercising Power?

In the larger picture, national security directives, czars, and signing statements are but a small portion of presidents' efforts to expand their power. Indeed, we could have filled this book with nothing but examples of presidents guarding their information, expanding their influence over the budgetary process, fortifying their control over the U.S. military, remaking the federal bureaucracy, and the like. Opportunities abound to witness presidents seeking power. To document their efforts to shape and inform public opinion, we could further examine the many forms of public appeals that presidents issue. And we could also explore the ways in which presidents manipulate networks and new media in order to influence Congress and the courts once in office.

The three cases offered here, though, illuminate a range of ways in which presidents attempt to augment their power. In the case of national security directives, we find successive presidential administrations using a new policy tool in ways never intended by the original Congress that delegated the relevant authority. Rather than use the tool to help rationalize national security policy, presidents have issued national security directives in all manner of policy domains. And because these directives are classified, Congress, the courts, and the larger public are ill equipped to monitor their issuance. Indeed, they typically do not learn about their contents until years or even decades after their issuance.

With policy czars, we find presidents reorganizing key aspects of a federal bureaucracy that is not of their own making, and hence is not especially suited to advance their policy agenda. When taking office, presidents inherit agencies serving policy missions with which they disagree, staffed by appointees whose interests they do not share, and retaining duties and obligations that overlap with all sorts of other administrative units. From the get-go, then, presidents have cause for genuine concern that the policy advice they receive will reflect others' interests, and that the policy directives they issue will not be implemented at all to their liking. Rather than throw up their arms, however, presidents have sought all sorts of ways to control the bureaucracy, whether through political appointments or reorganization authority. Czars represent the sine qua non of political centralization, whereby political appointees who report directly to the president oversee vast swaths of the administrative state. To be sure, czars constitute only a partial solution to the bureaucratic problems that presidents face. Still, as the auto bailout in 2009 makes clear, through czars presidents have managed to achieve policy objectives that otherwise would have been frustrated either by existing bureaucratic structures or Congress itself.

Finally, there are signing statements, which presidents have employed with greater and greater frequency to challenge policy provisions supported by other political actors—in this instance, laws enacted by Congress. Given the upset caused by Bush's use of signing statements, it is especially important to avoid hyperbole here. Nothing about signing statements is formally binding on either the bureaucrats who are charged with implementing laws or the judges who interpret them. Moreover, the jury remains on out whether these signing statements do in fact materially influence government actions. What is clear, however, is that presidents would like bureaucrats and judges to treat signing statements as if they were binding. Presidents employ these policy instruments for more than just expressive purposes. They seek to materially influence how legislative provisions with which they openly disagree translate into real-world outcomes.

How do we know whether presidents, in each of these settings, are exercising genuine power? The answer is not nearly as straightforward as it might seem. Simply because presidents are doing things, after all, does not mean that genuine power is being exercised. There is always the possibility that government outcomes of interest—such as the creation of new policies, administrative structures, and operational practices—might have turned out exactly the same had the president been altogether removed from the picture. Likewise, though, inaction on the part of the president does not obviously imply a lack of power. For in those instances when presidential inaction materially changes the behavior of other political actors, and hence changes the doings of government, power is obviously at play.

To understand the exercise of presidential power, indeed to understand the power of any political actor, one must think about counterfactuals—that is, outcomes that would result from the president's absence. It is useful to rule out two possibilities, which are regularly and altogether mistakenly utilized by political observers. The first concerns evaluating presidential power by observing whether the resulting set of policies or practices perfectly reflect the president's preferences. When gauging power by this standard, observers invariably miss the occasions when a president's actions meaningfully affect change, albeit not to the degree they might like. An observer in this instance also may make the opposite mistake, confusing the realization of the president's ideal outcome, which might well have occurred for reasons that have nothing to do with the president, with presidential power. Just because the president gets what he wants does not mean that the president is powerful. And just because he is frustrated does not mean that he is weak.

Similarly, the relevant counterfactual for assessing presidential power is not the change in a particular policy or practice that is observed over time. It will not do, for example, to observe the state of the world immediately before and after a presidential action and then attribute any observed changes to the action itself. Such changes may have originated by glint of other people's designs or, indeed, by a certain momentum all of their own. Likewise, it would be a mistake to attribute the lack of change to presidential inefficacy. For had the president not acted at all, substantial changes (particularly ones not to the president's liking) might well have occurred. Hence, temporal changes do not imply power, nor does stasis necessarily indicate impotence.

To assess power, we need to look elsewhere. The relevant counterfactual involves an entirely different state of being—namely, the hypothetical outcomes that would otherwise materialize in the president's absence. In this way, presidential power is measured by comparing these imagined outcomes to those that are actually observed. When searching for evidence that a president's veto augments his power, one must compare the newly enacted law to the policy that would exist had Congress not confronted a president with the ability to veto legislation—assuming either Congress overrides an issued veto or the president signs the bill into law. Alternatively, it must be compared to the status quo, assuming a veto is issued and an override fails. The key to this exercise lies in examining outcomes. Where the realized and the imagined outcomes are one and the same, then power clearly has not been exercised.

Consider, for instance, the power associated with a successful presidential veto, that is, one in which Congress fails to override it. On the one hand, it could well be the case that the veto authority translated into genuine power by blocking a bill that majorities within Congress would have like to see enacted into law. It also is possible, however, that the president's political enemies in Congress passed the bill *knowing* that the president would veto; perhaps they wanted to force him to veto, thereby taking an unpopular stance on an issue in an election year. If that is true, then the assertion of presidential power is less clear. For if the president had not had any veto power in the first place—the hypothetical situation—then Congress would never have passed the bill. In this case, the outcomes are the same (both in reality and in the hypothetical, the bill never becomes law) and the president's veto did not actually empower him. The president may have acted, indeed he may have realized his most preferred policy outcome, but he did not wield power, per se. The hallmark of power is the observation of differences between the relevant factual and counterfactual universes. And the amount of such power is appropriately measured in proportion to the size of such differences.

According to this standard—and, it bears emphasizing, this is the only credible standard—evidence of presidents acting would appear to outstrip evidence of presidents exercising genuine power. In the preceding case studies, we found a fair amount of evidence that presidents—through inaction or action, through tools transferred or fabricated anew—exert genuine power, either persuading or ordering the government to change course. But not always. In some instances, such as in signing statements, presidents' claims to power remain aspirational. And in others, such as in the creation of policy czars, the historical record simply does not support unmitigated claims about the exercise of presidential power.

In every instance, though, presidents' *interest* in power is plain for all to see. Indeed, it is altogether unmistakable. Through national security directives, presidents are clearly writing and implementing policy initiatives that would not withstand the legislative process. If nothing else, policy czars reveal the longstanding interest of presidents in centralizing authority within the White House. And though signing statements may yield limited influence over the implementation and interpretation of enacted laws, presidents would undoubtedly like bureaucrats and judges to treat these signing statements as though they were formally binding. Rather than make do in a political universe that is stacked against them, presidents adapt existing powers for their own purposes, create altogether new administrative positions to oversee the bureaucracy, and reassert their views even after their persuasive powers fail them. The results of these efforts, to be sure, are mixed. That presidents seek power does not mean that they acquire it. But seek it they do—persistently, tenaciously, and unabashedly.

CHAPTER 3

Constitutional Foundations

The Founders who wrote and ratified the U.S. Constitution endowed the president with but a handful of enumerated powers. And yet, consecutive presidents over the nation's history have enjoyed a great deal of leeway to augment these powers, and by extension, the power of their office. Though Congress and the courts have willingly ceded substantial authority to the president, a good deal of executive influence comes from the ambiguity of the Constitution itself. Indeed, the very Constitution that created the limited presidency also established the basis for its historical growth. In this sense, the Constitution both spawned and nurtured the president; it served as both embryo and yolk to the presidency.

A President's Assumed Intemperance

The men who gathered in Philadelphia in May 1787 for the Constitutional Convention arrived there with different opinions about how to create a robust republican system of government. On two points, though, they nearly all agreed: first, the new constitution had to prevent power from accumulating in a single branch of government; and second, the way to accomplish this balance was not by counseling prudence but by erecting institutional impediments that pit men against men. An appropriate balance of powers and, with it, the protection of individual liberties, would be realized through procedural safeguards rather than appeals for responsible stewardship. Instead of disciplining or reforming the president's will, the Founders thought, they must discipline its imposition.

James Madison took the pulse of his Founding brethren and found that "separate and distinct exercise of the different powers of government . . . is admitted on all hands to be essential to the preservation of liberty." This fear of accumulated authority stemmed from distrust that those in power would faithfully act for the benefit of the body politic, a belief that itself was rooted in a universal skepticism of human nature. George Washington, who contemporaries viewed as the embodiment of virtue, summed up this skepticism eloquently:

> The spirit of encroachment tends to consolidate the powers of all the departments in one, and thus to create whatever the form of government, a real despotism. A just estimate of that love of power, and proneness to abuse it, which predominates in the human heart is sufficient to satisfy us of the truth of this position.

Sharing this view of human nature, the Founders expressed consistent suspicion that good government might result from the inherent goodness of political leaders. The Founders wanted to create a political system that relied on the sound legal framework of its founding document. As Thomas Jefferson wrote, "In questions of power . . . let no more be heard of confidence in man, but bind him down from mischief by the chains of the Constitution."

This restraining of leaders would be achieved, the Framers thought, by a system of checks and balances. In order to ensure that no one branch would accrue too many of the different powers of government, the system was designed such that each branch had the authority to regulate actions of the others. As Madison explained it, "Great security against a gradual concentration of the several powers in the same department consists in giving to those who administer each department the necessary constitutional means and personal motives to resist encroachment of the others." Note Madison's emphatic insistence on the utility of personal motives in curbing ambition—yet it is individual actors checking the ambition of *other* actors, not virtuously restraining themselves. Ambition is not meant to be quashed so much as harnessed. The ambition of each negates the ambition of others. The prevention of tyranny could not be left to the hope that popularly elected leaders would, by virtue of their character and good will, stick to their prescribed constitutional roles. Rather, the institutional system itself had to ensure that potentially overreaching politicians would be set straight by the determination of other politicians with interests and powers of their own.

In Federalist No. 51, Madison laid this argument out in grand terms, which are so important that they warrant quoting at length:

> Ambition must be made to counteract ambition. The interests of the man must be connected with the constitutional rights of the place. It may be a reflection on human nature that such devices should be necessary to control the abuses of government. But what is government itself but the greatest of all reflections on human nature? If men were angels, no government would be necessary. If angels were to govern men, neither external nor internal controls on government would be necessary. In framing a government which is to be administered by men over men, the great difficulty lies in this: you must first enable the government to control the governed; and in the next place oblige it to control itself.

Human beings are fallible—their knowledge is limited, their passions can overcome their reason, and their best interests do not necessarily coincide with the broader public's. The solution to man's ambition, however, lies not in its eradication but its dispersal and, concomitantly, its proliferation. Ambition is both cancer and cure. When building a political system, one must take man's qualities as immutable. In the words of Washington, "We must take human nature as we find it, perfection falls not to the share of mortals." When designing a system of government, one must not revel in the great possibilities of man, writ large, but take men, all men, as they are.

To the extent there is any evidence at all that the Founders did put faith in the virtue of men in office, it can be found in Federalist *No. 77*. Here Hamilton describes not the presidency, but rather the Senate, in virtuous terms: "[The] institution of delegated power implies that there is a portion of virtue and honor among mankind, which may be a reasonable foundation of confidence." Hamilton, in this passage, argues that the president's power to appoint federal officials will be checked in part by virtuous senators: "The supposition that he could in general purchase the integrity of the whole [Senate] would be forced and improbable." This argument, however, in no way negates the Founders' broader conviction that a politician's virtue cannot be counted on to curb his own ambition. At the time, senators were chosen not by direct popular vote, but by state legislatures whose members represented the elite. In this paper, we find

Hamilton arguing merely that the appointment power is unlikely to lead to presidential tyranny. To substantiate this minor point, Hamilton openly doubts that the president could corrupt a majority of senators into blindly supporting his appointments. This line of reasoning—which represents some of the only evidence that the Founders counted on the basic goodness of men—still does not lean particularly heavily on the inherent virtues of political leaders. More important, to the extent that it does rely on "independent and public spirited men," it merely assumes that these men would work to prevent power accumulating in the hands of the president. It does not assume that the president or the Senate would willingly forsake power for themselves.

Though Hamilton, perhaps more than any other Founder, favored a strong unitary executive, he is nevertheless quick to point out in the *Federalist Papers* all the constitutional constraints on executive power. Since the Constitution prohibits the president from holding any additional offices, or from having his salary raised or lowered by Congress, the president will "have no pecuniary inducement to renounce or desert the independence intended for him." From the Senate, he faces checks on his power ranging from the previously mentioned confirmation of appointments to impeachment and the possibility of being thrown out of office. And from the people he faces a constant democratic check on his power in the form of regular elections every four years. Ultimately, Hamilton shared Madison and the other Framers' view that executive power needs some limit—and that this limit cannot simply take the form of electing great men and hoping for the best. The checks therefore had to come from outside the office, not from within it.

MISREADING WASHINGTON'S SIGNIFICANCE

The Founders, to be sure, cared a great deal about republican notions of virtue (for more on classical conceptions of republican virtue, see chapter 5). They simply did not believe that an individual's virtue could be counted on amidst institutional defects of government. From the nation's beginning, the office of the presidency was meant to be fully capable of withstanding individual ambition, avarice, and perfidy. In fact, the men who wrote the Constitution had a great leader in their midst—a leader whose virtue, modesty, and temperance they greatly admired. Yet, just because the first president exhibited these qualities did not cloud their—and should not cloud our—understanding of either the constitutional project the Founders themselves believed that they were undertaking, or the status of self-restraint within the presidency itself.

When the constitutional delegates convened in Philadelphia, their first order of business was to unanimously elect George Washington as president of the convention. It was a smart, if obvious, selection. As commander in chief of the Continental Army during the Revolutionary War, Washington had developed a national reputation as the ideal American leader: a gentleman of dignity, modesty, and valor. His presence at the convention gave the proceedings legitimacy, and his support of the drafted Constitution made it more palatable to state legislatures. Indeed, many observers at the time noted that without Washington's support for the Constitution, it never would have been ratified by the states. James Madison claimed that Washington's leadership was "the only aspect of the new government that really appealed to the people." And James Monroe wrote to Thomas Jefferson, "Be assured, [Washington's] influence carried this government."

Though Washington's importance to the ratification process is clear, his impact on the actual drafting of the Constitution remains more ambiguous. As president of the convention, his role was to gavel sessions to order and otherwise remain "above the fray." Washington therefore abstained from the other delegates' heady and often heated deliberations. Indeed, he only spoke on record twice at the convention: once to thank the delegates for the honor of serving as president of the proceedings; and again during the last session of the debates, to give his input on a fairly minor matter of representation.

In spite of this relative silence, some historians have argued that Washington was an important influence on the way the Framers of the Constitution articulated presidential powers in Article II. According to these historians, Washington's immense popularity and unimpeachable humility served as the model on which the American president was created. But how important was Washington in the creation of the office of the president? To what extent did expectations that Washington would become the first president actually inform the Framers' decisions about what the institution of the presidency would look like? And more generally, to what extent do individual personalities inform the way political institutions in America are created and function?

Historians of the Constitutional Convention appropriately emphasize the apparent contradiction between the Framers' deep distrust of anything resembling a monarchy and the broad executive powers that they ultimately enshrined in Article II. Washington's persona, some argue, resolves this perceived tension between belief and action. By this account, the former general, as the "living embodiment" of "classical Republican virtue," assuaged the Framers' concerns that their presidency would lapse into a kingship. Washington's familial relations also played their part, for lacking an heir, he could not establish a dynasty of his own. As one noted biographer summed up, "In a world frightened by a long history of kings, the convention decided on one President and allowed him an amazing amount of power. . . . The impress of Washington's prestige remains in the strength allowed the President of the United States." Or as the popular historian Joseph Ellis concludes, in a Constitutional Convention rife with disagreement and discord, "Washington demonstrated that one man provided a symbolic solution acceptable to all sides."

The most compelling evidence on this score comes in the form of a letter written by South Carolina delegate Pierce Butler. In the letter, which is quoted by nearly every historian writing on the subject, Butler admits that the executive branch's powers ended up being "greater than I was disposed to make them," adding that he doubts "they would have been so great had not many of the members cast their eyes toward General Washington as President; and shaped their Ideas of the Powers to be given to a President, by their Opinions of his Virtue." This quote lays a strong claim to Washington's legacy as a motivating factor in the formulation of the presidency.

However, it is not at all clear that the Framers found in Washington the balm they needed to design a strong, independent presidency. Indeed, Butler's letter stands nearly alone amidst a sea of inferences and conjectures. One line of argument, for example, notes that some Framers remained deeply ambivalent about how the executive branch should be constructed. Just weeks before the convention, James Madison wrote to Washington about the executive office, confessing that he had "scarcely ventured to form my own opinion either of the manner in which it ought to be constituted or of the authorities with which it ought to be cloathed." Madison also writes in his notes on the convention about how, when James Wilson first made a motion "that the Executive consist of a single person," the delegates delayed discussion of the matter, "seeming unprepared for any decision on it." According to this line of argument, Madison's expressed uncertainty, to the extent that it can be generalized, establishes that the Framers had no real conception of how to institutionalize executive power. Into this void, then, they posited the most obvious example of executive authority they could find: the restrained and singular General Washington. In this portrayal and others, it is simply taken for granted that the Framers would never have settled on a strong, unitary presidency had Washington not been sitting in their midst.

In contrast to Butler's pronouncement and Madison's admission of uncertainty, however, many of the most influential delegates harbored clear conceptions of how the institution of the presidency ought to be constructed. Before the convention began, John Jay wrote to Washington describing what he saw as the ideal form of government: a three branch federal system in which "the executive branch should stop short of a monarchy, but only slightly." Alexander Hamilton and John Dickinson likewise expressed their admiration for Britain's system of limited monarchy. And during the convention debates themselves, many delegates expressed their trepidation that the executive would be too weak, not too strong. As historian Jack Rakove writes, "The nearest thing to a first principle or independent variable [in the debates] was the desire to enable the executive to resist legislative 'encroachments.'"

From the outset, the delegates recognized that their charge was to build a nation's government anew. As such, they took the long view of the American presidency and executive power. They were committed institutionalists, set on building a legal document for posterity. As Federalist No. 10 makes clear, Madison himself fully appreciated that "enlightened statesmen will not always be at the helm"; and hence, that institutional precautions must be set in place to "control the effects" of their individual ambitions. Deliberations at the convention did not wallow in some vague comfort that Washington would be the first president, but were steeped in legal-historical analysis. And crucially, at the heart of the model of government that the Framers would create lay a belief in the importance of institutional checks and balances: the idea that one cannot depend on individual virtue to combat vice; but rather, that checks must be found externally, while the office itself—the institution and its powers—further disciplines the whims of individual actors.

This core tenet of the American Founding was eloquently summarized by none other than Washington himself: "Men are very apt to run into extremes . . . it is a maxim founded on the universal experience of mankind, that no [man] is to be trusted farther than [he] is bound by [his] interest; and no prudent statesman or politician ventures to depart from it." Without wanting to appear alarmist, Washington nonetheless admonished his colleagues not to trust in him, not to trust in anyone, lest this fragile system of republican governance service individual wants and desires rather than channel the competing interests and visions of a polity.

The Framers put little faith in the willingness of men to restrain themselves. Why, then, would they allow themselves to build an institution based on one man's reputation for humility? To do so would have been antithetical to their entire project of checks and balances. For even if Washington did project, in character and temperament, their notion of the presidential ideal—an executive who "would rise above party turmoil to embody a disinterested notion of the public good"—they also recognized that the heroic general was *exceptional* in this regard. Even John Adams, who was one of Washington's few contemporary critics, marveled that "he seeks information from all quarters and judges more independently than any man I ever knew." The Framers fully recognized that they could not count on men such as Washington always winning the presidency in the future—nor on Washington's precedent to constrain future presidents where institutions could not.

Constitutional Ambiguity

If a preoccupation with power does not accompany them into office, then presidents quickly acquire it. For both their short-term political survival and their long-term legacy depend on the seizure and protection of executive power. What provides the principled basis for presidents to act on their base desire for power? The answer, or at least a crucial element of it, involves the ambiguity of Article II of the Constitution. As Edward Corwin has written at length, it is the Constitution's obscurity, rather than any specific enumerated power, that has delivered the richest endowments of influence to the presidency.

On the one hand, Article II is quite precise. Available as an appendix to this book, Article II specifies exactly how the president and vice president are to be elected. It identifies who can run for office, and who can vote. It identifies the exact day that a newly elected president will take office. It lays out the specifics of the treaty ratification process. And it discusses the terms by which presidents' salaries can be adjusted. Indeed, Article II provides ample evidence of the Founders' intent that the executive branch be held in check by the other two branches, especially Congress. The Constitution requires two-thirds of the Senate to ratify a treaty, allows two-thirds of Congress to override a presidential veto, and insists that all presidential appointments to the Supreme Court and the cabinet be confirmed by the Senate. The Constitution does contain some clear descriptions and limits of presidential power, which cannot be explained away and must not be ignored.

On the other hand, on those issues about which the Framers disagreed most, and on those matters that would prove most consequential for the subsequent evolution of the office, Article II remains vague. Indeed, ambiguity may well be the defining feature of Article II. The Constitution does not so much confer a complete, well-delineated list of powers on the president—which Article I does for Congress—as it recognizes the president's claim to an array of broad titles and responsibilities. And depending on how one chooses to read these titles and responsibilities, one can draw radically different conclusions about the constitutional bases for either a strong or weak presidency.

What does it mean, for instance, to vest the president with the "executive power"; and then to require the president to "take care" that the laws of the United States are "duly and faithfully executed"? This question, of course, implies other ancillary ones. Given a relatively clear law, how quickly must the president implement it? If the president believes that a law is unconstitutional, is he still bound to implement it? What if Congress enacts a law that the president vehemently disagrees with? Meanwhile, how much discretion does the president have to interpret vague laws? And as outside observers, how are we to know when the president has gone too far?

The ambiguity of the "take care" clause does not end there. Presidents, after all, are not merely responsible for implementing one law at a time; they are tasked with implementing the entire corpus of statutory law. Further questions, therefore, naturally follow. Given one law that delegates powers to the president to oversee the domestic economy, and another that requires the president to set clean air standards, what is the president to do when the two conflict? Should he select the law that was enacted more recently? The one that is more precise? The one that, by the president's judgment, better serves the nation's interests?

Although the "take care" clause is notoriously vague, other elements of Article II present ambiguities of their own. Consider the president's foreign policy powers. In the case of a sudden attack against the United States, presidents, all concede, have a fair measure of discretion to exercise military force as they see fit. Indeed, this is the one area of American foreign policy—first identified in Madison's notes on the constitutional convention, and later codified by the courts—in which presidents command significant constitutional authority to exercise military force unilaterally. It remains an open question, though, just how far this authority can take the president. When are presidents "repelling sudden attacks" and when are they using force unconstitutionally? If U.S. vessels are attacked on the high seas, for instance, does the president have the power to command an immediate military response? If so, how much force can he exercise? Does it matter whether the vessel belongs to the U.S. government or a private corporation? Can the vessel then pursue a fleeing enemy? Can it seize the aggressor ship, its crew and bounty? Can it pursue adjacent ships that might pose further risks? Does it matter whether these ships hail from same nation as the original aggressor?

Such questions are not hypothetical. Over time, an incredibly detailed set of rules of military engagement has been devised—one which traces its origins back to events at the very beginning of the nation's history. Consider just two episodes from American's early decades, the first of which occurred in 1801. Upon receiving fire from a Tripolitanian ship in the Mediterranean, an American naval schooner promptly responded in kind, as all would admit it had the right to do. President Thomas Jefferson subsequently confessed to Congress, however, that the schooner's commander was "unauthorized by the Constitution, without the sanction of Congress, to go beyond the line of defense." Jefferson then went on to express his grave concern that "whether, by [giving Congress strict authority to] authorize measures of offense also, they will place our force on an equal footing with that of its adversaries." No longer serving in govern-ment, Alexander Hamilton chastised the president on this account, won-dering whether Jefferson was seriously proposing "that one nation can be in full war with another, and the other not in the same state."

Fast forward, then, to 1817, when Seminole Indians were conducting raids into American territory. At the time, President Monroe chose not to consult Congress before ordering General Andrew Jackson (later President Jackson) to chase the raiding parties back into Florida, a territory that had not yet entered the Union. This decision, no doubt, fell within his right-ful authority. But rather than stopping at the border, Jackson pursued his enemy into Florida; and once there, he found himself "fighting Spaniards and hanging Englishmen—actions that might conceivably embroil the country in serious war." Was Monroe's decision to support Jackson uncon-stitutional? Should he have ordered Jackson to stop at the Florida border? Or, sooner still, should he have insisted that Jackson halt his attack the moment that the Seminole Indians turned in retreat?

Article II of the Constitution does little to clarify these questions. Although it is possible to derive some broad principles from within the Constitution, politicians invariably must look beyond the founding doc-ument for answers. Moreover, and this is the critical point, presidents actively participate in the construction of such answers. They do not—indeed, they cannot—rely on the letter of preexisting law. But herein lies the rub. In formulating answers of their own, presidents have demon-strated an uncanny ability to provide principled justifications for actions that the Framers could hardly have imagined. As Richard Pious recog-nizes, presidents tend to read vast powers into the silences of Article II. Presidents interpret the absence of a prohibition as an explicit endorse-ment, as Article II rather quickly becomes a springboard for presidential interventions into any manner of policy disputes.

DIVINING INTENT

What are the origins of Article II's ambiguity? Did the Framers, to a man, head to Philadelphia with the expressed intent of designing a presidency whose central powers would support radically different interpretations?

Was this ambiguity the object of mindful choice, or instead, the accidental product of political deliberation?

Both possibilities have something to say for them. Ambiguity, after all, is a necessary part of any constitution. For constitutions to last, for future generations to continue to respect their basic principles when confronting challenges that their authors cannot possibly have anticipated, founding documents must be flexible. In Federalist *No. 22,* Hamilton recognized that "it is impossible to foresee or define the extent and variety of national exigencies, or the correspondent extent and variety of the means which may be necessary to satisfy them." Hence, Hamilton reasoned, the Founders ought not to shackle future generations with a Constitution that was too rigid and limiting to meet the challenges of their day. For it would be up to them to fashion, or more exactly refashion, a federal government that ensured a lasting tranquility, upheld the requirements of justice, and provided for the common defense.

In part, this required flexibility is achieved through the establishment of a formal amendment process, wherein politicians can clarify and correct constitutional provisions that no longer suit their generation. More often, though, flexibility is realized through ambiguity. It is pliability that allows a Constitution to operate in normal times as well as crises, on issues involving domestic and foreign affairs, on challenges and contingencies that lay well beyond the visible horizon. To accommodate the inevitable stretching and pulling that awaited the fledgling American republic, the Framers knew they needed to allow for some give in the constitutional apparatus. As Supreme Court Justice Oliver Wendell Holmes wrote in 1904, "Some play must be allowed for the joints of the machine." Protecting the "liberties and welfare of the people," Holmes recognized, required a great deal more than careful textual readings of the Constitution. For the government to function, the elected branches of government would have to muster their own spirited defense.

As an explanation of the Framers' intentions regarding the presidency, though, intentional ambiguity can take us only so far. While rigidity is to be avoided in any Constitution, the clarity of Article I (which lays out Congress's formal structure and powers) and Article III (which defines the judiciary's) stands in stark relief to Article II. Moreover, there are plenty of constitutions in other countries that contain far more specific language about the formal powers of the executive. Indeed, the U.S. Constitution, coming in at 4,602 words in its original form, is roughly a third of the size of the international average of 13,368 words, and a tiny fraction of the world's longest constitution (India's, established in 1949) of 74,971 words. Likewise, a good number of U.S. States—notably California and Louisiana—have longer constitutions than their national counterpart.

Perhaps, then, the ambiguity that is such a defining feature of Article II was born from political compromise. The Constitution, after all, was not merely a product of institutional engineering. It also was a political document written by and for individuals with very different interests and ideologies. The Framers, unable to agree on specifics, reached compromise through ambiguity, which allowed advocates of a strong federal government and champions of states-rights, for instance, to both return to their constituents claiming victory. The Framers, by this account, recognized the essential need to rehabilitate the federal government; a return to the Articles of Confederation was simply not acceptable. And so rather than hammer out a solution to every disagreement, they sought compromise in vague prose—effectively passing some issues off to other politicians as well as judges and justices, who would be required to make sense of the language in Article II.

As alternative explanations of the Framers' intentions, however, various claims about compromise also have their limitations. For starters, they presuppose that the Framers could not forecast the trajectory of an argument they had just begun; and that, aware of their own cognitive limitations, they then opted to play a lottery in which one side was bound to lose. By this account, each side in the debate about the presidency anticipated not only that others would pick up where it left off, advancing its views with due precision and vigor, but also that its arguments would, over time, ultimately prevail.

If such an account is true, then one of two conclusions follows. In one, those who originally argued on behalf of a limited presidency simply miscalculated. Having bet that their side would eventually win out, they were proven wrong; and given the opportunity to do it all over again, these individuals surely would insist that their views find a fuller hearing in Article II. Or else, in a second possibility, the Founders might well have stuck with the original text even if their powers of foresight had been equal to their powers of hindsight. Under this view, both sides in the original debate about the American presidency were intent on enjoining the views of others, come what may. The Framers simply wanted to grant each generation the discretion to refashion the American presidency anew.

It is difficult to know how to reconcile these dual possibilities. If the Framers were laying bets on the future, then surely some would want to take them back, what with the extraordinary changes in the American presidency that have since unfolded. But if they were passing along a constitutional artifice with which subsequent generations could do their will, then perhaps none of the Framers would have lamented their willingness to endorse Article II as written. Given that each possibility rests on a counterfactual that, by definition, cannot be observed, our own ability to divine the Framers' true intentions are sadly limited. Unable to send our Framers through time so that they might see the consequences of their decisions, and then back in time to their original seats in Philadelphia, we cannot know whether political compromise took the form of wagers under conditions of uncertainty or a positive endorsement of intergenerational delegations of power.

Challenges to the view that Article II's ambiguity derived from political compromise do not end here. In other contested domains, after all, the Framers eschewed ambiguity in favor of painstaking detail. Recall, for instance, the creation of the Electoral College, which settled the dueling concerns of small and large states, as well as the dictates of popular sovereignty on the one hand and a distrust of average citizens' ability to govern on the other. On matters involving presidential selection, the Framers did not wave their hands about vague governing principles, nor did they adopt wholesale one of the existing models of executive selection. Rather, with great specificity, they concocted a system of elections wherein: states would be assigned electoral votes on the basis of their population; state legislatures would select electoral delegates, who in turn would vote for two presidential candidates; the candidate with the most votes would be president; the runner-up would be vice president; and should no candidate win a clear majority, Congress would choose the president from among the top five contenders.

In spite of this attention to detail, of course, much about presidential elections has changed. With the advent of parties and the fiasco between Aaron Burr and Thomas Jefferson in the 1800 election, Congress in 1804 proposed and a supermajority of states ratified the Twelfth Amendment, which provided that separate ballots would be cast for president and vice president. Not since 1824, when it opted for John Quincy Adams rather than the more popular Andrew Jackson, has the House of Representatives selected the winner of a presidential election. And following Franklin Delano Roosevelt's four terms in office in the 1930s and 1940s, presidents were permitted to run for office and win only twice.

For our purposes, though, what is noteworthy is not that the structures of presidential elections have changed, but rather the detail and care that the Framers originally took in designing them. Facing extraordinary political and ideological divisions, the Framers nonetheless saw fit to construct a well-defined set of processes that would accommodate them. Such was not the case when it came to the most essential provisions of Article II that defined the duties and powers of presidents once in office. The most consequential arguments about presidential power have less to do with the operability of the "take care" clause, and more to do with its appropriate interpretation.

But there is a third explanation for the Founders' intentions concerning the presidency, one that attempts to split the difference between intent and happenstance. According to this account, the essential vagueness of Article II constitutes an invitation to presidents to pursue their interests in ways that do not find a strictly constitutional basis; ways that do not require a dependence on Congress and the judiciary, or even the broader public, to check the capricious exercise of presidential power. The Framers, in this view, had little interest in promoting gridlock, as the Progressives would later lament. Rather, the men who wrote the Constitution believed that though institutional tensions and roadblocks were necessary to foster deliberation, there were circumstances that called for action—action that could only come at the behest of executive initiative. As Gordon Silverstein notes, "Ambiguity would help make it possible for the government to act, possible for the branches to cooperate—but not easy. Providing gray, ambiguous limits and boundaries was one of the most important ways to make sure that the American system would be able to respond to unexpected developments, and yet make equally sure that power would not consolidate in a single branch for too long." Presidential power, the Framers anticipated, needed limits; but it also needed to allow for presidents to take action in ways and in circumstances that the men writing the Constitution could not hope to predict.

It is difficult to know just how far to push this line of argument. At its extremes, it suggests that all presidential actions are in some sense consistent with, or at least permitted by, the Framers' political science. Moreover, such an argument still relies on the notion that the Framers had a unified set of intentions and expectations, which motivated their ambiguous framing of Article II. If that were the case, then why did Hamilton and Madison promptly square off against one another about the proper meaning of Article II in the Pacificus-Helvidius debates, so soon after the Constitution's ratification? And why, within just a matter of years, did the other Framers so quickly divide into two major parties, the Federalists and Antifederalists, in large part over their vehement disagreement about the powers of the federal government and the presidency within it? At the same time, it is clear that opponents of broad presidential power agreed to sign a constitution that did not set forth unmistakable outer limits to executive authority. Thus it is difficult to believe that the ambiguous language all the delegates eventually agreed on was not at least *somewhat* intentional.

If the origins of this ambiguity are themselves unclear, however, other matters are not: the ambiguity of Article II in the U.S. Constitution was not a foregone conclusion. The Framers of the U.S. Constitution could have specified with a great deal more exactitude what they meant by the executive power and the take care clause. Moreover, their failure to do so had stark consequences for the future development of the office of the presidency, which produced clear winners and losers in the initial debate over presidential power. Though it took some time, champions of a strong presidency eventually won out. If there were delegates in Philadelphia who hoped that subsequent deliberations would lead to a consensus on a moderate interpretation of Article II, then those Framers simultaneously overestimated the ability of members of Congress to speak with one voice and, in the process, to guard their own institution's prerogatives; and underestimated the consistency with which consecutive presidents of very different ideological commitments and partisan affiliations would undertake a common project: that of interpreting the Constitution to suit their own institutional interests, of stretching the language of Article II ever more expansively, of reading into ambiguity nearly unconditional approval of their grandest designs, all in an effort to meet the extraordinary expectations set before them.

CHAPTER 4

Contrasting Conceptions of Executive Leadership

The authors of the modern executive quite consciously designed a system of government that did not look to a president to regulate himself. Instead, assurances that presidential power would not lapse into despotism were to be found in the institutional restraints that reside beyond the president's reach, and that do not require his cooperation for their effective operation. Governing harmony, Madison recognized, was achieved through the design of political institutions, each set in opposition to one another, not through the fine character of those individuals chosen to work within them.

It is worth remembering just how radical a notion this was—how patently it rejected a classical conception of politics that depended largely on individual temperament and morality. For centuries, the Western canon of political thought had vested a great deal in the character attributes of leaders—their knowledge, wisdom, experience, and virtue. Precisely because such qualities were in scarce supply, and precisely because a state's leaders were chosen on the basis of having them, external checks on power—according to the likes of Plato onward—necessarily degraded all that was potentially good about government. For if a state's leaders were the wisest and most virtuous citizens, who but the less wise and the less virtuous citizens would be available to restrain them?

This is not to say that ancient Greek and Roman political philosophers were blind to the practical need for auxiliary precautions against men's baser instincts. Cicero, in particular, went to great lengths to laud the legislative and judicial claims to independent government powers. And all of these philosophers recognized, even predicted, that idealized forms of politics might well disintegrate.

Nor did the ancient and early modern political philosophers uniformly agree about the proper design, powers, and selection of their leaders.

Rather, they harbored radically different views about the purpose, or *telos* of government, and envisioned altogether different forms and functions of leaders within them.

For the most part, however, these philosophers worried equally that a government might fall into the hands of either a despot or a jealous public. Moreover, when the stakes of government action were highest—that is, during times of crisis—these philosophers took their chances with despotism. That a temperate and wise consul might save the Republic, Cicero argued, external checks must altogether evaporate.

Cicero's way of thinking did not die off with the Roman Empire. Centuries later, it figured prominently in the political counsel that Machiavelli offered his Prince. It also was resuscitated in the Progressive Era with the likes of Woodrow Wilson, who pled that the president might be freed from his constitutional shackles. A great deal distinguishes these two figures, of course. Machiavelli taught prudence in the service of self-interest, whereas Wilson sought to refashion the presidency in order to advance the larger public good, as embodied in his New Freedom platform. For both, though, the reach of government crucially depended on the character and temperance of the single individual in charge, be he a Prince or president.

What sets the Founders apart from these other conceptions of leadership, then, is not the existence of restraints, but their origins. In the modern era, restraints reside exclusively outside of the president; and when deployed, they are imposed on him. But for Plato, Cicero, Machiavelli, and Wilson—each of whose views we consider in this chapter—such restraints necessarily beckon from within.

PLATO'S PHILOSOPHER-KING

For Plato, the ideal form of government is the philosopher-kingship. As he asserts in his masterpiece, *The Republic*, "Until philosophers rule as kings in cities or those who are now called kings and leading men genuinely and adequately philosophize . . . cities will have no rest from evils." For all citizens to flourish within the ideal city-state, the *kallipolis,* and for justice to be served, leadership must emanate from the "best man": the philosopher who, by distinguishing apparition from truth, has achieved genuine enlightenment; the virtuous individual whose wants and desires, rather than being in the service of the self, are grounded in the larger public good.

Plato was perfectly aware of the perils of arguing on behalf of philosopher-kings. In ancient Athens, as in modern society, philosophers were often seen as impractical, head-in-the-clouds daydreamers: "The greatest number become cranks," or worse, "completely vicious" individuals. Yet Plato insists this poor reputation arises because many people who call themselves philosophers are not in fact true philosophers. A true philosopher, for Plato, is someone who desires the whole of wisdom—they are "lovers of wisdom and knowledge." Such a person "will be guided by the truth and always pursue it in every way," for "it is the nature of the real lover of learning to struggle toward what is, not to remain with any of the many things that are believed to be."

Truth, for Plato, means something very specific. Central to Plato's philosophy is a conviction that there exist ideal "forms," which do not so much represent as they constitute the essential nature of things. These forms are distinct from the sensory world, which is the world as we perceive it. When we describe the world around us, we think we are articulating knowledge about the world. But in fact, says Plato, we are merely expressing an opinion. This opining is something more than ignorance, as it is grounded in appearances; but it is something less than true knowledge, which requires an ability to countenance forms. The pursuit of this true knowledge of forms, of things as they are, is the avocation of philosophers.

The true philosopher's love of learning does not arise from practical wants, but from a visceral hunger for knowledge. Hence, the true philosopher "must be without falsehood—[he] must refuse to accept what is false, hate it, and have a love for the truth." In addition to having an honest character, the true philosopher's commitment to wisdom must fixate his attention on "the pleasures of the soul itself by itself," leaving him to "abandon those pleasures that come through the body." He (or she, Plato allows that women can be philosophers as well) is not motivated by money or any other material desires. Rather, the true philosopher's sense of purpose will always and only be to better understand the truth of things in the world.

To make his case for philosophers being the best rulers, Plato utilizes his famous ship analogy. Imagine a ship, Plato instructs, in which the owner is the biggest, strongest person on board. However, the owner also is hard of hearing, poor of vision, and does not know all that much about sailing. The sailors on the ship, who themselves have never learned the art of navigation, are nevertheless constantly trying to persuade the owner to let them steer: they beg him, cajole him, flatter him, even drug him if necessary, in order to gain control. And whichever one of them succeeds in gaining control the rest call "captain"—at least until he is thrown overboard and a new sailor takes the helm. Meanwhile, all of these sailors dismiss as "a stargazer, a babbler, and a good-for-nothing" the person who Plato calls the "true captain": that is, the person who pays attention "to the seasons of the year, the sky, the stars, the winds, and all that pertains to his craft." The analogy to society is clear: the owner is the public; the sailors are members of the elite, who attempt to grab money and power for themselves by using rhetoric to fool the public; and the only true captain, the true philosopher, is dismissed as a fool, even though he alone has acquired the knowledge needed to set the ship on its proper course.

If he works hard enough, the true philosopher's passion for understanding will ultimately lead him toward a knowledge of the forms of all things, including people and the society in which they live. In this way, the philosopher will understand what is best for the society and its citizens more than citizens themselves. Knowledge, however, is not enough. In order to be an ideal ruler, the philosopher also must have two additional qualities: he must understand things as they are perceived by others (the existing social and political order); and he must love his city and desire to bring it closer to its ideal form. Plato does not assume that either of these qualities comes naturally. Rather, both must be learned. To ensure that philosophers have the knowledge required to rule effectively, the society should support a vital and demanding educational system. Plato therefore devotes a significant portion of The Republic (including his most famous analogy, that of the Cave) to outlining the rigorous educational regimen that is required of those who exhibit a natural inclination toward true philosophy—that is, toward the intrinsic rewards of learning. In this education, students are to be inundated with music and poetry, physical training, mathematics, and dialectic. As Plato lays it out, the process will take more than twenty years. At each phase in their education, only the most successful students (those who exhibit the strongest commitment to understanding true forms) are to graduate to the next level. And as part of their training, at every step these students "must show themselves to be lovers of their city."

Having proven themselves successful in and committed to the pursuit of the truth and the preservation of the city, the would-be philosophers undergo a final education: fifteen full years of practical political train-ing. Only by completing this final challenge are they fit to be instated as philosopher-kings of the kallipolis. In this way, Plato heads off potential concerns that his ideal rulers lack the practical faculties to understand how to institute their ever-so-enlightened policies. Plato's true philosophers understand things as they appear to be and things as they really are in their true forms. And having demonstrated their loyalty to the city and their desire for the public good time and again, they are ready to become members of the class of philosopher-kings.

Their training behind them, the philosopher-kings are "compelled to lift up the radiant light of their souls" to what is good and true in the world. Each does so, however, only temporarily. Philosophers are not to be kings for life—nor do they desire as much. Understandably, since their goal is truth and knowledge, these individuals would prefer to devote all of their time to philosophy. Yet because they also love their city and want to bring their fellow citizens as close as possible to the good, and because they have proven themselves to be the best possible leaders of the city, they are compelled to serve. Thus Plato imagines philosophers comprising a sort of aristocratic class in which individuals take turns being king. Once each completes his duties, he may return to his true calling as a full-time philosopher.

For Plato, there is no outside check on the philosopher-king's rule. Why should there be? After all, there is no danger of philosopher-kings (who care only for the pursuit of wisdom and truth) abusing their power or mis-leading the public. This point is underscored in how they become kings. Philosophers do not seek power. Rather, they are compelled to relinquish their true passion for knowledge in order to lead the city they love. They serve out of a sense of duty, not ambition. As a result, there need not be any check on the philosopher-king's desire for power. By definition he has none, else he is not a true philosopher.

For Plato, an outside check on executive power isn't merely unnec-essary—it is counterproductive; dangerous even. Under the reign of philosopher-kings, the rulers will be the wisest and most beneficent men and women. Their actions, unexceptionally, will do the most to advance the public good, which only they can fully comprehend. As a result, they must assume complete control of the government. There can be no democratic check on the executive since, in contrast to the philosopher-king's enlightened virtue, the "moods and pleasures" of the city's populace will inevitably fail to reflect "the reality of each thing itself." Rather, the public must turn over the keys of the city to the philosopher-king. He becomes the lawgiver, and citizens must have faith that his proven understanding of what is most true and most right for society will lead him to create just laws: laws that will cultivate a happy populace, in which each person fulfills a function closest to his own ideal form.

For all the trust he places in philosopher-kings, however, Plato does not ignore the possibility that his model government will devolve into tyranny. Yet, importantly, he does not attribute this propensity to the philosopher-kings themselves, whose judgments are beyond reproach. Rather, Plato argues that it is the natural tendency of all things to decline, including societies. There is no force that can prevent this from happening, and granting lesser men the power to check the philosopher-kings only hastens a society's decay. The best that can be hoped for is that citizens will not meddle in the affairs of the philosopher-kings, so that the kallipolis may endure for another generation.

Plato's characterization of philosopher-kings is one of the earliest conceptions in Western political thought of a model political leader. It also remains one of the most oft-cited and controversial. The political philosopher Karl Popper famously argued that the notion of philosopher-kings was inherently totalitarian, and that the origins of totalitarianism in twentieth-century Europe could be traced all the way back to Plato's political thought. Perhaps. But taken on its own terms the rule of the philosopher-king conveys a simple concept: the most just society is the one in which the most just people rule. If a society can identify its most just citizens, then it would do well to hand control over to them. People are best off when they give power to those who know and love them best. And the state, as a whole, can be only as just as its most educated citizens are wise.

The equation of societal strength with individual wisdom would not languish in Plato's philosophy. Quite the contrary. It would find expression in the political science of many others who more directly informed the Founders' thinking—including Cicero.

Cicero and Cincinnatian Restraint

After the Greek city-states fell from power, and then the Macedonian Empire under Alexander came and went, the Roman Republic was the next great civilization to rise in the Western world. Rome was also one of the first and most important examples of popular government, and, not coincidentally, America's Founders were steeped in Roman history and thought. Cicero stood out as Rome's most influential political theorist.

In important ways, Cicero's *On the Commonwealth* builds on critiques of *The Republic* leveled by Plato's own student, Aristotle. Like Aristotle, Cicero had little patience for idealized forms of government. Recognizing the practical challenges of governance, having himself participated in Roman politics, Cicero placed executive power squarely within a "mixed" republican framework of government, replete with all the checks and balances with which we are familiar today. Cicero's theory of executive power, as such, is far closer to the American model than any previous articulation. But as we shall see, Cicero heartily endorsed the Roman conception of dictatorial authority in states of emergency. As a result, his model of the executive, like Plato's, ultimately draws on notions of virtue, wisdom, and a public spiritedness that are averse to ambition, crudely understood.

Drawing on Aristotle's distinctions between the rule of one, few, and many, Cicero identifies three types of commonwealth: "monarchy," "aristocracy," and the "popular state" (i.e., democracy). Cicero further argues that any one of these types may be tolerable for a time. There might be a "wise king," for example, or rule by "selected leading citizens" of virtue, or even (though Cicero is highly skeptical of this) a "just and moderate" state in which the people rule. Yet each of these pure types of government, in Cicero's accounting, present two fundamental flaws. First, each is inherently unstable. In a monarchy or aristocracy, the people are deprived of their liberty. As a consequence, Cicero argues, the people will move to violence and revolt: "It is not easy to resist a powerful populace if you give them no rights or very few." On the other hand, when the people them-selves rule, something approaching absolute equality and absolute liberty exist within the state. Yet this, for Cicero, displays all the instability of the other two forms of government, if not more. Absolute equality "is itself inequitable, in that it recognizes no degree of status," he writes. Since the best and wisest men do not enjoy more power than the worst and most ignorant, the state will inevitably be governed poorly, and the government will crumble. Moreover, Cicero argues, absolute liberty is dangerous, since it allows individuals who are "bold, corrupt, [and] vigorous in attacking the people" to acquire unchecked power through freedom of action. In this way, "extreme liberty, both of the people at large and of particular individuals, results in extreme slavery."

And this leads us to the second flaw of all pure types of commonwealth: they are just as fallible as the men who govern them. While all three types can potentially hold to the best principles a society has to offer, each type also has "a path—a sheer and slippery one—to a kindred evil." Beneath a "tolerable and even lovable king," there "lurks, at the whims of the change of his mind," a cruel tyrant who places his own desires above the interests of the people. Likewise an aristocracy ruled by the best men may become, through the avarice and greed of individuals, an oligarchy ruled by a selfish few. And within any purely popular government lies the inherent threat of the violent mob. In this way, "the primary forms are easily turned into the opposite vices" by individuals within the commonwealth who lack virtue. Cicero therefore argues for a fourth type of commonwealth, one in which the first three are "blended and mixed." Only such a mixed type can avoid instability and the fallibility of individual actors. And for Cicero, the apo-theosis of this type is the Roman Republic itself.

Cicero calls the Roman system "mixed" with good reason. During the Republic, a highly convoluted state apparatus governed Rome and its colonies. Legislative, judicial, and even executive power was divided among numerous governmental institutions and groups. The preponder-ance of legislative and judicial powers were located in a Century Assembly, Tribal Assembly, Senate, and Tribunes, each of which represented differ-ent segments of society and wielded competing and overlapping powers.

Collectively, these four institutions provided the needed checks on each other's authority, such that no one individual or societal faction could assume control over the whole system.

Within this fractured framework of power, a preponderance of executive authority lay within the fifth institution: the magistrates, who executed the day-to-day operations of the government. By construction, the executive branch was both hierarchical and subject to numerous internal and external checks on its power. There were five ranks of magistrates: *consul, praetor,* and *censor* (the higher, more powerful magistrates), as well as *quaestor* and *curule aedile* (the lower magistrates, largely responsible for administrative functions). Consuls, as the highest-ranking magistrates, served as the primary leaders of the executive branch, and they held one-year terms. Acting as both civic and military heads of state, they also presided over meetings of the Senate and the two assemblies. Officially, the power of the consuls to execute laws was called the *imperium*—the power of command. Any executive order issued by a consul was immediately backed by the full authority of the state. In this way, consuls enjoyed a significant amount of power over the functioning of the government, including complete control over the lower, more administrative magistrates.

There were, however, several important checks on consular power, of which Cicero certainly approved. According to the established hierarchy, any magistrate could veto a decision made by any other magistrate of equal or lesser rank. Thus the primary internal check on a given consul's power was the veto of his fellow consul. In addition, the Senate's authority over funding further restrained consular power. Lastly, Tribunes elected by the Plebeian Council exercised a limited veto over any member of government, including the consuls.

Under normal circumstances, therefore, Roman executives enjoyed considerable yet constitutionally limited power, similar to the president in the U.S. Constitution. In the Roman Republic, however, one important exception to checked executive authority loomed large. In the event the Senate issued a *senatus consultum ultimum* declaring a state of emergency, it appointed a special temporary magistrate to oversee all governmental functions. This magistrate was formally called *magister populi,* but more often assumed the title of *dictator.* The dictator was appointed for a term of six months, after which point he was required to abdicate all authority and step down from office. During this six-month period, however, he wielded absolute, unchecked executive authority. While ordinary government institutions continued to operate, they were all subordinate to the dictator. Neither the Senate nor the consuls or tribunes had the power to overrule the dictator as long as he remained in office.

Cicero's ideal system of government closely mirrors the actual design of the Roman Republic, which he felt sustained an appropriate "balance in the state of rights and duties and responsibilities." This balance, Cicero argued, promotes stability by allowing the best men to rule while still granting the rest of the population sufficient liberty and freedom.

This mixed system, however, is specifically constructed for peace: its aim is to placate the competing desires of the aristocracy and the plebeians, and its success depends on a perpetual "tranquility" among "both individuals and classes." In times of war or revolt, in contrast, the challenge of balancing competing domestic interests is displaced by larger security concerns. And safety, for Cicero, requires a much simpler hierarchy of authority, one in which a single leader commands over all classes and factions. "In major wars," Cicero argues, "our people [want] all the power to be in the hands of one individual without a colleague, whose very title indicates the extent of his powers: he is called dictator because he is appointed, but in our augural books . . . he is called 'master of the people.'"

Like most of his political science, Cicero's advocacy for a dictator matches the constitutional construction in the Roman Republic. Yet in the centuries leading up to Cicero's time, the Republic had few dictators. In fact, by the time Cicero set to writing, the office had largely been phased out. Despite this historical record, Cicero repeatedly underscores the value of a unitary executive: "If authority is exercised by several people, then . . . there will be no controlling power; and unless power is undivided it is nothing at all." In an ideal commonwealth, "the rule of a single person, so long as he is just, is best," just as "it is better to trust a ship to one helmsman, and a sick man to one doctor (assuming that they are competent in their professions)." The only issue, for Cicero, is that unchecked executives such as kings can all too easily become tyrants. Thus the best commonwealth places executive authority within a more stable, equitable system, whereby "no one [is] allowed to grow used to power and be either too slow in surrendering it or too prepared for maintaining it." In the dictatorship, however, Cicero seems to find an ideal embodiment of the broad, unitary executive authority he generally admires.

Though he does not explicitly elucidate the qualifications for becoming a dictator, Cicero writes at length about what constitutes a good leader in general. The ideal leader of the commonwealth would be a "great and very learned man," someone who is "wise and just and temperate." This great figure must be "eager to learn about justice and the laws," and he must care above all about the people's welfare. Cicero's leader agrees that serving his commonwealth is "the greatest and best [task] among mankind." Presumably, these are the same ideal characteristics Cicero would guide the Senate to when naming a dictator.

It is of some consequence, then, that Cicero's allowance of dictatorial authority within the Republic implicitly relies on this archetypal notion of a "just and temperate" leader. As he makes clear in his discussion of monarchy, Cicero was well aware that an unchecked executive could all too easily morph into an unjust tyrant. Yet he fails to mention this possibility when praising the dictator as a republican institution. The only formal mechanism in place for limiting the dictator's power was the office's brief term limit: after six months, the dictator was expected to step down. It is unclear, however, how the Senate would enforce this requirement—especially given that the dictator maintained complete control over the armed forces. Cicero, for his part, does not outline a constitutional mechanism for ensuring the passage of dictatorial power. To the contrary, he dismisses concerns about taming the emergency executive and mentions in passing that during the brief reigns of dictators, everything was still "in the hands of the aristocracy." Thus, at precisely the moment that the greatest amount of executive authority is being wielded, the notion of wisdom and virtue is seen as most crucial. Cicero places his trust in the Senate's patricians to select a dictator who will faithfully carry out their will. This trust, in turn, is predicated on the idea of a self-restrained dictator: a man whose better nature will guide the "mixed" constitution of the Republic safely through its state of emergency—and will then promptly compel him to relinquish his power.

In a contemporary republican context, Cicero's lack of concern for potential dictatorial abuse of powers would seem to necessitate some sort of defense. In the context in which he was writing, however, Cicero could rely on the firmly established myth of the virtuous Roman dictator. This myth was embodied in the person of Cincinnatus, an early hero of the Roman Republic whose name was synonymous with republican virtue. As Cicero himself alludes to, Cincinnatus was a highly respected aristocrat and former consul who, after serving his one-year term, retired to work on his small farm outside the capital. A few years later, however, Rome fell into a costly and dangerous war, and the Senate called a state of emergency and subsequently asked Cincinnatus to come out of retirement and take over as dictator. Cincinnatus, a brilliant tactician, came to Rome's rescue and quickly led the army to victory. Yet his service was of the most selfless nature: immediately after saving Rome, he disbanded the army, handed power back to the Senate, relinquished control over all military and civil authority, and returned to his farm in the countryside. For Romans in the first century BCE, Cincinnatus embodied the true executive ideal. Only belief in such a model could allow someone as cautious of absolute authority as Cicero was to wholeheartedly embrace the existence of an unchecked dictatorship.

In its form, then, Cicero's ideal government with its mixed constitution resembles the American system far more than Plato's kallipolis ruled by philosopher-kings. Yet in his advocacy for dictatorial power in states of emergency, Cicero is actually closer to Plato than he is to the Founders. By prescribing absolute rule, even if temporarily, Cicero leaves open the possibility that such power might persist. Against the danger of tyranny inherent in his proposition, Cicero can only call on the dictator's sense of self-restraint.

The Founders, for their part, agreed that restraint was an exceedingly admirable executive quality. George Washington himself was esteemed by his peers as the "American Cincinnatus." Yet unlike Cicero, the Founders were unwilling to assume executive self-restraint. Checks on presidential power, they insisted, must come externally.

MACHIAVELLI'S PRINCE

The modern executive finds its first articulation in Niccolo Machiavelli. Though Machiavelli's *Discourses on Livy* paid due tribute to Republican forms of government, his most shocking, and exhilarating, writing on executive rule is found in *The Prince*. These late-fifteenth-century writings are intended to advise the executive—the Prince—on how best to survive and prosper. In the immediate instance, the Prince took the form of Lorenzo de Medici. It is clear, though, that Machiavelli intended to speak for the ages, and in that sense, Machiavelli wrote as an advisor not just to one Prince, but to all princes.

With its publication, *The Prince* represents a clear break from the past. Much of Machiavelli's counsel, after all, not only justifies but even demands violence and deception. Of necessity, Machiavelli argues, the Prince must instill fear, gratitude, and acquiescence in the public. Unlike Plato, Machiavelli recommends a set of strategies, qualities, and convictions that stand the best chances of securing the best interests of the Prince himself. It is the Prince's fortune, not justice, that Machiavelli attends to. Machiavelli provides no assurances that what is good for the Prince is necessarily good for the public—indeed, he openly admits many occasions when the two are patently at odds.

The differences we find in Plato's philosopher-king and Machiavelli's Prince stem from a basic disagreement about the criteria by which we are meant to evaluate executives. For Plato, these criteria centrally involve the public good, the material and spiritual well-being of a populace. The philosopher-king, Plato argues, is uniquely suited to protect and promote the general principles that are meant to govern a Republic.

Machiavelli, however, reveals little patience for Plato. From his vantage point, it is impossible to divine, much less assess, the public good outside of the people it ostensibly represents. Virtue cannot be understood except by reference to the objectives it serves. Hence, Machiavelli's "vertu"— sometimes translated as vigor rather than virtue—is unavoidably pragmatic in nature. Rather than being esteemed, virtue is harnessed. For Machiavelli, the Prince is to be judged not by some distant morality, traditionally understood, but rather by "looking to the end" and evaluating the outcomes he brings about. Virtue is known where prosperity is observed; and its absence is detected only where ruin befalls the Prince.

Machiavelli recognizes that the Prince retains certain responsibilities to his people; and that by not fulfilling these responsibilities, he invites insurrection. It is because of the material costs of neglecting his subjects, however, and not some moral obligation to care for them, that the Prince must fulfill these responsibilities. Indeed, Machiavelli goes to some length to caution the Prince against "liberality." It is possible to do too much on behalf of one's subjects, Machiavelli warns. Should the Prince bestow unnecessary gifts on his people at one moment, he will be obliged to do so at every subsequent moment as well, or else invite their hardened disapproval. Gifts may be given, to be sure. But they should only be given to an acquiescent, approving public.

Machiavelli looks on utopian thinking and "imagined republics" with a good deal of scorn. When jealous, scheming parties threaten him, the Prince who remains preoccupied by the way things should be, rather than the ways things unmistakably are, "learns his ruin rather than his preservation." The Prince must not pine for the ideal. Rather, he must always select the least offensive option before him, even when doing so evokes horror from his would-be allies. He must do so, what is more, without apology or hesitation.

How does the Prince best ensure his preservation? The people's love has its place, Machiavelli recognizes. But it is through fear that the Prince finds his salvation. Whereas wicked men will forsake love for their own gain, they cannot escape fear. Hence, the Prince must behave in ways that both strike and stoke fear in his subjects.

To do so, the Prince may need to act cruelly at times, according to the proviso that such "cruelties [be] well used." He must know "how to enter into evil, when forced by necessity." He must learn "to be not good, and to use it and not use it according to necessity." Hence, by turn, the Prince must engage in all sorts of nefarious activities: capricious violence, the concealment of political decision making, secrecy, even tyranny, if for a time. When necessary, the Prince must turn on those who once supported him. He must destroy, publicly and painfully, those who would betray him. At every instance, he must judge his relationships and actions not for their own worth, but for what they will deliver now and in the future.

Machiavelli is not interested in evil per se. He is interested in its utility. He is teaching a Prince, not a sadist. Hence, Machiavelli's teachings do not invite indulgence. Quite the opposite, in fact. The Prince must not be beholden to his baser instincts. He must not show himself to be saturnalian in spirit or hedonistic in character. He must not be consumed by passion or pride, and he must steadfastly reject rapacious and licentious behavior.

In Machiavelli's political science, the Prince must be disciplined in everything he does. It is the "prudent" Prince, Machiavelli repeatedly intones, who avoids ruin. And by prudent, Machiavelli does not mean cowering, accommodating, or cautious. Rather, prudence "consists in knowing how to recognize the qualities of inconveniences, and in picking the less bad as good." The prudent Prince is discerning, exacting, and restrained. He therefore does not burden his people unnecessarily. For just as great dangers await the Prince who gives too much, so too does ruin follow the Prince who takes excessively from his subjects.

To flourish, Machiavelli argues, the Prince must nurture fear with care. For when fear turns to hatred, the spell is lost. Hence, the Prince "should proceed in a temperate mode with prudence and humanity." Vigilantly, he must walk a line between confidence (which breeds incaution) and diffidence (which renders him intolerable). Though he may covet his subjects' property and women, the Prince must curtail the temptation to plunder. Though he invariably will kill individuals both within and outside his kingdom, the Prince must provide ample justifications for these acts, even when his subjects do not demand he do so. Parsimony, temperance, even chastity have their place in the Prince's rule.

For the Prince to flourish, however, he himself must learn Machiavelli's teachings. The Prince must be "wise by himself." Though admitting the need for help, whether from counselors or from armies, the Prince must recognize that the only lasting and sure defenses are those that depend exclusively on him. The fate of his kingdom cannot be left to his advisors or armies (who have interests of their own) or to fortune (which can shift at a moment). When kingdoms fall, then, they fall because of the failures of man, and a single man at that.

As a consequence, Machiavelli shares a good deal in common with both Plato and Cicero. Though they envisioned different governments serving different objectives, they all—in one way or another—vested the endurance and strength of the state in the qualities of individual men. For Plato, the state's resilience was to be found in the philosopher-king's unending wisdom and love; for Cicero, in the temperance of the dictator who, when called on, would rescue the Republic; and for Machiavelli, in the Prince's prudence. For all, the life of the state and the character of the ruler were closely entwined.

WILSON'S CONSTITUTIONAL CRITIQUE

Though the Framers of the U.S. Constitution rejected the strain of Western political thought that placed the state's fate in the hands of a virtuous leader, this line of thinking did not disappear from the nation's intellectual landscape. Indeed, a variety of important American thinkers eschewed the Founders' conception of a constrained executive in favor of a more vigorous presidency endowed with moral authority. In the case of Woodrow Wilson, the thinker in question also happened to become president himself.

Among U.S. presidents, Woodrow Wilson stands alone for having written rather extensively on the proper forms of executive, legislative, and judicial powers before taking office. In his first major publication, *Congressional Government*, Wilson heralded Congress's supremacy—albeit, a Congress remade in the image of Britain's parliament. As he put it, "Our constitution . . . practically sets [Congress] to rule the affairs of the nation as supreme overlord." For Wilson, executive (and by implication presidential) independence merely frustrated Congress's practical capacity to address contemporary challenges, and of "making [Congress's] authority complete and convenient." To guard against such eventualities, Wilson enlisted extraconstitutional institutions, in particular strong parties. The discipline imposed by such parties, Wilson thought, would temper executive independence and allow Congress to dispose of the "ever widening duties and responsibilities" appropriately laid before it as the federal government's first among unequal branches of government.

In a series of lectures he delivered in 1907, which were later published as *Constitutional Government*, Wilson would repudiate such claims. Concerned about a variety of emergent problems—particularly foreign threats to U.S. security interests—and the capacity of the federal government to respond to them, Wilson shifted his institutional allegiances from Congress to the president. As the only elected individual representing a truly national electorate; as the only individual with the gravitas needed to allay the concerns of foreign states; as the leader of his party; and as the administrator of executive powers that are at once personal and absolutely essential to all matters of governance, the president was uniquely equipped to lead the nation—by assembling in common purpose the various institutions of government that the Founders worked so hard to separate. For Wilson, the president alone could provide the vision that the country needed in order to meet the challenges of its day: a rapidly expanding industrial force, the assimilation of millions of new European immigrants, and soon enough, the advent of total war. Hence, notes Sidney Pearson in his introduction to *Constitutional Government*, "Presidential leadership occupied the most exalted position in Wilson's hierarchy of political virtues."

In *Constitutional Government*, as in *Congressional Government*, arguments about one branch's primacy are embedded in a more general critique of the Constitution. This critique, whether levied on behalf of the president or Congress, was largely at odds with the view of Abraham Lincoln, another president notable for his extensive writing on constitutional issues. For Lincoln, wars strained the constitutional order, beckoning presidents to act in ways that are best thought of as extra constitutional. When taking such actions, Lincoln insisted, presidents owed Congress and the citizenry something of an apologia. Having temporarily abandoned the Constitution in service of the nation's and perhaps the Constitution's survival, presidents must submit themselves to the judgment of their peers, who had every right to renounce their actions and, perhaps, throw them from office.

For Wilson, by contrast, wars (and other urgencies that warranted a government response) demanded revisions to the constitutional order itself. Wilson did not agonize about the relaxation of constitutional limits of presidential power during war. Rather, he felt that these limits, and the Constitution more generally, must be understood within the historical context in which presidents ruled. Representing the entire citizenry, presidents must reinterpret, and thereby remake, the Constitution to serve a larger public good. Whereas Lincoln viewed the Civil War as something of an interruption to the everyday business of presidents, who must protect the larger constitutional order, Wilson aligned himself, in the words of his fellow Progressive Henry Jones Ford, with "the work of the people, breaking through the constitutional form." Or as the historian Richard Hofstadter put it, "Modern humanistic thinkers [i.e., progressives] who seek for a means by which society may transcend eternal conflict and rigid adherence to property rights as its integrating principles can expect no answer in the philosophy of balanced government as it was set down by the Constitution-makers of 1787."

In Wilson's political science, then, a system of governance based on mechanistic checks and balances and a fixed conception of constitutional strictures was unsustainable. The world would not wait on political institutions working against one another or a constitution written by men long since dead. Rather than adhere to outdated constitutional notions, Wilson insisted, government must adapt to its surroundings, reconstituting itself and its relation to the citizenry according to the dictates of material wants and needs. "Government is not a machine, but a living thing. It falls, not under the theory of the universe, but under the theory of organic life. It is accountable to Darwin, not Newton. It is modified by its environment, necessitated by its tasks, shaped by its functions by the sheer pressure of life." And should it fail in this regard, Wilson thought, the government would suffer the fate of the ammonites, trilobites, and mastodon. To survive, the federal government, with the president at its helm, must evolve—remaking itself "from age to age by changes of life and circumstance and corresponding alterations of opinions." The presidency must be whatever the people and the times require of it.

Of course, evolution and teleology are not synonymous. The executive's ascendance in the hierarchy of government, though eminently justified, is not assured. To correct both the Founders' and his own past errors, Wilson recognized, presidential foresight and initiative would be crucial. Having rejected a static and highly constrained view of the presidency in favor of a "machinery of constant adaptation," Wilson encouraged presidents to view their office as "anything [they have] the sagacity and force to make it."

And here is the kicker. Such a system, in Wilson's view, would not disintegrate into tyranny precisely because presidents could be counted on to abide the public good and, with it, the strictures of limited government. From where Wilson sat in academia, a whole host of institutions in American society were expressly designed to inculcate virtue, temperance, and modesty in the country's future leaders. What were public schools and private universities if not training grounds for future politicians? And having placed great faith in the effectiveness of primary, secondary, and higher education, we must grant presidents the flexibility they need to pursue the public good. Having invested in civic institutions, we must rest assured that executive power will not reawaken in the educated man whatever selfishness and intemperance he was born with. And in the off chance that it does, we can count on the larger public to reveal the errors of his ways.

Wilson remained convinced that the moral fiber of a president, as a true "man of the people," would guard against tyranny. Tyranny, by Wilson's account, invariably follows from pretense. Leaders must be free to speak their mind, to ignore convention, and to avoid mimicry. Only with transparency, public engagement, and mutual trust can a government, with the president at its helm, hope to function effectively. Granted such discretions, however, it will surely flourish. In fact, Wilson argued that almost any method of control—such as independent commissions—represented "opportunities . . . for political influence and individual tyranny" that were avoided only by the good fortune of having been run by "men of some wisdom and great honesty," and "public opinion has watched the process of control with a constant critical scrutiny." If a government stood any chance of solving trenchant social problems, the public must be trusted to select men of good character to the office of the presidency.

In Wilson's rejection of the system of checks and balances created by the Framers, we find a deeper disagreement about the nature of man. Though Wilson (like Plato) denies that man is by nature wise, Wilson does believe (again like Plato) that man has at least the capacity for wisdom. And rather than persist with a government system that is expressly designed to frustrate this wisdom, we should look to institutions that support and nurture presidents whose "particular qualities of mind and character" might rally the larger polity behind reforms that augment the public good.

For Wilson, that which is virtuous and wise about presidents arises from, just as it contributes to, the larger public. The president, Wilson writes, represents "an embodiment of the character and purpose [the public] wishes its government to have," for it is the president who "understands his own day and the needs of the country, and who has the personality and the initiative to enforce his views both upon the people and upon Congress." Through their dialectical relationship with the public, virtuous and wise presidents will win elections and then seek power only insofar as power is needed to govern. A president's interest in power, after all, is merely incidental to his commitment to the larger public good.

Locating Temperance

To guard against despotism, our nation's Founders did not call on the wise to set aside their philosophical pursuits in order to lead the nation. During times of crisis, the Founders did not look to a dictator who could be counted on to relinquish all the powers that he had been granted. The Founders did not trust in man's prudence, virtue, and temperance— though they admired these qualities in individuals. Nor did they call on civic organizations—churches, schools, and the like—to produce a brand of leaders who would assume office reluctantly, exercise powers cautiously, and defer to the judgment of others. Not at all. The Founders fully expected self-interested individuals to seek the presidency; and once in power, they anticipated that these individuals would pine for the very powers that King George had wielded over the thirteen colonies.

For the Founders, the central challenge in creating leaders lay not in how to empower them, but in how to constrain them; and the remedy was to be found not in psychology but in political science. The nation's Founders placed executive power within a constitutional system with multiple branches of government wielding independent—albeit overlapping— powers. Through staggered elections and the separation of legislative, judicial, and executive powers, this system set interest against interest and ambition against ambition. Rather than residing quietly within the executive, despotism's disavowal was to be heard from afar. The failure of government would no longer be a failure of man. If it occurred, it would be a systemic failure.

Plato, Cicero, and Machiavelli show that the president did not have to be thusly situated, thusly constituted. When the Founders gathered to design our government, they could have taken an altogether different tack—one that Wilson, at least, would have much preferred. But rather than building a government on the principles of virtue, prudence, and limited government, they designed one that offered the greatest protections against their opposites: vanity, recklessness, and despotism. As Wilson's constitutional critique makes clear, though, avoiding sin does not necessarily deliver virtue. As a consequence, many political theorists, like Harvey Mansfield, lament the "obsolescence of Republican virtue" in the modern executive. For a government premised on the positive affirmation of what is good and possible just might render a more mature polity and more effectively governed state.

Though Madison and the Founders did not dismiss the benefits of an aristocracy of true philosophers—indeed, they considered themselves members of such—they put little faith in a system of government premised on wisdom and virtue. To create a stable system of government, they argued, one must not only account for human weakness, folly, and venality—one must build a governing system that would thrive amidst them. The central challenge of government lay not in the eradication of vice or elevation of virtue, but rather than in setting vice against vice, and thereby realizing a delicate balance of mutual frustrations.

Perhaps our government would have been better off had our Founders seen the possibilities in allowing unfettered executive leadership. Perhaps not. Whether for good or ill, though, the Founders quite consciously rejected the models of leadership outlined by Plato, Cicero, and Machiavelli, which relied on either a leader's selfless rule (in the case of the former two) or the prudence not to exercise powers fully within his command (in the case of the latter). In so doing, however, the Founders unmistakably designed a presidency whose officeholders have every incentive to seek, guard, and expand their power.

CHAPTER 5

Misguided Entreaties

That other models of executive leadership were considered and rejected by our nation's Founders has not kept any number of politically interested parties from invoking them. Indeed, we regularly hear calls for presidents to "do the right thing," abide their personal conscience, and curtail their behavior. "Yes, Mr. President," the critics exhort, "*you could* take this action that advances your policy interests, and perhaps the larger public's as well. But you must not. For to do so would disrupt the delicate balance of powers originally achieved by constitutional design and then preserved by a succession of responsible, selfless presidents. Power has been entrusted to you. But only so much power—and it is your sacred duty to use only that which was originally given."

Again and again such entreaties are made—by libertarians, public administration scholars, and blue-ribbon commissions of one sort or another. And again and again such entreaties are ignored. This should hardly surprise us. Such entreaties, after all, address presidents who have no interest in checking themselves, who look outward rather than inward when deciding how far or how fast to push in politics, and whose primary incentives are defined by the material expectations laid before them and not some higher, moral order.

Baying for a "Responsible" President

Pundits and politicians have long attempted to shame presidents into relinquishing their power—indeed, such public shaming might be considered something of a national pastime. When Abraham Lincoln suspended habeas corpus and restricted freedom of speech during the Civil War, his political opponents publicly attacked his use of "arbitrary power."

As Representative Clement Vallandigham cried on the House floor, "[You] have made this country one of the worst despotisms on earth for the past twenty months." Rather than mobilize Congress to counter Lincoln's power grabs, Vallandigham urged the president to desist his abuses. Lincoln responded by having Vallandigham jailed for the remainder of the war.

As the executive branch grew over the course of the twentieth century— and as executive power grew alongside it—the intensity of such appeals has only increased. On a regular basis, political observers call on presidents to recognize and abide the constitutional limits of their own office. These observers see the antidote to presidential power in presidential restraint. And curiously, a great number of them invoke the Founders to buttress their claims.

In *The Imperial Presidency*, a landmark 1973 study of the evolution of presidential authority, Arthur Schlesinger argued that presidents have become too powerful in the realm of military and foreign affairs—far more powerful than the Founders had intended. The recourse, as he saw it, was for presidents to work toward diminishing their own importance. "The men who become presidents in the last quarter of the twentieth century," Schlesinger advised, must "begin by ridding themselves of honest misconception about the nature and power of the office." These "Future Presidents" would also have to "admit Congress to genuine, if only junior, partnership in the foreign policy process." Only in this way—by presidents reconfiguring their own relationship to power—might balance in the federal government be restored.

Echoing Schlesinger, Jack Goldsmith has recently made similar arguments about the need for presidents to check themselves. A former assistant attorney general in the George W. Bush administration, Goldsmith saw firsthand what he felt was a problematic exercise of executive power. By consistently taking "unilateral action" to fight terrorism, Goldsmith argued, President Bush deprived the nation of "public debate." This debate "is one of the strengths of a democracy at wartime, for it allows the country's leadership to learn about and correct its errors." In Goldsmith's view, the root of the problem stems from a simple misunderstanding concerning the nature of the presidency: "The administration's conception of presidential power had a kind of theological significance that often trumped political consequences." Presidential overreach would be eliminated, therefore, if future presidents chose to follow the example of FDR, a strong president who nevertheless took pains to "consult widely and to receive consent from important American institutions." Roosevelt's "pragmatic" approach, Goldsmith asserted, was "premised on the notion that presidential power is primarily about persuasion and consent rather than unilateral executive action." Sometimes, Congress might not want to fulfill its constitutional role, preferring to "inquire and complain but not make hard decisions." Yet if Congress could not always be counted on to check the president, it would be left to future presidents themselves to "forc[e] Congress to assume joint responsibility" for policy decisions.

Whereas Schlesinger and Goldsmith see presidential restraint as a sort of philosophical necessity, a significant body of public administration and organizational management literature, much of it from the 1980s, emphasizes the necessity of presidential moderation for good governance. In *Managing the Presidency*, Colin Campbell argued that the most effective presidents work within the institutional framework of the presidency, rather than choosing "to ignore the state apparatus and do whatever they can get away with politically." Presidential effectiveness depends on a personal commitment to check one's own ambition, which in turn depends on strength of character. According to Campbell, "personalities play a huge role in how [presidential] administrations actually function." A president with the right temperament and leadership style will understand that by delegating his authority to the institutional bureaucracy, he can better achieve his preferred policy goals.

More recently, the *New York Times* offered this advice to President Bush on the morning of his 2004 reelection: "Only a president can create a new mood [of bipartisanship], and he can do it only by sacrificing his own short-term political advantage on occasion for the common good." Rather than emerging from the interactions and contestations between the various branches of government, the "common good" is to be nurtured and preserved within just one branch. Never mind the extraordinary challenges put before you, the *Times* implored the president—you must relinquish the powers at your fingertips so that an era of bipartisanship might be restored.

Four years later, in the run-up to the 2008 election, the *Times* editorial board sought to shame the American *people* into electing a leader who would restrain himself. "We can only hope that this time, unlike 2004, American voters will have the wisdom to grant the awesome powers of the presidency to someone who has the integrity, principle and decency to use them honorably." If an existing president cannot be rehabilitated, the *Times* argued, then the public must replace him with another who will govern with all the humility and self-sacrifice that the Constitution ostensibly requires.

The troubles wrought by a power-seeking president, however, are not confined to Bush. In the summer of 2011, President Obama faced intense criticism for his decision to involve the United States in NATO military operations in Libya without requesting congressional authorization for such actions. This unilateral exercise of power, critics argued, was an affront to the Constitution—and only the president himself could prevent it. Legal theorists Bruce Ackerman and Oona Hathaway wrote that "the only way to keep faith with the Founders' commitment to checks and balances" was for the president to honor his "constitutional responsibility." It was the president's job, Ackerman and Hathaway intoned, to "belatedly heed the War Powers Resolution" and to "press Congress" to authorize the military use of force.

Obama's unilateral decision to intervene militarily in Libya raised all sorts of hackles in Congress. Various members called it "an affront to our constitution" and "illegal," while others called publicly for a court injunction. In the main, however, members opted to plead with the president rather than assert their own, independent powers over military affairs. A bipartisan House Resolution to remove troops from Libya fell short by more than fifty votes after Republican Speaker John Boehner said the "resolution goes too far" and instead requested that Obama willingly inform Congress about his goals and strategy in Libya. House Foreign Affairs Committee chairwoman Ileana Ros-Lehtinen pushed for a resolution requesting Obama explain his strategy so Congress could "get the attention of the White House" without destabilizing "our standing, our credibility and our interests in the region." Despite the veneer of outrage, the collective message coming from Congress was one of supplication.

When beseeching presidents to rein in their own power, these critics frequently invoke the Founders. And yet the Founders did not expect that presidents would check themselves. As we have seen, they explicitly repudiated such a notion. The limits of presidential power, they decided, would not be secured through the beneficence of the men who filled the office. Rather, all of the checks on the presidency were to be found outside of the executive branch, and the benefits of limited government would be secured through the mutual frustrations of each politician's ambition. It is with unintended irony, then, that calls for presidential restraint are usually made in the name of recovering some understanding of constitutional government that supposedly has been lost in the practice of politics. But of course the Constitution was written with the assumption that personal appeals to reason could not be counted on to restrain political leaders.

WHY LIBERTARIANS MAKE BAD PRESIDENTS

Some of the most consistent and principled arguments for presidential self-restraint come from politicians and pundits who self-identify as libertarians. In a normative sense, libertarians may well be right to denounce presidential overreach and to demand that presidents take action to limit the powers of their office. We as a country might be better off if they did. But when it comes to presidential politics, libertarians are tone-deaf, for the ideals and principles they espouse doom any presidential candidate who might follow their counsel.

Libertarians believe in constitutionally limited government. They deeply distrust centralized, unchecked authority. They fight for basic individual liberties and freedoms, particularly against what they perceive to be government encroachments. Political valor, for libertarians, constitutes a willingness to stand up for constitutional principles precisely when the national mood holds them in least regard. They assert that the letter of the Constitution must always trump the creedal passions and calls for action that sometimes dominate the day.

In March 2007, a band of respected libertarians called on candidates in the upcoming presidential election to sign a "Freedom Pledge," which obligated them to honor ten restrictions on presidential power—including renouncing signing statements and allowing journalists to print state secrets without punishment. The pledge received coverage, much of it favorable, in outlets as diverse as the *New York Times*, *San Francisco Chronicle*, and Reuters. Advocates for the pledge feared the presidency was becoming "chilling, reminiscent of the kingly abuses that provoked the Declaration of Independence," and that "liberty is disemboweled" in the face of executive overreach during the War on Terror. Presidential actions specifically forbidden by the pledge included warrantless surveillance (wiretapping) of Americans and torturing foreign combatants.

Outside of the presidential race, the Freedom Pledge attracted support from many leading libertarians. The organization that wrote the pledge, the America Freedom Agenda, was formed by Bruce Fein, Bob Barr, John Whitehead, and Richard Viguerie. These were not small names in the world of politics and policy. Fein had served as a lawyer in the Department of Justice, the Federal Communications Commission, and on congressional and America Bar Association committees; he would later serve as senior legal advisor to Ron Paul's 2012 presidential campaign. Barr had served as a four-term congressional representative from Georgia and a U.S. attorney under President Reagan. Whitehead had founded the Rutherford Institute, "one of the nation's premier civil liberties organizations," according to the *Village Voice*; he also had argued before the Supreme Court and been awarded the Hungarian Medal of Freedom. *Politico* had named Viguerie the "Funding Father of the conservative movement" for his innovative techniques in reaching voters and soliciting money.

Two Libertarian candidates for president signed the Freedom Pledge within a month of its release: Steve Kubby, best known for his main platform of legalizing marijuana, and George Phillies, who had twice run for and lost a seat in Congress. Ron Paul, the staunch libertarian congressional representative from Texas who caucused with the Republican Party, also signed on. But that was it. Tellingly, no mainstream Democrat or Republican who stood any chance of securing a party's nomination for president signed the pledge. Paul, for his part, formally introduced the pledge as a legislative bill, the American Freedom Agenda Act (AFAA) of 2007. Yet while the bill was hailed by some conservatives as a "beautifully argued document [that] feels historic and has the ring of great power to correct great injustice," the AFAA garnered only two cosponsors: Representative

Dennis Kucinich (who did not sign the pledge as a presidential candidate) and Representative Peter Welch. It died without so much as a single committee hearing. Ironically, the pledge was such a flop that by the time one of its authors, Bob Barr, was elected as the 2008 Libertarian candidate for president, he decided not to sign it.

Libertarians brandish the Constitution as both sword and shield. And they may be right to see virtue in respecting constitutional strictures and, when appropriate, relinquishing power. But when it comes to executive politics, libertarian entreaties badly miss the mark. In today's politics, presidents can ill afford to repudiate any power that might enable them to address the onslaught of expectations put before them. For when they do, as the next chapter demonstrates, they suffer mightily for it. Our nation's Founders did not place any faith in the possibility that an appropriate balance of powers would be achieved through presidential self-restraint. Neither should we.

Whistling Commissions

Every so often, a blue ribbon commission of experts and former politicos is formed to right some perceived wrong in the operations of government. Earnest and well meaning, the individuals who participate in these commissions and author their reports posit the existence of some problem—such as an unwillingness of one branch of government to fulfill its constitutional obligations, the inefficiencies and waste associated with bureaucratic redundancy, or the displacement of neutral competence with politicking—and then set about offering a set of policies designed to fix it. Often, though, these suggestions treat those who would ratify and implement such reforms not as political creatures operating within well-defined institutional settings, but as the sort of people who make up the commission itself: thoughtful, reflective, and socially conscious individuals devoid of any clear institutional attachments. Not surprisingly, the primary contributions of these reports are to landfills.

Such was the case with the 2008 National War Powers Commission, which represents one of the most concerted efforts of the last quarter century to reform the domestic institutional machinery of war. Rather than lambaste an imperial president and feckless Congress, as so many had done before, the commission sought to lend a more measured tone and constructive voice to ongoing debates about the domestic politics of war. Substantively, the commission aimed to clarify the obligations of presidents and members of Congress during the lead-up to war, to calm the partisan bickering that so often accompanies military deployments, and crucially, to promote reforms that bipartisan majorities could accept.

The specific changes promoted by the commission were packaged as a legislative proposal: the War Powers Consultation Act (WPCA). The principal objective of the WPCA, which the commission hoped Congress would enact into law, was to augment the quality and frequency of interbranch dialogue. As the commission's members put it, their primary objective was to establish "a constructive, workable, politically acceptable legal framework that will best promote effective, cooperative, and deliberative action by both the President and Congress in matters of war." Hence, the WPCA set forth guidelines—some binding, others not—for how the president and Congress ought to communicate with one another during the lead-up to war. These guidelines were intended to strengthen Congress's ability to extract from the executive branch information about a prospective military venture but also to require members of Congress to take a clear position for or against an impending war. The WPCA promised to replace secrecy with forthrightness, obscurity with transparency, happenstance with order. Because the act did not meaningfully alter the basic impetus for presidents to seek power, however, there was little reason to expect that it would materially change how we, as a country, go to war. And so it hasn't.

Yet it was on precisely this possibility that the commission's final report took pride. The report repeatedly states the commission's intention to offer a "pragmatic approach" for how Congress and the president can work out their differences about war. As their guiding principle the members of the commission sought to develop a proposal that would "maximize the likelihood" that the president and Congress would more productively consult with one another. The commission had no interest in offering symbolic reform. Rather, the commission's legislative proposal intended to deliver results.

But to deliver results, the WPCA had to be self-enforcing. Certainly the commission's members could not count on the judiciary to police either

Congress or the president. Although it cited the judiciary's unwillingness to affirm the constitutionality of the existing War Powers Resolution as among that statute's central failings, the commission offered no reason to expect things to be any different under the WPCA. The WPCA's success, therefore, depended on the inclination of both Congress and the president to abide by its central provisions.

The members of the commission certainly recognized the self-serving ways in which presidents interpret laws. When making their case against the War Powers Resolution, the members pointed out that "presidents have regularly involved the country's armed forces in what are clearly 'hostilities' under the terms of the statute, while claiming the statute is unconstitutional or not triggered in that particular case." The commission, though, gave us no reason to believe that things will be especially different under their new statutory framework. Nothing about the WPCA fundamentally altered the core incentives of presidents to seize and control the federal government's war powers.

It is of some note, then, that the War Powers Consultation Act offered plenty of ambiguities of its own, each ripe for presidential exploitation. Take, for instance, the requirement that the president consult with Congress in cases of "significant armed conflict." When is an armed conflict "significant"? Does every military deployment represent a "conflict"? Answers to these questions are hardly straightforward. Recall that Truman labeled America's involvement in Korea a "police action." In the 1960s, first Kennedy and then Johnson insisted that they were deploying U.S. military personnel only to "train and advise" local Vietnamese forces. According to Reagan, military excursions in Lebanon were a "rescue and peacekeeping" operation, and Grenada was a mere "rescue" mission. In each of these cases, presidents redefined their actions in ways that allowed them to avoid the very kinds of consultations that the commission hoped to foster.

The ambiguities within this act continue further still. Consider the expansive exceptions that the commission granted to presidents under the WPCA. Presidents, for instance, need not consult with Congress about "limited acts of reprisal against terrorists or states that sponsor terrorism." But as former legislators Paul Findley and Don Fraser rightly ask: "Who identifies 'terrorists'? Who defines 'terrorism'? Who determines which are 'states that sponsor terrorism'? Who defines 'limited'? The president alone." With both the freedom to define the law and powerful incentives to skirt it, it was not at all clear how the WPCA would compel presidents to substantially increase the quality or frequency of consultation with other branches of government.

Constitutionally, Congress already has the power to express its views about a war, either in support or opposition; to demand that the president provide information about either a prospective or ongoing war; and to pass bills that authorize, end, or otherwise govern a war. Yet Congress members regularly choose not to exercise these powers at their disposal. And when they do, their motivation has less to do with constitutional allegiance and more to do with partisan politics. A substantial body of research shows that Democrats within Congress regularly and predictably support Democratic presidents who are contemplating military action, just as Republican members of Congress back Republican presidents; and that it is nearly always across party lines that the deepest political cleavages erupt.

These facts have clear implications for the WPCA. Copartisans within Congress are unlikely to force the president to consult with them more regularly than they already do. Members of the opposition party, meanwhile, may well challenge the president. They will do so, however, not out of a shared sense of duty to defend laws enacted under previous presidents, nor (and this is crucial) out of a natural inclination to guard their institution against the encroachments of another. Though presidents seek and guard power tenaciously, members of Congress do not. Hence, their propensity to check the president has less to do with the power claims he asserts than with the ways in which his policies and actions map onto their own reelection considerations.

When members of Congress are willing to resist the president on matters involving war, as with all sorts of other issues, they do so because they have powerful political incentives to criticize the opposition president who takes our nation to war. Because they recognize these political incentives, presidents tend to resist the demands for information sharing that follow. Implore as it might, the WPCA does nearly nothing to contain presidential ambition, bolster Congress's sense of self-efficacy, or restructure the relations between Congress and the president. Like so many other pledges, reports, and op-ed articles that fall under the rubric of "good government," the WPCA promises a great deal more than it can possibly deliver.

BUT DON'T PRESIDENTS CARE AT ALL
ABOUT THE RULE OF LAW?

Though politically naïve in their ambition, advocates of a more limited U.S. presidency may nonetheless hold some sway. Presidents, after all, do not usually flaunt their power. Occasionally, in fact, they show signs of restraint. Going out of their way to justify the legality of their actions, some presidents, at least some of the time, honorably eschew political exigencies in order to fulfill their oath to "preserve, protect and defend the Constitution of the United States." Presidents' gestures toward the rule of law, what is more, may not be entirely for show.

Take, by way of example, William Howard Taft's expressed views about the presidency. In a famous series of lectures at Columbia University in 1915–16, Taft argued that "the president can exercise no power which cannot be fairly and reasonably traced to some specific grant of power" in the Constitution or a law passed by Congress. Throughout his tenure, Taft counseled, the president must retain a continual and meticulous awareness about his actions' legality. And those actions that are not explicitly authorized under the Constitution or the corpus of statutory law should not be taken.

This view, which stood in stark contrast to his predecessor Teddy Roosevelt's stewardship theory of presidential power, made Taft something of a hero among libertarians. It also turned the president into a middling advocate of the policy changes, such as a reduction of national tariffs, on which he had run in the 1908 election. After assuming office the following year, Taft promptly convened a special session of Congress to tackle the issue. That, though, was as far as he could bring himself to rustle up support for his policy initiative. In his opening address on the subject, Taft "laconically mentioned the conditions that made it necessary" to address the issue and "pleaded for speedy action" from Congress, without even mentioning his actual goal of reduction. Thereafter, Taft refused to apply any direct pressure on Congress. The president's principled inaction allowed Representative Sereno Payne and Senator Nelson Aldrich to significantly dilute the provisions Taft had campaigned on; the final bill, the Payne-Aldrich Tariff Act, contained substantially fewer reductions and, in some instances, actually raised some tariffs. Though his fellow Progressives encouraged him to veto the bill, Taft claimed that it was the result of a fair legislative process as envisioned by the Constitution. He signed the bill and then defended it in later addresses to Congress.

Taft was among the most reluctant presidents in U.S. history. He much preferred an appointment to the Supreme Court, a wish that President Warren Harding granted him in 1921. But he was not the only president to harbor legal interpretations of a limited American presidency. Indeed, such concerns infuse the public rhetoric and private deliberations of the nation's most esteemed—and, not coincidentally, most powerful—president, Abraham Lincoln. Long recognized as a "constitutional dictator," Lincoln twice suspended habeas corpus during the Civil War, including once against the explicit order of the federal judiciary in *Ex parte Merryman*, just as he jailed many Americans merely for expressing antigovernment sentiment. Still, Lincoln insisted that there existed an upper limit to what his principles would allow.

In 1864, Lincoln faced the prospect of another presidential election. It was not altogether clear, though, that a proper election could be held while the civil war continued to rage. Anticipating defeat, Republicans from across the nation, as well as Treasury Secretary Salmon Chase and former secretary of war Simon Cameron, urged Lincoln to delay. Though he might well have gotten away with it, Lincoln nonetheless refused such counsel, later writing that "if there is anything which it is the duty of the whole people to never entrust to any hands but their own, that thing is the perseveration and perpetuity, of their own liberties, and institutions." Though he already had demonstrated a clear willingness to curtail civil liberties, Lincoln felt a profound moral duty to follow the laws regarding elections—so much so, in fact, that he required his entire cabinet to sign a pledge vowing that "although it seems exceedingly probable that this Administration will not be re-elected . . . it will be my duty to cooperate with the President-elect" to ensure a smooth transition.

Some presidents, then, do have it in them to deny their own interests and curtail their own power. Yet while the examples of Taft and Lincoln have their place, we must not take the point too far. Both Lincoln and Taft, after all, held office during times when the public did not expect nearly as much of the president as it does today. Independent of political costs and calculations, the rule of law remains a second-order consideration among modern presidents. When forced to choose between paying sanctity to the law and steadfastly pursuing the public interest, modern presidents nearly always choose the latter. And when they do privilege the rule of law over the public interest, as we shall soon see, presidents pay a steep political price.

Publicly, presidents tend to give legal considerations their due when they are married to the political mobilization of those branches of government that stand in their way. Absent a judicial, legislative, or public rebuke, whether administered contemporaneously or in the near future, presidents can be expected to gather unto themselves all the power within their reach. This is the regular course of presidential politics. As we have discussed at some length, our very system of government is predicated on the notion that ambition must be made to check ambition, that constraints on presidential power depend on legislative and judicial will, and that neither the law nor Constitution alone could be counted on to reign in an especially entrepreneurial president. Reflecting on the Bill of Rights in Federalist No. 48, James Madison declared that it would be unsafe "to trust to these parchment barriers against the encroaching spirit of power." The various institutional components of government must stand ready to check each other without usurping one another's duties, lest any one branch "everywhere extend the sphere of its activity, and draw all power into its impetuous vortex"—and for what it is worth, Madison saw Congress as the most likely offender.

For still more reasons, legal considerations tread lightly on the exercise of presidential power. Precisely because the Constitution and the corpus of law are collectively so vague, presidents can often cobble together arguments on behalf of most power moves. Such arguments may not be especially persuasive to a disinterested party. But in the absence of legislative or judicial reprobation, which is precisely when legal constraints are needed most, such arguments may suffice for a president bent on expanding his power. We should not underestimate a president's capacity to read into the Constitution and law powers that neither the Founders nor enacting coalitions intended to confer.

During times of crisis, meanwhile, the fibers of legal constraints are stretched to their limit. Sometimes they snap. A growing body of empirical research documents the expansions of presidential power that occur during times of war. And among constitutional law scholars, who are particularly concerned about the status of legal constraints, the liberating effects of war on presidential power are widely recognized. Indeed, a massive literature on "crisis jurisprudence" directly repudiates the notion, often expressed by judges themselves, that the government cannot change "a constitution, or declare it changed, simply because it appears ill-adapted to a new state of things." Quite the opposite, crisis jurisprudence insists that the Constitution, if it is to survive, must adapt and evolve. The material context in which presidents operate crucially determines the legality of their actions. And as contexts go, war legitimates presidential power like no other. As Justice Felix Frankfurter argued in *Korematsu v. United States,* "The validity of action under the war power must be judged wholly in the context of war. That action is not to be stigmatized as lawless because like action in times of peace would be lawless." Plainly, the president cannot round up thousands of citizens of a particular national background on a whim, as Roosevelt did to Japanese Americans in World War II. But as long as the nation's security is at risk, Frankfurter reasoned, the courts ought to grant presidents a measure of deference that appropriately eludes their peacetime associates.

Of greatest relevance, though, is that presidents pay a steep political price when they even so much as appear indifferent to the public interest. As the next chapter illustrates, presidents who fail to act, even when the statutory or constitutional basis for action is dubious, face the prospect of a substantial political backlash against them and their party. As a practical matter, therefore, concerns about the rule of law do not bind especially tight. Unlike cultural and political constraints that function as outside and independent checks on presidential power—which we discuss at some length in this book's final chapter—legal considerations must burrow into the conscience of presidents. And we, like the nation's Founders, should be highly skeptical that a principled commitment to the rule of law will reliably and consistently guide presidents as they try, largely in vain, to manage the extraordinary demands and expectations placed before them.

CHAPTER 6

What Failure Looks Like

We have seen how presidents accumulate more power for themselves, building on the authority of their predecessors and adapting the tools of the office to suit their own agenda. That the American public has allowed presidents to accrue such power speaks to what novelist and essayist Joan Didion calls "that divergence between our official and our unofficial heroes . . . the apparently bottomless gulf between what we say we want and what we do want." Superficially, we want presidents who act within the constraints of office and duly recognize the authority of Congress, the courts, and the larger constitutional order. In practice, however, the public esteems presidents who break constitutional rules and find ways to exercise their will in the face of institutional checks on their power. The Founders expected presidents to seek power. The American people demand as much. We harbor high expectations for our commanders in chief, and our desire to see those expectations fulfilled consistently outweighs our concerns for constitutional or legal checks on presidential power.

Nowhere is this gap between our official and unofficial expectations more clear than when presidents fail to exploit powers that are there for the taking. Nothing invites censure like failing to utilize the full extent of authority to meet a crisis head-on. The greatest disgrace a president can commit is to sit idle while the world unravels around him. Presidents who advance normatively bad policy, who patently pursue their own private interests, or who engage in corrupt or even criminal behavior will usually receive their due admonishments. But when refusing to act—or worse yet, proving unable to act precisely when action appears called for—presidents invite all sorts of ridicule on themselves. It is the neutered president, forceless and frail, who becomes the laughing stock of late night television.

Lest you doubt this, consider the round condemnations that persistently surround nearly all recounting of Jimmy Carter's attempts to free the Iranian hostages, George Bush's nonchalant flyby over New Orleans in the immediate aftermath of Hurricane Katrina, and Barack Obama's mishandling of the debt crisis in the late summer of 2011. In each of these instances, the presidents then in office did in fact take active steps to address the challenge at hand. Yet in the end, public perceptions of executive impotence and indifference cut through to the bones of their reputations.

CARTER AND THE IRANIAN HOSTAGES

On November 4, 1979, a group of young Islamic militants stormed the U.S. embassy in Tehran by force, taking 66 Americans hostage; 444 days later, the last of the hostages were released unharmed—thereby concluding one of the most tumultuous periods in American foreign policy. Throughout it all, the eyes of Americans remained locked on the news out of Iran. "From the moment the hostages were seized until they were released," writes historian George Gaddis Smith, "the crisis absorbed more concentrated effort by American officials and had more extensive coverage on television and in the press than any other event since World War II, including the Vietnam War." The Iran hostage crisis helped topple the presidency of Jimmy Carter, just as it aided the unlikely ascendancy of conservative hero Ronald Reagan from actor to president of the United States. Carter returned to Georgia in disgrace, despite having successfully negotiated a peaceful resolution to the crisis just before his term expired. His legacy never fully recovered.

Tragically, perhaps, Carter's failures derive not from an unwillingness to act, but rather from a lack of viable options for action. In hindsight, it is unclear that Carter could have handled the situation much differently than he did; indeed, he ultimately achieved his ideal outcome of a safe hostage return without spilling blood or caving to enemy demands. But while "waiting out" the crisis, an overwhelming public perception set in that Carter was a weak and ineffective commander in chief who avoided military conflict at all costs. By the time the hostages finally came home, the perception had hardened into a widely accepted fact. It was Carter's failure to act—even when no obvious course of action presented itself—that ultimately proved to be his downfall.

In the Iranian Revolution of January 1979, Islamists deposed the regime of the shah of Iran and brought Islamic cleric Ruhollah Khomeini back from exile to lead the country. The shah had been an ally of the United States throughout the Cold War, and his overthrow was seen as a desta-bilizing factor in the Middle East, where other countries such as Egypt and Afghanistan functioned under Soviet influence. More hawkish ele-ments within the Carter administration, such as national security advisor Zbigniew Brzezinski, urged the president to crush the Islamic uprisings with military force. The State Department, in contrast, argued that Carter should work with the revolutionaries to build a new government, thereby ensuring that America retained its influence in the region. Faced with two difficult options—commit U.S. troops to a violent foreign civil war or sup-port the consolidation of power by violent and disorganized militants—Carter chose neither. The Islamists promptly gained control of the country and began chastising the United States as an enemy of the Iranian people. The result proved utterly damning for the president. As Gaddis Smith puts it, "President Carter inherited an impossible situation—and he and his advisers made the worst of it."

By failing to respond immediately and decisively to the Iranian revolu-tion, Carter left himself open to criticism that he was weak willed: a damn-ing label in any era, but especially so during the height of the Cold War. Within the Carter administration, officials recognized the importance of projecting a strong will in the international arena. In a top secret internal memo at the time, Brzezinski warned Carter that he needed to convince Americans he was a strong chief executive: "For domestic political reasons you ought to deliberately toughen both the tone and substance of our foreign policy. The country associates assertiveness with leadership." Less than eight weeks later, events conspired to give Carter another chance to test his assertiveness. Iranian militants had taken American citizens hos-tage, and Iran's new leader, Ruhollah Khomeini, endorsed their actions. How would the president react this time?

In the immediate aftermath of the embassy takeover, President Carter strove to calm the nation's fears, even as he met around the clock with advisors to develop a plan of action. Once again, though, it was not immediately clear what legitimate options for action there were. The United States had never faced a foreign state-sanctioned hostage situation. And national policy experts lacked a comprehensive understanding of the Islamist militants' background and demands. There were simply no existing policies in place for dealing with such a crisis: it was "a problem which is so novel that appears entirely without precedent." In an eerily prescient interaction, Carter had actually asked his advisers months earlier, after a previous threat on the embassy in Tehran, how the United States might deal with such an attack in the future. As Vice President Walter Mondale later recalled, "[Carter] said, 'And if [the Iranians] take our employees in our embassy hostage, then what would be your advice?' And the room just fell dead. No one had an answer to that. Turns out, we never did." Whereas during the Iranian revolution, Carter was presented with two clear options and embraced neither, during the hostage crisis he was given no clear plans for how to assert himself.

Despite this uncertainty, Carter kept busy during the early stages of the crisis. The president first met with military leaders, who detailed the high levels of risk involved in any attempt to liberate the hostages by force. Fearing that the hostages would be executed should anything go wrong, Carter and his team turned to diplomacy. The president moved quickly to organize a boycott of Iranian oil, the nation's primary export and main source of revenue. He also froze all Iranian assets housed in U.S. banks, further undermining Iran's financial stability. As he took these actions, Carter addressed the American public repeatedly, unveiling a "Rose Garden Strategy" that essentially promised the president would not leave the White House until the hostages had been brought home safely. The public, for its part, rallied behind their president. Before the hostages were captured, Carter's approval rating had plummeted to a lowly 32 percent. In the three weeks after the embassy takeover, his approval rating soared past 50 percent, and before long it climbed toward 60 percent.

The media coverage was all encompassing, as television channels scrambled for any morsel of new information out of Iran. The image of blindfolded American hostages being led about by their captors filled the nightly news. CBS news anchor Walter Cronkite signed off each broadcast with a running counter of the number of days since the hostages were first captured. Not to be outdone, ABC aired a late night news program called *America Held Hostage,* which focused entirely on the fate of the hostages held at the embassy. Hosted by Ted Koppel, the show aired nightly, even as breaking developments were few and far between. Undeterred, the program's producers began resorting to increasingly sensational tactics. In one memorable episode, the show staged an on-air exchange between an unsuspecting Iranian diplomat and the wife of one of the hostages. Critics found the event "cheaply theatrical, mawkish and self-promotional," but the public ate it up. All this hyperactive media coverage fueled an ongoing overflow of patriotism among average Americans. People began buying yellow ribbons in record numbers, which they tied around trees, fence posts and articles of clothing. In a more troubling trend, Americans also purchased a record number of Iranian flags for the purposes of burning during public demonstrations.

This nationalist fervor helped buoy President Carter's approval ratings in the early days of the crisis. But as time wore on, the days kept getting counted off, and Americans kept turning on their televisions to discover that nothing had changed. The stasis eventually took its toll on the president's image. Whereas most Americans were initially satisfied with Carter's insistence that no viable military options were available, steadily there emerged a renewed sense that the commander in chief was holding back. As one citizen wrote in the *Denver Post*: "These Iranians have committed an act of war against the United States and all Carter wants to do at the moment is talk. It is time to speak with the power and the might of a first rate country instead of the wishy-washy language of diplomatic compromise."

With his approval ratings dropping—in an election year, no less—and pressure mounting for him to instigate an end to the crisis, President Carter finally embraced aggressive action. On April 24, 1980, he ordered a rescue attempt known as Operation Eagle Claw, an option that the administration had previously rejected after military leadership deemed it too risky. The covert mission called for helicopters to drop off troops in Tehran in the dead of night for an assault on the embassy. It proved to be a disaster. Halfway through the operation, two of the helicopters suffered technical malfunctions, causing Carter to call off the mission. Meanwhile, a third helicopter crashed into a transport vehicle, killing eight U.S. troops in the middle of the desert. On the news the next day, Americans were greeted by footage of Iranians gleefully pointing to the smoldering remains of a U.S. helicopter: a symbol of the great military power's inability to free its citizens from the clutches of a small band of poorly armed militants.

President Carter's popularity did not plummet in the wake of this catastrophe; in fact, his approval rating actually increased from 39 to 43 percent. Citizens across the country penned letters to their local newspapers applauding Carter for finally ordering a brave military action—even though the action failed. "My thanks to Mr. Carter and to those who volunteered," one man wrote the *Tampa Tribune*. "I wouldn't have voted for Carter before but I will now." A woman in Birmingham agreed, writing, "I'm sad that it didn't work [but] I think it was very important to try. . . . I think everyone in the United States should stand behind James Carter, and I'm not a Carter fan." And in a letter to the *Denver Post*, a man took the media to task for second-guessing the president: "It turned out unfortunately sad and tragic, but I am proud that it was at least attempted."

The president's orders played out in the worst way possible: he lost American lives, failed to rescue the hostages, and publicly embarrassed the U.S. military on an international stage. Yet at home, this was actually seen as a slight improvement over the president's previous decisions to impose sanctions and negotiate for the hostages' eventual release—decisions that seemingly betrayed an incapacity for firmer action. The lesson is clear: presidents face powerful incentives to assert their authority first and sort out the consequences later. In the public's eye, action is nearly always superior to inaction. Action reveals bold and strong leadership, whereas inaction betrays cowardice and debility.

Unfortunately for Carter, after this failed military rescue mission, there were no more bold actions left to take. Unwilling to risk further casualties and with little recourse to impose further sanctions, the president resolved to negotiate his way to the bitter end. His approval ratings suffered as a consequence. For the next eleven months, Carter used diplomatic channels to fulfill his promise of bringing the hostages home. Ultimately, he was successful—but by that time, he had already lost the presidential election by a full 10 percent of the popular vote. Just as Ronald Reagan was giving his inaugural address, the Americans who had spent more than a year as hostages at the Iranian embassy were put on a plane headed for home. Looking back on the events years later, Carter opined that the crisis had cost him a second term in office.

In the three decades since the hostage crisis, President Carter's name has largely become synonymous with ineffective presidential leadership. Ted Koppel, the former host of *America Held Hostage*, characterized the perception of Carter during the crisis as "sort of wimpish, feckless." It is a characterization that has stuck. In recent years, it has become common for critics of the Obama administration to pejoratively compare the current president to Carter. "Jimmy Carter's Legacy of Failure," read one 2006 op-ed headline. During the 2008 presidential debates, John McCain argued that voting for Obama would be like voting Carter into a second term. In 2010, Walter Russell Mead declared that "the worst scenario" would be for Obama to replicate Carter's "weakness and indecision" in foreign policy. And during the midterm elections of that year, MSNBC host Chris Matthews wondered if Democrats up for reelection would "run away from President O'Carter."

It is ironic that Carter's lasting legacy of weakness stems from his inability to take strong action in a situation that was largely out of his control. There were few viable courses of action during the Iran hostage crisis. Yet public perception is not based on how prudently presidents think through decisions to act or not to act—or even what action means. The public sees only presence and absence, and it punishes absence with a vengeance. Pleading the constraints of circumstances does not fly, for nothing is ever considered fully outside the president's control. The journalist Elizabeth Drew, herself no ally of Carter, summed up President Carter's predicament thusly: "Fairly or not, [the hostage crisis] came to symbolize the question of whether Carter was a leader, whether he was competent, whether he was strong. . . . In some ways this was unfair. It happened. Things happen on presidential watches. In the end, though, it undid him." For presidents, passive admissions that "things happen" are untenable. Presidents must *make* things happen. And when they fail in this regard, their leadership credentials are predictably called into question.

BUSH'S CATASTROPHIC FLYBY

"George Bush doesn't care about black people." With this accusation, uttered live before a national television audience, rapper Kanye West helped cement a lasting public perception that the devastation wrought by Hurricane Katrina in the summer of 2005 might have been prevented had the president done more. Later, Bush would say that he remembered West's comment as "one of the most disgusting moments of my presidency." At the time, however, the popular music artist was not the only one raking Bush over the coals for his response to the tragedy, which was seen as "a monumental failure of leadership." Indeed, even politicians within the president's own party viewed Bush's response as wildly ineffectual: Republican senator Susan Collins claimed it undermined his "reputation for competence and compassion," adding that the president's demeanor appeared "hesitant and halting when it should have been crisp and competent." A year after the storm, polling found that only 34 percent of Americans approved of how Bush handled Katrina's aftermath.

Unquestionably, government responses to the crisis in the Gulf Coast were mismanaged at the federal, state, and local levels. Yet the disapproval directed at President Bush was particularly acerbic; and its origins involved a great deal more than just policy failure. At its heart, the public's anger stemmed from the perception that Bush had failed to uphold the obligations of his office. Americans expect their commander in chief to be commanding: strong, decisive, unflappable. Bush, by contrast, appeared addled, aloof, out of his element—not so much powerless as incapable of authoritatively asserting his power. In the days immediately following Katrina's landfall, the president himself neglected to appear on scene. Infamously, he chose the comforts of Air Force One rather than stopping to assess the damage in person. This became the iconic image of Bush and Katrina. Despite numerous visits to Louisiana and Mississippi in the weeks and months that followed, Bush could not shake this initial characterization as a "flyover" president. He learned the hard way that the public punishes presidents who fail to project an image of authority, while rewarding those who solidify their powerful reputations with speeches and photo-ops. Whatever the president *does*, he must *appear* in control of events at all times.

In times of crisis, Americans tend to rally around their leaders, lending their fealty to a president who both embodies and guards the nation's honor. During the Iran hostage ordeal, as we have seen, the public initially supported President Carter, despite the fact that Carter did not actually take any strong action to save the hostages. What Carter did do was immediately position himself front and center before the American public, holding press conferences and giving televised speeches to calm people's fears. For a time, these public appearances projected an image of a president in control, for which he was rewarded politically.

President Bush, in contrast, failed to get out in front of Hurricane Katrina. Before the storm even arrived on the Gulf Coast, it had already been declared a Category 5 hurricane. Two days before landfall, the governors of Louisiana and Mississippi had already declared states of emergency, and FEMA had formally recognized the possibility of massive flooding. A day before landfall, New Orleans mayor Ray Nagin had issued the first-ever mandatory evacuation of city residents. But the day Katrina finally arrived and the first levee was breached, Bush made three public appearances completely unconnected to the hurricane: two visits, to an Arizona resort and a California senior center, promoting his Medicare drug benefit legislation; and a birthday photo-op with Senator John McCain, which pictured the two smiling men holding a big cake. The next day, the president spoke at a naval base about the war in Iraq and posed for a publicity photo in which he played guitar with country singer Mark Willis. He then returned to his ranch in Texas to finish off a nearly five-week-long vacation. The next day Bush finally returned to Washington and held his first press conference on Katrina.

The president's activities during this period contrasted sharply with the images of the unfolding disaster that Americans witnessed in newspapers, on television, and on the Internet. On August 30, the *New York Times* ran a huge front-page headline: "Hurricane Katrina slams into Gulf Coast; Dozens are Dead." The following day, the paper's headline was more drastic still: "New Orleans is Inundated as 2 Levees Fail; Much of Gulf Coast is Crippled; Toll Rises." The nation watched in horror as hundreds of thousands of people streamed out of the region. The photos of the flooding were dramatic and devastating: people stranded on roofs, their homes completely underwater; children and families huddled in the streets as rioters rampantly looted local stores. Mayor Nagin told reporters that rescue boats had no time to fish out the corpses floating through the city: "We're not even dealing with dead bodies. . . . They're just pushing them to the side." A gruesome *Los Angeles Times* story depicted the conditions in the Superdome, the local stadium transformed into a refugee camp:

> A 2-year-old girl slept in a pool of urine. Crack vials littered a restroom. Blood stained the walls next to vending machines smashed by teenagers . . . At least two people, including a child, have been raped.

At least three people have died, including one man who jumped 50 feet to his death, saying he had nothing left to live for. There is no sanitation. The stench is overwhelming.

Amidst these unfolding terrors, the product of what the media was calling the "greatest natural disaster" in U.S. history, the president was nowhere. In the public's eyes, Bush's absence from the scene was unconscionable. That Bush failed to benefit from a rally effect after Katrina—that, indeed, he suffered a significant drop in public support—can be attributed primarily to his activities during the gap between when the storm struck and when he issued his first public statements more than two days later. The degradations of average Americans taking place across the Gulf Coast frightened a country in which the horrors of September 11 were still fresh in the national consciousness. In the wake of this tragedy, people longed for unity and leadership. By not immediately speaking out on the flooding and the subsequent death and destruction, the president failed to rally Americans around their flag. As a result, Americans failed to rally around their president.

With the publication of a photo of Bush flying over the region on the way back from vacationing at his ranch, the public turned against the president for good. That Bush happened to be on vacation, and not in Washington, when the storm struck was an unfortunate coincidence for the administration. The president's decision not to cancel his scheduled public appearances in the two days after Katrina made landfall was a severe political miscalculation. Yet even at that point, had Bush flown to New Orleans and consoled the victims, had he personally surveyed the damage on the ground, had he met with the local police and rescue teams, it is possible that he might have salvaged his reputation. Instead, White House staffers invited reporters and photographs to visit with the president on Air Force One and take pictures as the plane flew over—not to—New Orleans.

The resulting uproar set the tone for nearly all media coverage that followed. "Instead of looking out the window of an airplane, [Bush] should have been on the ground giving the people devastated by this hurricane hope," railed Democratic senator Frank Lautenberg. Another Democrat, Representative Harold Ford, accused the president of having a "cavalier attitude": "Now is not the time in the face of pain, anguish and death to be weak and uncertain," he said. In the media, pundits lambasted Bush for the words he supposedly uttered while surveying the wreckage out of the plane's window: "It's devastating. It must be doubly devastating on the ground." Liberal commentator Arianna Huffington wrote, "Hey, here's an idea, Mr. President: maybe you should, y'know, get off the plane and see for yourself?" Huffington extended the incident into a metaphor for Bush's entire tenure in office—"The Flyover Presidency of George W. Bush"—which she described as "detached, disconnected, disengaged." The label stuck, and public vitriol against the president hardened.

In the days following the flyover, the Bush administration scrambled to salvage the president's image as a strong, engaged leader. Bush spoke regularly about the crisis, assuring the nation that federal departments such as FEMA were working "to save lives," and expressing confidence that, "with time . . . the great city of New Orleans will be back on its feet." On Friday, September 2—four days after Katrina first hit—Bush visited the region in person, holding a press conference and posing in front of demolished homes and flood victims. He returned to the Gulf Coast again the following week. At first, the administration was hopeful Americans would come around and lend their support to the president. As one White House official told a reporter, "Normal people at home understand that it's not the president who's responsible for this, it's the hurricane."

When Bush's approval ratings fell to the lowest of his presidency, his administration kicked things into high gear. Political advisor Karl Rove and communications director Dan Bartlett directed executive branch officials not to respond directly to attacks on the president's handling of Katrina. Instead, they were instructed to shift blame onto local levels of government in their public remarks—as Secretary of Homeland Security Michael Chertoff did, when he argued on television that "the responsibility and the power, the authority . . . rests with state and local officials." Meanwhile, the White House continued to orchestrate the federal response after the initial tragedy, diverting a total of $109 billion federal dollars in the year after Katrina to families and communities in the Gulf Coast. But while these political and policy moves may have helped divert some heat away from Bush, they ultimately failed to dispel the public's image of the president looking down on the wreckage of Katrina from thousands of feet in the air. As Senator Collins later reflected, "Unfortunately, it may be hard to erase the regrettable photo of him on Air Force One. . . . That's a searing and very unfortunate image that doesn't reflect the president's compassion."

To be fair, the president's decision not to land in New Orleans probably had little material effect on the ongoing relief efforts. If anything, as White House officials subsequently argued, there were credible reasons to think that landing Air Force One on the Gulf Coast in the midst of a massive emergency relief situation would have done more harm than good. In 2010, Karl Rove wrote in his memoirs that landing in New Orleans "would have been disruptive" to relief workers and security forces trying to maintain order, adding that the decision not to stop "was right for the relief effort but wrong for President Bush's public standing." Realistically, the president was not about to swoop in and start pulling victims from the flood with his bare, outstretched hands. And when Bush finally did arrive on the scene two days later, critics accused the president of diverting Coast Guard helicopters to stage a photo-op.

The president's seeming indifference to Katrina distracted attention from a more suspect culprit: the Bush administration's long-term policy decisions in the years leading up to the catastrophe. As some observers pointed out, the federal failure after Katrina could potentially be traced to the president's decision in March 2003 to downgrade FEMA from a cabinet position and fold it into the newly formed Department of Homeland Security, where it garnered less attention. Fingers also could be pointed toward President Bush's repeated slashing of agency budgets. In the summer of 2004, FEMA denied Louisiana a predisaster funding mitigation request. That same summer, and again in June 2005, the budget for the New Orleans district of the Army Corps of Engineers, part of which was allocated for levee construction and repairs, was cut. At that time, one local emergency management chief was quoted as saying, "It appears that the money has been moved in the president's budget to handle homeland security and the war in Iraq, and I suppose that's the price we pay." These were legitimate policy decisions the president had a hand in, which ultimately might have exacerbated the aftermath of Katrina. As liberal critic Kevin Drum noted at the time, "I don't blame [Bush] for being on vacation when Katrina made landfall. I don't blame him for a certain amount of chaos in the initial response. . . . Nor do I think that Bush doesn't care about national disasters." Instead, wrote Drum, the media attention should focus on the true nature of Bush's failure: "What happened was the result of a long series of decisions, all flowing out of Bush's natural conservative governing instincts, that added up to make Katrina more damaging than it had to be and at the same time eroded our ability to react to its aftermath." But while Drum and a handful of others raised these substantive points, most fixated on the optics of Bush's flyover. By and large, the president was harangued less for his policy decisions or even his governing philosophy than for the perception that he did not care enough to act.

For proof, contrast the public's treatments of Bush after Katrina and 9/11. While Hurricane Katrina is considered one of Bush's greatest failures, his presence at Ground Zero in the aftermath of the September 11 attacks is remembered as perhaps his finest hour. Bush, standing alongside a New York City firefighter, spoke through a megaphone from atop the rubble of the fallen Twin Towers and assured those around him, "I can hear you. The rest of the world hears you. And the people who knocked down these buildings will hear all of us soon." Like Katrina, 9/11 shined a spotlight on bureaucratic failure in departments under the executive branch's purview. Like the levees breaking, there is evidence that the terrorist attacks on New York and Washington, D.C., could have been prevented beforehand with more careful and considered planning. And like the federal response to the plight in the Gulf Coast, America's initial response to being attacked was characterized largely by fear and confusion. Both tragedies occurred while George W. Bush was president. Yet one portrayed an aloof and overwhelmed president, the other a commander in charge and on the scene.

It is conceivable that, had Bush landed that day in New Orleans—had he stood amidst the wreckage, had he shaken relief workers' hands, had he prayed with the victims' families—the public's memories of Bush's involvement in Katrina might have been radically altered. But he didn't. From a safe perch above the city, the president flew over the ruin below; the moment was captured for posterity, and no amount of subsequent photoops or federal dollars could turn public opinion back in his favor. Repeated polling found that Bush was never able to return to the approval ratings he had enjoyed pre-Katrina. "I might argue that this was the worst thing that's happened to George Bush in the whole six years of his presidency,"

Democratic senator Charles Schumer told reporters a year after the storm. "It was a perception-altering event." Once a president is labeled weak or indecisive—either because of an action he fails to take, a decision he reverses course on, or even a perception of disengagement—the political damage is often irreversible.

After leaving office, Bush conceded that his response to Katrina was a "huge mistake," and that he considered it one of the lowest points of his presidency. Tellingly, however, the former president did not focus his regret on his decisions concerning when and how to commit federal resources to the region. Rather, it was his handling of public perception that Bush wished he had navigated better: "I should have touched down in Baton Rouge, met with the governor and walked out and said, 'I hear you. We understand,'" Bush lamented, adding that he now realized the flyover in Air Force One had made him appear "detached and uncaring." Bush learned from his experience with Katrina the lesson he seemed so in command of after 9/11: in times of crisis, the public wants—indeed, seems to viscerally need—a strong, decisive leader who unhesitatingly takes command, who projects power and authority, and who offers reassurance that someone is in control.

OBAMA LEAVES HIS LEVERAGE ON THE TABLE

President Barack Obama learned the price of inaction during the debt deal standoff in the summer of 2011. That May, Treasury Secretary Timothy Geithner announced that, in order to avoid reaching the country's existing $14.29 trillion limit on borrowing, the Treasury would be forced to take "extraordinary measures" to fund government agencies' existing obligations. Geithner warned Congress that unless the debt ceiling was raised by August 2, the federal government would officially be out of money and thus in danger of defaulting on its loans and shutting down key programs such as social security. Despite this sense of urgency, negotiations in Congress stalled: liberal Democrats refused to cut funding to many agencies and insisted on generating new revenue through tax increases, while newly elected conservative Republicans with Tea Party allegiances vowed to vote down any compromise that raised taxes, asserting that all budget relief must come from spending cuts. As the stalemate dragged into June and then July, all eyes turned to the president to see how he would handle the emerging crisis. Specifically, pundits and politicians wondered aloud whether Obama would step into the breach and unilaterally lift the debt ceiling himself.

As it turned out, President Obama did not flex his muscle in the debt ceiling debate, at least not publicly. And he was excoriated for it. Attacks on his leadership were ubiquitous, and they came from both sides of the partisan divide. On the left, the president's inability to dictate the terms of the debate was interpreted as a Republican victory. And with cause. The eleventh-hour agreement to raise the debt ceiling came with $2.1 trillion in government spending cuts and no increases in taxes. Liberal pundit Lincoln Mitchell complained that "Obama's silence" on the debt ceiling was "depressing" and represented "a failure to take moral leadership in the face of the grave and surreal threat posed by the far right." In a *New York Times* op-ed, professor Drew Westin analyzed the president's failure to lead in psychological terms, arguing that the "constraints of his character" compelled Obama to choose "bipartisanship" over "confrontation" with congressional Republicans. Conservatives, for their part, rather abruptly turned from criticizing the president's overreach on health care reform to criticizing the president's inability to take decisive action on the debt crisis. "The ultimate failure of President Barack Obama," noted John Mariotti, "is that he is unable or unwilling to lead." Obama, it was agreed by all, was too passive during the crisis. He abdicated his leadership responsibilities, rather than meeting the challenge head on.

In point of fact, Obama was not idling at this fateful intersection. His administration spent much of that time pushing for a debt deal, both publicly and behind closed doors. On July 7, the president convened talks with congressional leaders from both parties at the White House, where he pushed them to embrace his ambitious plan to cut the federal deficit by $4 trillion over the next decade. On July 21, Obama informed Democratic leaders in Congress that he and Republican Speaker John Boehner were close to achieving a deal that would cut spending and overhaul the tax structure to increase future revenue. And finally, after those and other talks broke down, President Obama brokered a last-minute deal with party leaders that led to the debt ceiling increase passed by Congress on August

1. Throughout this bargaining process, the president lambasted Republicans for their failure to compromise. He also repeatedly clarified for the American people the likely fallout of any failure to raise the debt ceiling.

For all these efforts, however, there was a widespread perception that Obama could have done more. Specifically, critics pointed out that the president could have bypassed a stalled Congress and taken matters into his own hands, giving the order to raise the debt ceiling himself. A July 22 op-ed by legal scholars Eric Posner and Adrian Vermeule laid the groundwork for this course of action. "Mr. Obama needs to make clear," they argued, "that he will act unilaterally to raise the debt ceiling if Congress does not cooperate." Their opinion was echoed by leading members of the president's own party in Congress, who urged the executive to take action if the legislature would not. "I believe that [unilateral action] will bring calm to the American people and will bring needed stability to our financial markets," said Representative James Clyburn, the third highest-ranking Democrat in the House. Senator Barbara Boxer opined, "I think [the president] should seriously look at whatever options he has." Even former president Bill Clinton entered the fray, suggesting that if he were in office, he would raise the debt ceiling unilaterally, "without hesitation, and force the courts to stop me."

Once a debt deal was reached, many lamented that the president did not "seriously look" at all his options, that he did not act promptly and forthrightly. Obama should have "been more adamant in dealing with Republicans . . . threatening to use constitutional powers to [raise] the debt ceiling if Congress abrogated its responsibility," chided the *New York Times* editorial board. In the paper's op-ed section, columnist Paul Krugman blamed the president for allowing conservative members of Congress to hijack the agenda of the debt debates, secure in their knowledge that Democrats had to go through them to get any deal legislatively. "At the very least," Krugman lamented, "Mr. Obama could have used the possibility of a legal end run to strengthen his bargaining position [with Republicans]. Instead, however, he ruled all such options out from the beginning."

For all the calls for Obama to threaten unilateral action, the available legal justifications for ordering that the debt ceiling be raised remained murky. Congress has the exclusive constitutional authority to authorize the federal government to borrow money. Since the Second Liberty Bond

Act of 1917, Congress has authorized government debts by creating a "ceiling"; rather than approving each individual bond, the debt ceiling establishes a legal limit on the total dollar amount of all bonds issued. For most of the twentieth century, approving the debt ceiling was something Congress did regularly and without controversy. Since additional bonds are issued to pay for government spending that Congress has already authorized, some observers believe the ceiling is actually legally redundant, and should be abolished. So long as the debt ceiling does exist, however, raising it would seem rather clearly to be Congress's prerogative.

Proponents of a presidential incursion into the legislative realm made arguments along two contrasting lines. Most advocates found legitimacy for presidential action in Section 4 of the Fourteenth Amendment, which states that the "validity of the public debt of the United States . . . shall not be questioned." If Congress allowed the country to run out of money, the argument went, it would be within the president's rights, and his Constitutional obligation, to order the Treasury to continue paying off existing debts as a means of ensuring that those debts were not called into question. Yet relying on the Fourteenth Amendment, as Congressman Clyburn and others urged the president to do, remained a shaky legal proposition. As former federal judge Michael McConnell observed at the time, upholding Section 4 was not inconsistent with abiding by the debt ceiling: "For Congress to limit the amount of the debt does not 'question' the 'validity' of the debt that has been 'authorized by law.' At most, it means that paying the public debts and pension obligations of the United States, as they become due, has priority over all other spending." Even after the government had reached the debt limit, it would have still continued to make approximately $175 billion in new revenue each month—enough to pay off existing obligations. To invoke the Fourteenth Amendment, the president would have had to prove that even after cutting spending on all other government programs, there still was not enough money to pay back debts. This was an impossible proposition. Thus President Obama no doubt spoke with veracity when, in his brief public comments on the possibility of using the Fourteenth Amendment, he dismissed the option's legality: the president had "talked to my lawyers," and they were "not persuaded that that is a winning argument."

Specific legal justifications were one thing. But students of executive authority who wanted the president to raise the debt ceiling also elucidated an alternative, more political, way forward. Posner and Vermeule, who had recently published a book called *The Executive Unbound*, thought that those looking at specific constitutional language were chasing a red herring. "Our argument," they wrote, "is not based on some obscure provision of the 14th amendment, but on . . . the president's role as the ultimate guardian of the constitutional order, charged with taking care that the laws be faithfully executed." From Lincoln to FDR, explained Posner and Vermeule, Obama's predecessors had already established a time-honored legal justification for the president acting unilaterally during times of crisis: the executive may violate a single law if it is necessary in preventing the upheaval of the entire constitutional order. With the country on the verge of bankruptcy, with the nation just coming out of a recession, with Standard and Poor's threatening to downgrade the U.S.'s credit rating (and they subsequently would), with cuts already in place for important government programs, and with Congress unable to produce a stabilizing debt deal legislatively, was it not within the president's purview to use his executive authority—to ensure that the laws of the land were executed?

If the president had chosen to threaten to raise the debt ceiling himself, he could have justified it to the American people. He might have put it as follows:

We are facing an economic crisis in this county of historic proportions. We did not create this dire fiscal situation; but together, we can get out of it. That is, if we take bold action now, today.

I have repeatedly stated my preference that both parties in Congress work to achieve a solution legislatively. I have repeatedly expressed a personal willingness to compromise with Republicans. I have even followed through on those promises of bipartisanship by making concessions on spending cuts to entitlement programs—a decision that earned me lots of criticism from my friends on the left. But I knew that keeping our country solvent was our greatest priority, and I hoped we could achieve that outcome by working together.

Unfortunately, Republicans in Congress have remained unwilling to compromise now, when the economic well-being of our country hangs in the balance. Because of their intransigence, talks remain at an impasse.

Meanwhile, the hour of American bankruptcy is at hand. The time for talking is over. Now is the time for action—before it is too late. That is why I have decided that, if a deal is not struck by August 1 at midnight, I will fulfill my executive responsibility and order the Treasury to raise the debt ceiling.

I never wanted us to reach this point. I hope we still do not reach this point. But if Congress continues to fail in its responsibilities, I will be left with no choice. All of the top economic minds in our country tell us that raising the debt ceiling is necessary. Leaders of both parties agree that it is necessary. The American people know that it is necessary. And if Congress can't get it done, then I will.

But Obama never gave that speech, or any version of it. Instead, he let Congress pass a weak bill that neither provided long-term fiscal stability nor met his policy objectives. The consequences were not just financial, but also political: by the end of July, the president's job approval rating had sunk to a new low of 40 percent. The debt ceiling crisis marked itself as one of the lowest points of his presidency.

From the public's perspective, Obama failed not because he acted incorrectly, but because he did not act with sufficient authority. Past presidents have shown great willingness to claim broad powers for themselves, given even the slightest window to do so. Because of the ambiguities inherent in the president's Article II powers, that window is almost always open at least a crack. Certainly it was open to President Obama in this instance. And while we may firmly believe in checks on executive power in theory, Americans not only allow but actively demand that presidents exercise outsized authority in crises. Anything less is perceived as a failure to lead. By not threatening to unilaterally raise the debt ceiling, Obama thus betrayed the public: he did not do everything in his power to avert a crisis; he left his leverage on the table.

In the months after the debt-ceiling showdown, Obama showed signs of having learned his lesson. His administration ended 2011 by publicly stating that its new strategy would be to bypass Congress and act unilaterally. Josh Earnest, the president's deputy press secretary, acknowledged that failure on the debt ceiling had led to the administration's new strategy, which involved painting "the image of a gridlocked, dysfunctional Congress and a president who is leaving no stone unturned to try to find solutions to the difficult . . . economic challenges facing the country." As if to show off this new approach, Obama directly challenged Republicans in Congress to adopt his temporary extension of the payroll tax cut in December 2011. Though they at first refused, Republicans eventually caved in the wake of public pressure favoring the extension and Obama's insistence that he would act if Congress did not. Emboldened by this success, the administration then announced that it would no longer consider working with Congress to be "a requirement." This aggressive posture marked a clear shift from the president's first run for office, which had centered on changing the partisan tone in Washington. Since serving as president, Obama learned the hard way that although the public might say they want compromise and consideration, what they really reward is decisive action.

Failure as Failure to Act

Presidents' preoccupation with power, of course, is not deterministic. While in office, presidents do as they choose. But as Obama's, Bush's, and Carter's examples in this chapter show, opting not to act—indeed, merely being perceived as not acting—comes at a great political cost.

These three presidents are not unique. Throughout the nation's history, the most stinging rebuke to a president is the charge that he demurred at precisely the moment when action was most needed. And for some presidents, this perceived failure, fair or not, has come to define their entire tenure in office.

James Buchanan, who assumed office in 1857, will forever languish in the dustbin of forgotten presidents not because he tried to resolve the simmering challenges between North and South and failed, but rather because he refused to pursue a resolution to the conflict with sufficient vigor. Buchanan, an accomplished lawyer and legislator, repeatedly insisted that while Southern secession was illegal, so too was any concerted effort by the president to stop it; that though he would prefer that the Union remain whole, he simply lacked the power to stand in its defense. Where power was lacking, he, as president, proved unwilling to claim it anew. Hence, as the issue of slavery passed from simmer to boil, his Democratic Party fractured, and the economic panic of 1857 set in, Buchanan at every turn took a measured response, underscoring the importance of constitutional restraint and the benefits of limited government. As president, Buchanan embodied the balance that the Founders had sought to ensure across the various branches of government. Yet by disavowing ambition and power, Buchanan satisfied no one. His contemporaries held him in contempt, and future historians scorned his failings.

And then there is Herbert Hoover, perhaps the most ideologically sophisticated president of the twentieth century. Amid the greatest economic depression the nation has ever known, Hoover only reluctantly extended the arm of government power to intervene in the marketplace. His reticence reflected a well-defined worldview about the proper role of government and the president's place within it. Straddling laissez-faire economics and what would later be known as Keynesianism, Hoover was an adamant proponent of public-private cooperation. The market, Hoover firmly believed, could not be expected to work itself out of every downturn. But Hoover thought the government should not force businesses to act in ways they were not otherwise inclined to. While he supported a variety of public works projects, tariff reforms, and monetary policy as antidotes to the growing economic malaise, Hoover would go no further. And for this, his was a failed presidency. When historians rank the nation's forty-four presidents according to their greatness—a quality lacking a clear definition, to be sure—Hoover typically appears in the mid-to-upper twenties. By refusing to meet the spiraling crisis at hand, even to meet it ineffectively, Hoover turned against the dictates of his office and invited prompt defeat at the next election by a far less accomplished individual who was willing to act, and act decisively.

The converse is also true. As long as a president forthrightly pursues his notion of the public good, his place in history is reasonably secure—even when he, and those who work for him, behave in ways that are patently illegal. Consider, then, the muted effect of Iran-Contra on Ronald Reagan's legacy. High-ranking officials within Reagan's administration secretly sold arms to the Iranian government—the same government that was in power during the waning months of Carter's administration—in exchange for the release of six U.S. hostages held there. In a clear violation of the recently enacted Boland Amendments, portions of the proceeds of these sales were used to support the Contra rebels in Nicaragua, who were seeking to overthrow the communist-backed Sandinista government. When the details of this extraordinary scheme came to light in 1986, a massive government investigation ensued that ultimately led to the indictment of fourteen officials, including Secretary of Defense Caspar Weinberger.

What Reagan personally knew about Iran-Contra and whom he supported remains unclear. It is striking, however, just how little Iran-Contra did to tarnish the president's legacy. To this day, Reagan is touted as one of the nation's great presidents, and every four years candidates for the Republican presidential nomination routinely insist that they are his true heir. Reagan's presidency shines today as brightly as ever.

How is this possible? Why doesn't Iran-Contra cast a well-deserved pall over Reagan's presidency? A good part of the answer concerns the nature of the scandal itself. Though the actions taken were unquestionably illegal, a gross abuse of executive power, and a violation of even the most basic notions of democratic transparency, Iran-Contra, at a very basic level, presented a presidential administration bent on advancing its notion of the public good. By assuming such an uncompromising stance against communism in the Western Hemisphere, and by steadfastly refusing to bow to Congress, the Reagan administration courted controversy. But for exactly these same reasons, it inoculated itself against the kind of contempt that was directed at Carter, Bush, and Obama when they refused to exercise power and project command.

To survive politically, presidents must not assume a reactive posture. They must not appear indifferent to the plight of any citizen. They must never resign themselves to defeat. Rather, presidents must face the headwinds, as they emanate mastery and command of their surroundings. They will not always succeed. Their policies may not reflect their highest aspirations. But at every turn, presidents must push forward, passing off improvisation as fluency, compromise as realism, and act, always act, for all to see. And as the actions required proliferate, so too do presidential attempts to claim the power needed to carry them out.

CHAPTER 7

Limits

If what we claim is true, if presidents really do care so much about power, then why don't we see them pursuing it even more aggressively? Why don't we witness our presidents nearly every night claiming new powers over new policy domains—particularly when the signature of presidential failure, as we argue, is the disavowal of powers already at hand? Why don't concerns about power openly and unapologetically animate everything that presidents do?

The answer, it turns out, has more to do with the political environment in which presidents work than the underlying interests of presidents themselves. The very reason why presidents so doggedly pursue power also explains why they must do so strategically, cautiously, even prudently; and why, moreover, presidents do not acquire anywhere near the amount of power that they would like. Presidents have inherited a constitutional—one might even say a cultural—legacy that is deeply ambivalent about concentrated executive authority: in the one instance offering ample opportunities to read extraordinary powers into vague Article II provisions; and in the next expressing deep skepticism toward brazen claims to vast reservoirs of untapped governmental authority. Presidents also face a set of genuine legal constraints that regularly thwarts their policy ambitions. They operate in a system of government that is stacked against them, in which adjoining branches of government have ample resources and opportunities to contest both new and old claims to executive authority. And if that were not enough, presidents must continually adapt to circumstances not of their choosing and events not of their making.

For these three reasons—cultural ambivalence, political constraints, and an uncooperative world—presidents must take a measured approach to power. A good deal of their efforts to guard and amplify their power will occur behind the scenes. Having vanquished their political enemies, presidents will not boast that they are now even more mighty than before. And when laying claim to altogether new powers, or directing their powers at altogether new subjects, presidents are apt to move cautiously, lest Congress, the courts, or the larger public promptly snatch away that which has only just been acquired.

But do not be fooled. That presidents regularly compromise with their political opponents, that they pay homage to constitutional limits, that they avoid grand entrances to new policy domains does not signify that their appetite for power is diminished. There is not an immediate correspondence between what presidents want and how they behave. Indeed, somewhat ironically, presidents occasionally must act in ways that would appear anathema to their core underlying interests—until, that is, one appreciates the genuine cultural norms, political forces, and material obstructions lined up against them.

Presidents want a great deal more power than they can get. The relevant question, then, is not whether presidents interminably pursue power. They do not. The question is whether presidents lay claim to as much power as they can garner. And the answer, nearly always, leans toward the affirmative.

Cultural Misgivings

For reasons we have already discussed, the ambiguity of Article II invites presidents to justify even the most audacious power claims in the "take care" and vesting clauses. Such readings occasionally defy logic and patently violate the most basic understandings of original intent, but no matter. Successive presidents offer these readings with straight faces, and frequently the only segment of the American public objecting is constitutional law scholars.

An important strain of American political culture, though, tempers at least the expression of presidential power claims. It is a strain, moreover, that finds its earliest expressions in America's revolt against the reach of monarchical power across the Atlantic, and the subsequent efforts of a newly independent people to design a system of government that would protect against executive tyranny. Recognizing the need for greater energy in the federal government, the Framers designed a presidency that retained considerably more formal authority than the presidency found in the Articles of Confederation. That the Framers were willing to confer new authority on the presidency, however, did not signify an abandonment of their concerns about despotism. To varying degrees, all of the nation's Founders worked under the premise that when designing a presidency, the imperatives of effective, energetic governance must be weighed against the very real threat of concentrated, unchecked executive power.

As we have already seen, the Founders held little faith that raw, individual ambition might serve anything other than individual interests. Hence, they did not beckon virtuous men to come forward and serve their country. Their project was one of institutional design. It was not a casting call or seven-step program toward personal transformation. Well-designed institutions, Madison noted in Federalist No. 51, would ensure that "the interest of the man" would be "connected with the constitutional rights of the place." Through institutions, individual ambition might be channeled, redirected, intermittently stymied, but ultimately aligned with the larger public interest. As Madison put it, "The constant aim [of government] is to divide and arrange the several offices in such a manner as that each may be a check on the other that the private interest of every individual may be sentinel over the public rights."

In the same instance that the Founders endowed an office with new authority to act, they constructed a set of institutional safeguards meant to frustrate those who would fill the office. While hoping that they had created a system of government that could address genuine social problems, they simultaneously expected that such a system would endure the tenure of even the most venal and myopic presidents. Presidents were to act, but the basis for such action would always be contested. The larger system of government was to serve the public good, but not because of the good intentions and hard work of any single individual.

The resulting ambivalence about presidential power leads Americans to roundly condemn those presidential candidates who betray too much interest in holding the office. The candidate who lurches toward the presidency can be expected to have his outstretched hand slapped. In the nineteenth century, presidential candidates did not attend party conventions, lest the delegates perceive an unseemly appetite for power. Presidential candidates were to be called for service; and having been called, they were expected to express a good deal of reluctance to serve. Individual candidates often made a point of disavowing any interest—and certainly any long-standing interest—in holding office. And each disavowal only confirmed a presidential candidate's fitness for office.

As one example, consider James Garfield's extraordinary rise to prominence in the 1880 Republican convention. Garfield, a respected but little-known member of Congress, attended the convention in Chicago not to advocate on his own behalf, but rather to tout the credentials of his fellow Ohioan, James Sherman. As so often occurred at the time, however, no single candidate could attract a majority of the convention delegates. For thirty-three ballots, in fact, the delegates split the preponderance of their votes between Sherman, James Blaine, and former president Ulysses Grant. On the thirty-fourth, however, sixteen of the eighteen delegates from Wisconsin suddenly broke for Garfield. But rather than betray the least bit of flattery, Garfield openly protested their endorsement. Rising from his seat, he caught the attention of the convention's president and declared, "I challenge the correctness of the announcement. The announcement contains votes for me. No man has a right, without the consent of the person voted for, to announce that person's name, and vote for him, in this convention. Such consent I have not given." Rather than honor Garfield's request, the president stifled his outburst and insisted that he return to his seat.

Garfield's objections, however, only served to confirm the judgment of the Wisconsin delegates. With each subsequent ballot, the additional states of Indiana, Maryland, Minnesota, North Carolina, and Pennsylvania rallied behind Garfield, who, in turn, expressed greater and greater dismay. Sensing the gathering momentum, Garfield insisted that "if the convention nominates me, it should be done without a vote from Ohio." But such protestations were in vain, as even his fellow delegates from his home state rallied to his cause. Garfield's objections to becoming the Republican nominee may well have been sincere. Little in the historical record suggests that he came to the convention for any reason except to repay a political debt to Sherman, who had just backed him in a successful run for Senate. Still, his vocal and very public protestations did nothing to quell the mounting enthusiasm for his candidacy. To the contrary, they buoyed it onward.

Garfield was not the last to benefit—if "benefit" is the right term, given the fate that awaited him—from denying any great interest in the accouterments of public office. The dangers of embracing the trappings of ambition persist to this day. Charges that a candidate has structured his entire life around this single run for office—that the seedlings of presidential aspiration began to grow in him as a small child, and that every elected position he subsequently held was a calculated attempt to eventually win a major party's nomination for office—continue to sting.

Just ask Al Gore, who as the Democratic nominee in 2000 endured all sorts of heckling for being a professional politician whose lifelong goal was to assume the presidency. Meanwhile, Bush's Texas origins and long-standing disinterest in presidential politics were seen as very much a point in his favor. *Washington Post* correspondent David Broder derided Gore's convention acceptance speech for having carried "on about what he wants to do as president." In his speeches, George W. Bush regularly needled Gore for long-standing interest in the presidency. *New York Times* columnist Maureen Dowd perhaps best summed up the press coverage of the two candidates when she wrote, "Al is the Good Son, the early-achieving scion from Harvard and Tennessee who always thought he would be President. (So did his parents.) George is the Prodigal Son, the late-blooming scion from Yale and Texas who never thought he would be President. (Neither did his parents.)" Of course, both men came from extraordinarily powerful political families—they were the son of a senator and a president, respectively. Yet it was the *perception* of their different paths toward the White House that counted most.

Republican candidates also are vulnerable to the charge of wanting the presidency too much. Witness the lingering perception in the 2012 presidential race that Mitt Romney had charted a pathway to the presidency since his early days at Bain Capital. Romney's "vaulting ambition" may have paid dividends in securing the nomination, but it did little to win over the larger public wary of candidates who appeared just a bit too eager to sit in the nation's highest seat of power. Reflecting on Romney's weaknesses as a presidential candidate, Fred Davis, a Republican political strategist, had this to say: "All politicians are eager to win, but you mask it behind, 'I want to help the people, I want to give back. I don't think Mitt bothers with that. He's looked a little too eager to get the job.'"

Barack Obama, too, has endured his share of criticism, albeit for a slightly different offense: being too competitive and overly zealous. His incessant drive to win—not just in elections, but in bowling and basketball—coupled with his persistently high opinion of himself—on all matters, including his capacity to read children's books and direct a political staff—inflame our political sensibilities. We want to see our presidents occasionally letting their guard down, conveying modesty, demurring in the face of others' excellence. That Obama does not do so—perhaps cannot do so—nearly enough amounts to a political liability.

Expressions of what Harvey Mansfield calls the "ambivalence of modern executive power" challenge all presidents. While gathering unto themselves more and more power, presidents must at least tip their hat to the mantle of limited government. Precisely because this skepticism toward concentrated executive authority is so ingrained in American political culture, presidents go to great lengths to justify their actions as constitutional. It would be easy for a popular executive to renounce originalist understandings of the Constitution once and for all. Instead presidents argue, all facts to the contrary, that their decisions to unilaterally intervene in foreign military crises are perfectly consistent with the commander in chief clause; that even the most convoluted interpretations of enacted statutes naturally derive from their constitutionally assigned executive power; and that Lockean prerogative powers reside in the "silences" of Article II. Presidents make these claims not—or at least not entirely—because they have an abiding interest in obeying the Constitution. They do so because we expect them to adjure the very powers that they themselves have seized. We demand that our presidents honor the Constitution even as they nimbly extract themselves from its hold on them.

POLITICAL CONSTRAINTS

A great deal more than just cultural norms constrain the president, however. When asserting existing powers and claiming new ones, the president can expect to bump up against other political actors with constitutional powers of their own. Should the president proceed without statutory or constitutional authority, the courts stand to overturn his actions. Congress, too, may contest the president's power claims and the specific policies advanced under their auspices. Crucially, then, the president's pursuit of power can only be understood by reference to the larger institutional framework within which he operates.

The influences of Congress and the courts on presidential power certainly vary over time and across policy issues. Presidential power grabs tend to receive a warmer reception in foreign policy than in domestic, during times of crisis than during time of peace, in the early months of a presidential administration than during an election year. Likewise, when large numbers of ideological and partisan sympathizers inhabit the adjoining branches of government, objections to the president's power can be expected to abate.

Nowhere and at no time, however, is the president wholly immune from Congress and the courts. Even in those moments when presidential power reaches its zenith—that is, during times of war—judicial and congressional prerogatives may be asserted. Interbranch struggles over military decision making constitute a great deal more than just political theater. When presidents contemplate launching new military initiatives and/or staying the course on existing ones, they remain carefully attuned to the likely response in Congress, the courts, and the larger public. Anticipating vigorous hearings and investigations in the aftermath of military failure, cuts in military budgets, extra reporting requirements, and a chorus of public appeals against a military venture, presidents proceed with a great deal more caution than they otherwise would prefer.

And herein lies a basic lesson about the exercise of presidential power within our system of government. Though we occasionally witness adjoining branches of government rising up and then striking down the president, whether in war or peace, the deeper effects of judicial and congressional restraints remain hidden. Obama might like to increase financial assistance for job training programs, establish a single-payer health care system, and ensure that same-sex couples secure all the same federal benefits available to heterosexual couples through marriage. But he recognizes that he lacks crucial political support on these matters. So rather than tempt controversy, he does not push nearly as hard as he would like.

So it is with all presidents. Whether unilaterally or cooperatively, they do and claim as much as they think they can get away with. But in those instances when a policy initiative or power grab can be expected to spark some kind of political reprisal, presidents proceed with caution; and knowing that they will promptly be overturned, presidents usually choose not to act at all.

Presidential power crucially depends on the willingness and capacity of the adjoining branches of government either to support the president ex ante or check him ex post. A president's base interest in power may exist independent of the adjoining branches of government. But every action he takes with respect to this interest centrally involves strategic calculations about the likelihoods of judicial and legislative support or interference. Where resistance is likely, a president may temper his aspirations. But where he thinks he can prevail, the president usually will pounce.

Why have presidents been so much more successful in pursuing power on matters involving the U.S. military than they have on, say, policies with clear domestic distributive benefits? There is no reason to believe that presidents have a stronger preference for war power. Nor, most legal scholars recognize, do presidents enjoy an especially large amount of constitutional authority in this domain. Rather, key to understanding the presidents' success in expanding their war powers is the behavior of Congress and the courts, who, for reasons entirely of their own, have strong incentives not to get in the president's way.

Among the many base motivations of legislators and judges, two stand out as particularly relevant for understanding the growth of presidential war powers. As members of Congress care foremost about their reelection prospects, they tend to invest more of their resources into directing domestic policy benefits to their home districts and states, for which they can claim clear credit come election time, than in monitoring distant threats to U.S. security interests, which amount to a public good. Likewise, as judges worry about the perceived legitimacy of their institution, they are not nearly so likely to demand changes in a military operation, over which they have precious little information and exercise little to no control, than they are to plunge headlong into debates about domestic policy matters, over which they are more informed and their rulings are likely to be more binding. Presidents, therefore, can justifiably expect to encounter less legislative or judicial interference on matters involving war than on purely domestic issues, not because they have a special preference for these powers, but because other political actors are more willing either to grant them outright or simply to accede to the president's power claims.

Whether in war or peace, presidential powers need not be conceived in legislative or judicial bodies and then transferred to the executive. Entrepreneurial presidents are perfectly well equipped to lay claim to new powers entirely of their own making. However, the form of these powers, the duration with which they are held, and the opportunities they afford any particular president to advance a policy agenda all depend on how Congress and the courts receive them. And success during one administration or era does not guarantee success during another, any more than failure on one issue necessarily portends failure on others. As Madison would have it, the president, Congress, and the courts engage one another in a continual struggle over the appropriate boundaries of their powers, and each is equipped with tools to guard against the encroachments of others.

An Uncooperative World

With the federal government monitoring goings-on across the globe and involved in nearly every policy domain imaginable, presidents regularly confront scandals, crises, and natural disasters not of their choosing. Poised to announce a major policy initiative one day, a president may instead find himself addressing a plane crash killing dozens of U.S. diplomats, a tsunami wiping whole villages off the map, the media breaking a story about a prominent senator's sexual improprieties, or a young student killing his classmates in school. Prepare as they might, presidents must confront the world as it is, not as they would prefer. And as every president learns to appreciate, a great deal of the world is not especially interested in his plans for the country.

Many crises, to be sure, have the potential to augment presidential power. In the aftermath of September 11, Bush wielded extraordinary powers over the conduct of U.S. security policy. And as we have shown in other published work, Congress thereafter appeared substantially more deferential to both the president's foreign and domestic policy agendas. During the 107th Congress, members of both the House and Senate rallied behind their commander in chief and voted more conservatively on a wide range of bills after September 11 than they had before. Likewise, the economic meltdown of 2008 established the groundwork for both Bush and Obama to launch massive interventions into the economy, reconfigure the regulatory framework of the financial industry, extend large tax cuts, and enact massive public spending initiatives.

Unforeseen catastrophes, however, can take just as they can give. The time and resources spent consoling victims of a hurricane, giving speeches about the tragic loss of life, launching investigations into perceived political scandals, and the like are time and resources not spent on a president's most cherished policy objectives. Even when crises augment presidential power, the resulting influence may be narrowly confined. Presidents may find themselves working on policy initiatives about which they care very little. Worse still, such crises may demand executive action that violates their partisan or ideological commitments.

As a case in point, recall the final months of Bush's second term in office, when a declining economy suddenly transitioned to free fall. With the subprime mortgage crisis spreading havoc in nearly all sectors of the economy in the fall of 2008, many of America's major financial institutions seemed in danger of going under. Pressure mounted on the government from the private sector to do something to save these institutions, which were seen as "too big to fail"—too integral to the country's financial stability and well-being to be allowed to go bankrupt.

In the face of such pressure, fiscal conservatives and libertarians urged the president to remain firm and let the market sort itself out. By intervening into the private sector, they argued, the government could only turn bad to worse, racking up extraordinary debt while simultaneously establishing incentives for the financial industry to persist in making the risky bets that had helped create the crisis in the first place. Fully cognizant of the political dangers of inaction, though, the president decided to intervene and bail out the big banks. On October 3, Bush signed into law the Troubled Asset Relief Program (TARP), which granted the Treasury Department broad authority to purchase up to $700 billion of toxic assets and other equity from financial institutions, thereby saving them from bankruptcy.

The move, which constituted the largest government intervention into the private sector in U.S. history, was roundly denounced by Bush's former supporters on the right. In the *National Review*, commentator Deroy Murdock even went so far as to hurl at Bush the same epithet that Bush had once leveled against President Carter: socialist. "The 'far-right' George Bush of leftist lore," wrote Murdock in the wake of Bush's bailout policy, "will leave office as a cheerleader for constitutionally suspect, pro-labor socialism."

Murdock was right to point out the president's about-face. Before entering the Oval Office, Bush presented himself as an avowed opponent of government intervention in the marketplace. In the 2000 presidential campaign, he ran on an economic platform of free-market principles. He described what he saw as a presidential imperative to limit the role of government in the face of excessive legislative spending: "It's the president's job to make sure Congress doesn't have the money to spend in the first place." Attacking his opponent Al Gore's plans for new government programs, Bush insisted that "the surest way to bust this economy is to increase the role and the size of the federal government." And in his political autobiography, timed for release amidst the campaign season, the future president described the government's intrusion into the private sector under former president Jimmy Carter as having a formative effect on his own ideology. About the Natural Gas Policy Act and the Fuel Use Act of 1978, Bush wrote: "It seemed to me that elite central planners were determining the course of our nation. Allowing the government to dictate the price of natural gas was a move toward European-style socialism. If the federal government was going to take over the natural gas business, what would it set its sights on next?"

As it turned out, the federal government under President Bush set its sights on a great deal more. In his first two years in office, federal expenditures rose by 22 percent, and discretionary domestic spending on federal agencies such as education and labor grew by roughly 70 percent. Such extravagant spending led the conservative Cato Institute to dub Bush "the most gratuitous big spender to occupy the White House since Jimmy Carter." By the end of Bush's two terms in office, the size of the federal government—as measured by total expenditures in the federal budget—increased by 104 percent. By contrast, government spending during President Clinton's two terms increased by roughly 11 percent.

There are a variety of ways to make sense of the disjuncture between President Bush's free-market principles and his support for federal programs. The simplest is to downplay the former's significance. While giving lip service to free-market principles, the president was perfectly willing to sponsor and promote government largesse. Bush, as such, was a good deal more liberal than either his supporters or detractors thought. But if we take Bush at his word—to the very end of his time in office, the president continued to insist that "the greater threat to economic prosperity is not too little government involvement in the market, it is too much government involvement in the market"—then an altogether different interpretation is warranted. The bookends of September 11 at the beginning of the president's tenure and the economic meltdown at its conclusion demanded aggressive responses by the federal government. The president had no choice but to act, less he consign himself and his party to oblivion.

The president does not exercise power according to his own schedule. And he does not always exercise power in the service of objectives that fit neatly within his worldview. Try as he might, the president cannot rearrange his surroundings like so many pieces on a chessboard. The best laid plans of even a president fray on execution.

Power and Policy

To realize nearly every substantive goal they cherish—policy achievements, a lasting historical legacy, a strengthened party, and the approval of their public and professional peers—presidents need, and therefore pursue, power. But presidents' pursuits do not run at full throttle over the entire course of their tenure in office. A good deal of the reason why has to do with the various cultural, political, and legal factors that constrain presidents. The results from congressional elections, the opportunities to appoint Supreme Court justices, the existence of foreign crises, and the like all bear on a president's ability at any given time to expand his power. And to the extent that these factors vary over time and place, a president's pursuit of power may appear a good deal more sporadic than we might otherwise expect.

The president, like any politician, operates under something of a budget constraint, afforded only a limited amount of resources and time to build a legacy of his own. Political fights over power, however, drain these resources just as they complicate a president's schedule. Either because they mobilize the president's political opponents or because they divert scarce resources away from other endeavors, contestations over power can be costly. For all sorts of reasons we have discussed in previous chapters, a president is advantaged in these contests with Congress and the courts. But that he is advantaged in the fight over power does not mean that the president is impervious to its expenses, which may take the form of editorials decrying the abuse of presidential powers or calls from the halls of Congress for the dismantling of an imperial presidency. Though usually fruitless, such political appeals detract, if only temporarily, from a president's ability to define and realize a policy agenda.

The president who devotes all of his energy and resources purely to expanding his power will not realize the main goal of accruing that power: the policy achievements demanded of him by both the public and posterity. He will establish the groundwork for future presidents to do extraordinary things. But he himself will have little to show for the effort. Hence, for the sake of expediency alone, presidents may forsake political fights over power in order to pursue more immediate policy objectives.

That the pursuit of power introduces both direct political costs and opportunity costs has important implications for first- and second-term presidents. By investing in power, presidents lay the groundwork for subsequent policy achievements. But if presidents discount the future, as they assuredly do, then their willingness to pay these costs may vary over the course of their terms. In the waning years and months of a second term, therefore, presidents can be expected to devote much more of their energy and resources to advancing policy achievements through existing powers rather than trying to invent new ones. In order to establish a legacy of policy achievements, they may relax their vigilant defense of power. What appears as the weakness of a lame-duck presidency, therefore, may instead reflect an individual president's recognition of the declining marginal benefits of power investments.

As we have argued throughout this book, presidents' interest in power is primarily instrumental. Power is not an end in itself, but rather a vehicle to other more tangible objectives: changing public policy, responding to foreign crises, advancing the nation's interests abroad, building a historical legacy. From nearly the moment he assumes office, the most self-effacing presidential candidate will quickly be transformed into a great apologist for presidential power. He has no other choice. For as the brief case studies in chapter 6 make clear, the president who disavows power can expect to incur the wrath of those constituencies that matter most to him: contemporary publics and future historians.

Seeking Power: Humbly, Strategically, Pertinaciously

Working within a political culture long distrustful of the concentration of political power, and facing political and worldly obstacles at many turns, presidents do not possess anywhere near the amount of power that they would like. But nor do they wear their disappointment for all to see. To the contrary, as they present themselves to the public and plot their way forward, presidents go out of their way to demonstrate modesty, discipline, and above all, command.

Presidents rarely grab new reins of authority in lavishly orchestrated public displays. We do not find our presidents announcing radical new directives before hordes of reporters in Rose Garden signing ceremonies. When they do come forward to announce a change in policy that neither Congress nor the courts have formally endorsed, presidents speak as though their authority was perfectly well established, as though no new powers are being claimed at all. Presidents do not invite others to join in the deliberations about expanding executive power. Rather, power grabs are presented as a fait accompli—and even then, presidents may steadfastly deny that any grabbing occurred at all.

A president's ambitions are tempered by the political realities of the day and, particularly, by the extent to which Congress and the courts intend to thwart his intentions. When lobbying Congress, a president may advocate on behalf of modest policy changes; when exercising his unilateral powers, he may alter the existing policy landscape only incrementally; and when fabricating new powers for himself, he may appear especially conciliatory to the expressed wishes and concerns of Congress and the courts.

When asserting executive powers either in a new policy domain or through a new mechanism, the president will proceed cautiously. Initial forays are designed to avoid detection and thereby establish precedent for bolder intrusions later on. The president therefore quietly inserts himself into new policy arenas by reorganizing the bureaucracy, issuing arcane rules, devising new forms of unilateral directives, guarding his information, and resisting, as much as he can get away with, calls for greater transparency. Power, in this sense, is quietly nurtured and only obliquely referenced. The imprints it leaves on our policy and politics often are not discovered until long after a president has left office.

But don't be fooled. For all their self-effacement, their apparent willingness to compromise, and their invocations of the Constitution and the rule of law, presidents hunger for power. And given the boundless expectations set before them, it is difficult to imagine what it would take to satiate their appetite.

Before becoming president, Barack Obama was an avowed opponent of indefinitely detaining suspected terrorists. As a former constitutional lawyer turned senator, Obama stated in 2006 that "restricting somebody's right to challenge their imprisonment indefinitely is not going to make us safer. In fact, recent evidence shows it is probably making us less safe." Two years later, as a presidential candidate, Obama restated his position: he was committed to "reestablishing our credibility as a nation committed to the rule of law, and [to] rejecting a false choice between fighting terrorism and respecting habeas corpus." This position seemed to weaken slightly once Obama took office, as he did not immediately move to close Guantanamo Bay, the infamous U.S. detention center indefinitely holding terrorist suspects in Cuba. Finally, however, President Obama made a push at the end of 2010 to get Guantanamo suspects tried in the U.S. court system—only to have his move blocked by Congress.

The real test of Obama's position on detainees came in the form of 2011's Levin/McCain detention bill. The proposed legislation aimed to codify policies that had already become status quo under the Bush administration: the U.S. government would explicitly be authorized to hold terrorism suspects without trial, whether they had been captured "in the course of hostilities" or not. Additionally, the bill was silent on whether or not this applied just to foreign prisoners or whether it could be applied to U.S. citizens as well. The bill was attacked by a significant number of senators from both parties. Democratic senator Dianne Feinstein issued a statement saying, "Congress is essentially authorizing the indefinite imprisonment of American citizens, without charge. . . . We are not a nation that locks up its citizens without charge." Conservative Republican Rand Paul agreed: "Detaining citizens without a court trial is not American," he asserted, adding that if the law passed, then "the terrorists have won."

Initially, President Obama threatened to veto the Levin/McCain bill. After negotiating with senators on the Armed Services Committee led to a new draft, however, the president reversed his position and offered his support. What changed? No concerns about civil liberties were properly addressed by the revised legislation. Quite the opposite: the bill's cosponsor Carl Levin revealed that the White House had demanded removal of a provision in the original draft which would have exempted American citizens from military detention. In other words, the administration had essentially demanded greater detention power by removing one of the few constraints on who could be detained, and how. Obama had forced the senators to address "security concerns," but not the ones "related to civil liberties and the rule of law." Rather, the president had pushed to remove all language that might restrict his decision-making authority as commander in chief by codifying specific cases in which individuals could or could not be detained indefinitely. As commentator Glenn Greenwald wrote at the time, "The White House's North Star on this bill—as they repeatedly made clear—was Presidential discretion: they were going to veto the bill if it contained any limits on the President's detention powers, regardless of whether those limits forced him to put people in military prison or barred him from doing so."

Whatever Obama's preferred policy on detention really was, it mattered far less to him then his preferred level of authority: as close to absolute as possible. And in this regard, Obama stood in for all who came before him. Power is every president's North Star.

Article II of the U.S. Constitution

Section 1.

The executive Power shall be vested in a President of the United States of America. He shall hold his Office during the Term of four Years, and, together with the Vice President, chosen for the same Term, be elected, as follows:

Each State shall appoint, in such Manner as the Legislature thereof may direct, a Number of Electors, equal to the whole Number of Senators and Representatives to which the State may be entitled in the Congress: but no Senator or Representative, or Person holding an Office of Trust or Profit under the United States, shall be appointed an Elector.

The Electors shall meet in their respective States, and vote by Ballot for two Persons, of whom one at least shall not be an Inhabitant of the same State with themselves. And they shall make a List of all the Persons voted for, and of the Number of Votes for each; which List they shall sign and certify, and transmit sealed to the Seat of the Government of the United States, directed to the President of the Senate. The President of the Senate shall, in the Presence of the Senate and House of Representatives, open all the Certificates, and the Votes shall then be counted. The Person having the greatest Number of Votes shall be the President, if such Number be a Majority of the whole Number of Electors appointed; and if there be more than one who have such Majority, and have an equal Number of Votes, then the House of Representatives shall immediately chuse by Ballot one of them for President; and if no Person have a Majority, then from the five highest on the List the said House shall in like Manner chuse the President. But in chusing the President, the Votes shall be taken by States, the Representatives from each State having one Vote; a quorum for this Purpose shall consist of a Member or Members from two thirds of the States, and a Majority of all the States shall be necessary to a Choice. In every Case, after the Choice of the President, the Person having the greatest Number of Votes of the Electors shall be the Vice President. But if there should remain two or more who have equal Votes, the Senate shall chuse from them by Ballot the Vice President.

The Congress may determine the Time of chusing the Electors, and the Day on which they shall give their Votes; which Day shall be the same throughout the United States.

No Person except a natural born Citizen, or a Citizen of the United States, at the time of the Adoption of this Constitution, shall be eligible to the Office of President; neither shall any person be eligible to that Office who shall not have attained to the Age of thirty five Years, and been fourteen Years a Resident within the United States.

In Case of the Removal of the President from Office, or of his Death, Resignation, or Inability to discharge the Powers and Duties of the said Office, the Same shall devolve on the Vice President, and the Congress may by Law provide for the Case of Removal, Death, Resignation or Inability, both of the President and Vice President, declaring what Officer shall then act as President, and such Officer shall act accordingly, until the Disability be removed, or a President shall be elected.

The President shall, at stated Times, receive for his Services, a Compensation, which shall neither be encreased nor diminished during the Period for which he shall have been elected, and he shall not receive within that Period any other Emolument from the United States, or any of them.

Before he enter on the Execution of his Office, he shall take the following Oath or Affirmation: —"I do solemnly swear (or affirm) that I will faithfully execute the Office of President of the United States, and will to the best of my Ability, preserve, protect and defend the Constitution of the United States."

Section 2.

The President shall be Commander in Chief of the Army and Navy of the United States, and of the Militia of the several States, when called into the actual Service of the United States; he may require the Opinion, in writing, of the principal Officer in each of the executive Departments, upon any

Subject relating to the Duties of their respective Offices, and he shall have Power to Grant Reprieves and Pardons for Offences against the United States, except in Cases of Impeachment.

He shall have Power, by and with the Advice and Consent of the Senate, to make Treaties, provided two thirds of the Senators present concur; and he shall nominate, and by and with the Advice and Consent of the Senate, shall appoint Ambassadors, other public Ministers and Consuls, Judges of the supreme Court, and all other Officers of the United States, whose Appointments are not herein otherwise provided for, and which shall be established by Law: but the Congress may by Law vest the Appointment of such inferior Officers, as they think proper, in the President alone, in the Courts of Law, or in the Heads of Departments.

The President shall have Power to fill up all Vacancies that may happen during the Recess of the Senate, by granting Commissions which shall expire at the End of their next Session.

SECTION 3.

He shall from time to time give to the Congress Information on the State of the Union, and recommend to their Consideration such Measures as he shall judge necessary and expedient; he may, on extraordinary Occasions, convene both Houses, or either of them, and in Case of Disagreement between them, with Respect to the Time of Adjournment, he may adjourn them to such Time as he shall think proper; he shall receive Ambassadors and other public Ministers; he shall take Care that the Laws be faithfully executed, and shall Commission all the Officers of the United States.

SECTION 4.

The President, Vice President and all Civil Officers of the United States, shall be removed from Office on Impeachment for and Conviction of, Treason, Bribery, or other high Crimes and Misdemeanors.

Notes

Preface

Page

ix

"Narcotic" power: Robert Spitzer, "Is the Constitutional Presidency Obsolete," in Charles Dunn (ed.), *The Presidency in the Twenty-First Century* (Lexington: University Press of Kentucky, 2011), p. 61.

Chapter 1. On Being President

Page

2

Petitions to the president: Stephen Splane, "Dear President Obama: The President Reads 10 Letters a Day from the Public, With Policy Ramifications," *ABC News*, 23 February 2009, http://abcnews.go.com/blogs/politics/2009/02 /dear-president/; Henry Alder et al., open letter to Bill Clinton, 20 November 1996, http://www.mathematicallycorrect.com/clinton.htm; Mike Kelleher, quoted in Ashley Parker, "Picking Letters, 10 a Day, That Reach Obama," *New York Times*, 20 April 2009, A14; Avinash Bali, "Man Requests U.S. President to Ban Skyrim," *Tech2*, 26 November 2011, http:/www.moneycontrol.com /news/technology/man-requests-us-president-to-ban-skyrim_624820.html.

3

"Interest groups have buried the White House with . . . advice": Michael D. Shear, "'Mr. President, Say This on Tuesday Night,'" *New York Times: The Caucus*, 21 January 2011, http://thecaucus.blogs.nytimes.com/2011/01/21 /mr-president-say-this-on-tuesday-night/.

4

For critiques over the deficit, see: "The Union's Troubled State," *The Economist*, 27 January 2011, accessed online at: http://www.economist.com /node/18010469; "State of the Union Sets Big Objectives, Lacks Leadership on Debt," *USA Today*, 25 January 2011, http://www.usatoday.com/news /opinion/editorials/2011-01-26-editorial26_ST_N.htm.

On the president's lack of specificity, see: Ezra Klein, "Lots of Vision, but Few Policy Specifics," *Washington Post: Voices*, 25 January 2011, http://voices .washingtonpost.com/ezra-klein/2011/01/lots_of_vision_but_few_policy .html. For a critique on job growth, see: Zachary Roth, "Obama Slammed for Neglecting Jobs Crisis," *The Lookout*, 26 January 2011, http://news.yahoo .com/blogs/lookout/obama-slammed-neglecting-jobs-crisis-20110126 -123515-096.html.

On education, see: Valerie Strauss, "Obama's Faulty Education Logic: What he Said and Failed to Say," *Washington Post: The Answer Sheet*, 25 January 2011,

http://voices.washingtonpost.com/answer-sheet/poverty/obamas-stran
-faulty-educationge.html.
Other examples of critiques include Gary Shapiro, "What President Obama
Missed in His State of the Union," *forbes.com*, 31 January 2011, http://
www.forbes.com/2011/01/28/innovation-entrepreneurs-barack-obama
-opinions-contributors-gary-shapiro.html; Jenny Triplett, "Mass Incar-
ceration Needs More Attention by President Obama," *Prisonworld Maga-*
zine, 15 February 2011, http://prisonworldblogtalk.com/2011/02/15/mass
-incarceration-needs-more-attention-by-president-obama/.

4   "These days go by at their accustomed pace . . . .": Dwight D. Eisenhower
to Edward E. Hazlett Jr., 26 January 1954, *The Papers of Dwight David Eisen-*
hower (Baltimore, MD: John Hopkins, 1996), document #692. The schedule details are from "The President's Appointments: Friday, July 1, 1955,"
Dwight D. Eisenhower's Daily Appointment Schedule.

4   George Bush's schedule: *Public Papers of the President of the United States:*
George W. Bush, Book 2 (Washington, DC: GPO, 2005), p. 1907.

5   Presidents' travel: Brendan Doherty, "POTUS on the Road: International
and Domestic Presidential Travel, 1977–2005," *Presidential Studies Quar-*
terly (2009), p. 39; Mark Knoller, "Obama's 2010: By the Numbers," *CBS*
News, 31 December 2010, http://www.cbsnews.com/8301-503544_162
-20026885-503544.html; Mark Knoller, "President Bush by the Numbers,"
CBSNews, 11 February 2009, http://www.cbsnews.com/stories/2009/01/19
/politics/bush_legacy/main4735360.shtml.

5   Bush's visit to Afghanistan: Jim Angle, "Bush Makes Surprise Visit to Troops
in Baghdad," *Fox News*, 28 November 2003, http://www.foxnews.com
/story/0,2933,104246,00.html.

5   "While occasionally paying homage . . . .": As Lyn Ragsdale puts it, "The
image of a president is thus of a person who is omnicompetent (able to
do all things) and omnipresent (working everywhere)." Lyn Ragsdale,
"Studying the Presidency: Why Presidents Need Political Scientists," in
Michael Nelson (ed.), *The Presidency and the Political System*, 9th ed. (Wash-
ington, DC: CQ Press, 2010), pp. 36–37. See also: Fred Greenstein, "What
the President Means to Americans," in James Barber (ed.), *Choosing the*
President (New York: American Assembly, 1974), pp. 130–31; Gene Healy,
The Cult of the Presidency: America's Dangerous Devotion to Executive Power
(Washington, D.C.: Cato Institute, 2008).

5   Sources of demands for presidential aid: Richard E. Neustadt, *Presidential*
Power and the Modern Presidents: the Politics of Leadership from Roosevelt to
Reagan (New York: Free Press, 1991).

6   Functions of the president: Clinton Rossiter, *The American Presidency*, 2nd
ed. (New York: Harcourt, Brace, 1960), pp. 16, 42.

6   Bush's "takeover" of national security: Charlie Savage, *Takeover: The Return of the Imperial Presidency and the Subversion of American Democracy* (New York: Little Brown, 2007).

8   President's "authority over the administration": Rossiter, *American Presidency*, p. 246.

9   David Orentlicher, *Two Presidents Are Better Than One.* (New York, New York University Press, 2013).

10   "A substantial body of scholarship . . . .": See, for example: Charles Cameron, Veto Bargaining: Presidents and the Politics of Negative Power (New York: Cambridge University Press, 2001); Glen Krutz and Jeffrey Peake, *Treaty Politics and the Rise of Executive Agreements: International Commitments in a System of Shared Powers* (Ann Arbor: University of Michigan Press, 2010); David Lewis, *The Politics of Presidential Appointments: Political Control and Bureaucratic Performance* (Princeton, NJ: Princeton University Press, 2008).

12   James Kent, *Commentaries on American Law* (New York: O. Halsted, 1826), vol. 2, article 1, section 1.

17   Emergency powers: H. C. Relyea, "National Emergency Powers," *Congressional Research Service Report for Congress*, 2007, available online at: http://www.fas.org/sgp/crs/natsec/98-505.pdf.

17   Power considerations only weakly motivate: Terry Moe, "The Presidency and the Bureaucracy: The Presidential Advantage," in Michael Nelson (ed.), *Presidency and the Political System*, 5th ed. (Washington, DC: Congressional Quarterly Press, 1998), pp. 437–468).

CHAPTER 2. BEARING WITNESS

Page
20   "Use all necessary and appropriate force": "Authorization for the Use of Military Force," Joint Resolution of Congress, September 14, 2001.

21   Objectives of NSPD-9: "Testimony of the U.S. Secretary of Defense Donald H. Rumsfeld Prepared for Delivery to the National Commission on Terorist Attacks upon the United States," March 20, 2004.

22   Unification not a "partisan issue": "Unification at This Session," *New York Times*, 2 July 1947.

23   "The Council shall . . . make recommendations and reports": National Security Act of 1947.

24   "I, for one, have too much faith in the American people . . . .": 93 *Cong. Rec.*, 1947, pp. 8492-8505 and 9431-9456.

24   "Fashion a more definite . . . and effective military policy": Representative Lyle, *Cong. Rec., 1947*, 9427.

24   President Truman and the NSC: "History of the National Security Council, 1947–1997," http://georgewbush-whitehouse.archives.gov/nsc/history.html.

26   "Policy hill": "National Security Council [NSC], Eisenhower Administration, 1953–1961," http://www.fas.org/irp/offdocs/nsc-ike/index.html.

27   Eisenhower continued the policy of sequential numbering for NSC papers begun by Truman. Thus the first known security directive under the Eisenhower Administration was NSC 143. For more on this, see Cooper 2002, pp. 147–49.

27   "Best and the brightest": David Halberstam, *The Best and the Brightest* (New York: Ballantine Books, 1973).

27   Under Truman and Eisenhower, security directives were called National Security Council policy papers (NSCs). Kennedy and Johnson dubbed them National Security Action Memorandums (NSAMs); Nixon and Ford called them National Security Decision Memorandums (NSDMs); and so on down the line, all the way to the Obama administration's Presidential Policy Directives (PPDs). Since Nixon, presidents have also distinguished between decision directives—orders issued by the president—and review directives (requests for research into a given policy or issue). Review directives have also changed their names with each administration. After September 11, President Bush began issuing an additional type of directive, the Homeland Security President Directive (HSPD). HSPD-1, in conjunction with Executive Order 13228, set about organizing the newly formed Department of Homeland Security. It is unclear whether or not President Obama has continued this practice. What is clear is that directives do not appear to be in danger of going out of vogue anytime soon.

29   "Foreign and military policy-making": United States General Accounting Office, "The Use of Presidential Directives to Make and Implement U.S. Policy," *National Security*, January 1992, http://www.fas.org/irp/offdocs /gao-nsiad-92-72.pdf.

29   "Citing executive privilege": Harold Hongju Koh. "Why the President (Almost) Always Wins in Foreign Affairs: Lessons of the Iran-Contra Affair." The Yale Law Journal, Vol. 97, No. 7, (1988): 1255-1342.

33   Origins of the term *czar*: "What's With This 'Czar' Talk?" *All Things Considered*, National Public Radio, http://www.npr.org/templates/story/story .php?storyId=10215599.

33   "Czar of Prices": Obituary, "Leon Henderson, Penn Economist Who Became 'Price Czar' For FDR," *Philadelphia Inquirer*; see also Ben Zimmer, "Czar Wars," *Slate*, 29 December 2008, http://www.slate.com/articles/life /the_good_word/2008/12/czar_wars.html.

33   "Under the presidency of George W. Bush . . . .": These figures refer to top policy advisors who specifically did not go through a Senate confirmation process—other positions that are sometimes considered "czars" but are in fact subject to congressional oversight were not included in the counts.

34   "More czars than the Romanovs": Steve Holland, "Obama Fashions a Government of Many Czars," *Reuters*, 29 May 2009, http://www.reuters .com/article/2009/05/29/us-obama-czars-analysis-idUSTRE54S5U120090 529?pageNumber=2&virtualBrandChannel=0&sp=true.

34   "Czars belong in Russia": Michael A. Fletcher and Brady Dennis, "Obama Critics Say Policy 'Czars' Skirt Proper Oversight, Vetting," *Washington Post*, 16 September 2009.

34   "Darned if I can figure out all the czars": Steve Benen, "When You Wish upon a Czar . . . ." *Washington Monthly*, 11 July 2009.

34   Czars "undemocratic": Fletcher and Dennis, "Obama Critics Say Policy 'Czars' Skirt Proper Oversight, Vetting," 2009.

34   " . . . outside the Constitution and the authority of Congress": "Questions Raised Over Influence of Obama 'Czars,'" *FOXNews.com*, 13 July 2009, http://www.foxnews.com/politics/2009/07/13/questions-raised-influence -obama-czars/#ixzz1br1ml5pH.

35   Rapid accumulation of power threatening to the system of checks and balances: Benen, "When You Wish upon a Czar . . . ."

35   "I would hope that the White House lets Dr. Chu have the authority he needs . . . .": Zachary Coile, "Obama's Big Task: Managing the Best, Brightest," *San Francisco Chronicle*, 11 January 2009, A9.

35   "It will have the tendency to cause cabinet members to feel subordinate": Laura Meckler, "'Czars' Ascend at White House," *Wall Street Journal*, 15 December 2008.

36   Czars allow president to "hit the ground running": Ron Walters, quoted in Coile, "Obama's Big Task."

36   Benefits for GM employees: Jonathan Cohn, "An Interview with Steven Rattner," *New Republic*, 10 September 2010, http://www.tnr.com/blog /jonathan-cohn/77794/interview-steven-rattner?page=0,0.

37   Ramifications of bankruptcy for the Big Three: Harold Meyerson, "The Case for Keeping the Big Three Out of Bankruptcy," *American Prospect*, 24 November 2008, http://prospect.org/article/case-keeping-big-three-out -bankruptcy.

37   "D.N.C.'s A.T.M.": Louise Story, "Obama's Top Auto Industry Troubleshooter," *New York Times*, 5 April 2009.

38   "Came into this project with . . . less than zero knowledge": Cohn, "An Interview with Steven Rattner."

38   No prior experience in the auto industry: In his subsequent book on the auto bailout, Rattner explains why he chose Whitacre: "His reputation was for toughness. I remembered having once read a *Business Week* story that described him killing rattlesnakes on his Texas ranch (he would pin down the snake with a stick and crush its head with a rock). His flinty image was reinforced by his lean, six-foot-four frame, his full head of gray hair, and his laconic speech. Ed believed that we are born with two ears and one mouth

and we should use them in rough proportion." Steven Rattner, *Overhaul: An Insider's Account of the Obama Administration's Emergency Rescue of the Auto Industry* (New York: Houghton Mifflin, 2010), p. 221.

41   "Legislative efforts that impede the President's ability . . . violate the separation of powers": "Statement by the President on H.R. 1473," *White House Office of the Press Secretary*, April 15, 2011.

41   "We know what you wanted . . . to do, but we don't think it's constitutional": Devin Dwyer, "President Obama Issues 'Signing Statement' Indicating He Won't Abide by Provision in Budget Bill," *ABC News* Political Punch Blog, 15 April 2011, http://abcnews.go.com/blogs/politics/2011/04/president-obama-issues-signing-statement-indicating-he-wont-abide-by-provision-in-budget-bill/.

41   "The President does not . . . choose which laws he will follow and . . . ignore": Catalina Camia, "GOP Lawmaker Blasts Obama for Ignoring Congress on 'Czars,'" *USA Today*, 18 April 2011.

41   " . . . fierce critic of presidents who overreached . . . .": John Fund, "Obama vs. Obama," *Wall Street Journal*, 27 April 2011.

42   "Not going to use signing statements as . . . an end run around": Barack Obama, as seen in http://www.youtube.com/watch?v=seAR1S1Mjkc.

42   "There is simply no question that Obama is now asserting exactly the power that . . . he insisted was illegitimate": Glenn Greenwald, "Obama v. Obama on Signing Statements," *Salon*, 17 April 2011, http://www.salon.com/2011/04/17/signing_statements/.

      For other examples of Obama using signing statements to repudiate elements of legislation with which he disagreed, see: Charlie Savage, "Obama's Embrace of a Bush Tactic Riles Congress," *New York Times*, 8 August 2009.

42   President Jackson's signing statements: Louis Fisher, *Constitutional Conflicts between Congress and the President* (Lawrence: University Press of Kansas, 1997), p. 132.

42   Signing statements "an unusual method": Quoted in Christopher N. May, *Presidential Defiance of 'Unconstitutional' Laws: Reviving the Royal Prerogative* (Westport, CT: Greenwood Press, 1998), p. 930.

42   Prevalence of signing statements: Figures available in James P. Pfiffner, *Power Play: The Bush Presidency and the Constitution* (Washington, DC: Brookings Institution, 2008), p. 199.

43   "This bill is good for America": "Presidential Signing Statements Accompanying the Fiscal Year 2006 Appropriations Acts," Government Accountability Office Report, 18 June 2007, http://www.gao.gov/decisions/appro/308603.htm.

43   Charlie Savage: *Takeover*, pp. 231–232.

44   "Congress had used this episode to expand their power": Cooper 2002, p. 202.

44 " . . . signing statements assume their rightful place in the interpretation of legislation": Samuel A. Alito, Jr., "Using Presidential Signing Statements to Make Fuller Use of the President's Constitutionally Assigned Role in the Process of Enacting Law," Office of Legal Counsel Memorandum, February 5, 1986; quoted in Todd Garvey, "Presidential Signing Statements: Constitutional and Institutional Implications," *Congressional Research Service Report* January 4, 2012, p. 3.

44 Signing statements "underutilized and could become far more important": Savage, *Takeover*, 233.

45 Figures on presidential signing statements: Todd Garvey, "Presidential Signing Statements: Constitutional and Institutional Implications," pp. 3–5.

45 Bush and signing statements: Garvey, "Presidential Signing Statements"; Pfiffner *Power Play*, p. 203.

46 "The executive branch shall construe . . . .": "Statement on Signing the USA PATRIOT Improvement and Reauthorization Act of 2005," March 9, 2006, quoted in Savage, *Takeover*, p. 229.

46 "Unitary executive": Savage, *Takeover*, p. 240.

46 "It is not for George Bush to . . . decide he is above the law": Savage, *Takeover*, pp. 248–49.

47 "My constitutional authority supersedes the statute": "Recommendation: Task Force on the Presidential Signing Statements and the Separation of Powers Doctrine," *American Bar Association*, 2006.

47 News organizations call for an "end to signing statements": Savage, *Takeover*, 245.

47 "The Constitution is not what the president says it is": "Recommendation: Task Force on the Presidential Signing Statements," *American Bar Association* 2006.

47 "presidential signing statements have come to be . . . very dangerous": Cooper 2002, pp. 204, 230.

48 Signing statements "power tools": Dana D. Nelson, *Bad for Democracy: How the Presidency Undermines the Power of the People* (Minneapolis: University of Minnesota, 2008), p. 148.

48 "Expanding executive power at the expense of Congress and the courts": Pfiffner *Power Play*, p. 226.

49 "It's vastly preferable for a president to openly declare his intent to violate the law": Greenwald, "Obama v. Obama."

49 " . . . illegality is not augmented or assuaged by the issuance of a signing statement": Garvey, "Presidential Signing Statements," p. 16. See also Curtis A. Bradley and Eric A. Posner, "Presidential Signing Statements and Executive Power," Working Paper, July 2006.

53 " . . . the power associated with a successful presidential veto": This counterfactual is just as relevant for thinking about the mechanisms that

presidents fashion, and that Congress willingly delegates, for creating and implementing public policy. Take, for instance, the president's use of executive agreements: like treaties, these agreements formalize the outcomes of negotiations with foreign states; unlike treaties, they do not require the Senate's approval. One of the striking facts about the historical trend in executive agreements is the steep rise in their usage. What are we to make of such a fact? If executive agreements merely accomplish things that Congress otherwise could have (and would have) done on its own, then they cannot be said to contribute to the president's arsenal. On the other hand, if executive agreements establish policies that either would not exist at all, or that would look quite a bit different under a treaty, then they plainly do augment the president's power.

Chapter 3. Constitutional Foundations

Page

55   "Separate and distinct exercise of the different powers of government . . . is essential": *Federalist* No. 51.

56   George Washington's skepticism on human nature: Farewell Address, 19 September 1796.

56   " . . . let no more be heard of confidence in men": "The Kentucky Resolutions, Jefferson's Draft," in *The Papers of Thomas Jefferson*, Vol. 30, 1 January 1798 to 31 January 1799 (Princeton, NJ: Princeton University Press, 2003), pp. 536–43.

57   " . . . perfection falls not to the share of mortals": Washington, Letter to John Jay, 15 August 1786.

58   President's financial motivations: *Federalist* No. 73.

59   Presidency the "only aspect of the new government that really appealed to people": James Thomas Flexner, *Washington: The Indispensable Man* (Boston: Little, Brown, 1974), p. 214.

59   "Washington's influence carried this government": Monroe to Jefferson, 12 July 1788, in Boyd et al., *Papers of Jefferson*, Vol. 13, 35; quoted in Flexner, *Washington*, p. 211, and Gordon S. Wood, *The Radicalism of the American Revolution* (New York: Random House, 1992), p. 209.

59   Washington "above the fray": Joseph J. Ellis, *His Excellency: George Washington* (New York: Random House, 2005), p. 177.

60   "Living embodiment of classical Republican virtue": Wood, *Radicalism of the American Revolution*, p. 206; Flexner, *Washington*, p. 207. See also Carol Berkin, *A Brilliant Solution: Inventing the American Constitution* (New York: Houghton Mifflin Harcourt, 2003), p. 142.

60   Washington's lack of an heir: Wood, *Radicalism of the American Revolution*, p. 209.

60 "The convention decided on one president and allowed him an amazing amount of power": Flexner, *Washington*, p. 209.

60 " . . . one man provided a symbolic solution acceptable to all sides": Ellis, *His Excellency*, pp. 183–4.

60 Executive branch's powers "greater than I was disposed to make them": Pierce Butler to Weedon Butler, May 5, 1788, in Max Farrand, *The Records of the Federal Convention of 1787*, rev. ed. (New Haven: Yale University Press, 1937), vol. 3, p. 302; quoted in Jack N. Rakove, *Original Meanings: Politics and Ideas in the Making of the Constitution* (New York: Random House, 1997), p. 244 and elsewhere.

60 " . . . scarcely ventured to form my own opinion": Madison to Washington, Apr. 16, 1787, *Papers of Madison*, William T. Hutchinson et al., eds. (Chicago: University of Chicago Press, 1962–77), vol. 9, 385; quoted in Rakove, *Original Meanings*, p. 255.

61 Delegates ambivalent on whether "the Executive consist of a single person": *Records Records of the Federal Convention of 1787*, vol. 1, 64–66 and 66–69; quoted in Rakove, *Original Meanings*, p. 257.

61 "The executive branch should stop short of a monarchy, but only slightly": Ellis, *His Excellency*, p. 176.

61 Admiration for limited monarchy: Rakove, *Original Meanings*, p. 256.

61 " . . . desire to enable the executive to resist legislative encroachments": Rakove, *Original Meanings*, p. 259.

62 "Men are very apt to run into extremes": Washington to Henry Laurens, 14 November 1778, John C. Fitzpatrick, ed., *Writings of George Washington* (Washington, DC: 1931–39), vol. 13, 254–257; quoted in Joseph Ellis, *Founding Brothers: The Revolutionary Generation* (New York: Knopf, 2000), pp. 132–133.

62 Executive "would rise above party turmoil": Rakove, *Original Meanings*, pp. 247–48.

64 " . . . unauthorized by the Constitution": Jefferson, "First Annual Message to Congress," December 1, 1801.

65 " . . . that one nation can be at full war": *Papers of Alexander Hamilton*, Harold C. Syrett et al, eds. (New York: Columbia University Press, 1961–79), vol. 25, p. 455.

65 " . . . fighting Spaniards and hanging Englishmen": Arthur M. Schlesinger, Jr., *The Imperial Presidency* (New York: Houghton Mifflin Harcourt, 2004), p. 26.

65 Presidents read vast powers into the silences of Article II: Richard Pious, *The American Presidency* (New York: Basic Books).

66 Protecting the "liberties and welfare of the people": *Missouri Kansas & Texas Ry. Co. v. May* 194 U.S. 267, 270 (1904).

67 "there are plenty of constitutions in other countries . . . .": These figures come from the Comparative Constitutions Projects, which is housed online at: http://www.comparativeconstitutionsproject.org/.

69   "Ambiguity would help make it possible for the government to act": Gordon Silverstein, "U.S. War and Emergency Powers: The Virtues of Constitutional Ambiguity" (Berkeley: University of California Berkeley Typescript, 2011).

Chapter 4. Contrasting Conceptions of Executive Leadership

Page

72   "Until philosophers rule as kings . . . cities will have no rest from evils": G.M.A. Grube translation, revised by C.D.C. Reeve (Cambridge, MA: Hackett, 1991). All subsequent quotes from Plato's *Republic* also come from this translation.

76   Philosopher-kings inherently totalitarian: Karl Popper, *The Open Society and Its Enemies*, vol. 1, *The Spell of Plato* (Princeton, NJ: Princeton University Press, 1971).

77   And the "popular state" (i.e. democracy): These and other quotes from Cicero's *On the Commonwealth and On the Laws* that appear in this section come from James E.G. Zetzel's translation (New York: Cambridge University Press, 1999).

80   "Cicero's ideal system of government . . . .": Indeed, Cicero outlines much of the governmental structure above in *On the Commonwealth* and its sequel, *On the Laws*. However, much of those books—including many of the parts detailing the various offices and their powers—have been lost to history, or survive only as fragments in secondary sources. For fuller articulations of the Roman republican system of government, see Livy (*History of Rome*) and Polybius (*Histories*). A good modern description can be found in Gary Forsythe, *A Critical History of Early Rome* (Berkeley: University of California Press, 2007).

82   "As Cicero himself alludes to . . . ." :Cicero mentions Cincinnatus in passing in *On Old Age*, writing that he was "actually at the plough when word was brought to him that he had been named dictator." As Forsythe has argued, there are actually several varying myths about Cincinnatus and his dictatorial role, and Cicero subscribes to the "variant of the popular Roman tradition of Cincinnatus to the rescue" (Forsythe, *Critical History of Early Rome*, 240).

83   Niccolo Machiavelli, *The Prince*, ed. Harvey Mansfield, 2d ed. (Chicago: University of Chicago Press, 1998). All subsequent quotes from Machiavelli's *The Prince* also come from this translation.

86   "Our constitution . . . practically sets [Congress] to rule the affairs of the nation": Wilson, *Congressional Government: A Study in American Politics* (New Orleans, LA: Quid Pro, LLC, 2011[1885]), p. 115.

86   Executive independence frustrates Congress: Wilson, *Congressional Government*, p. 115.

87   "Presidential leadership occupied the most exalted position": Wilson, *Constitutional Government in the United States* (New Brunswick, NJ: Transaction Publishers, 2002[1908]), p. xlvi.

87   Wilson aligned with "the work of the people": Henry Jones Ford, *The Rise and Growth of American Politics: A Sketch of Constitutional Development* (New York: Macmillan, 1898), pp. 292–93.

87   "Modern humanistic thinkers . . . can expect no answer in the philosophy of balanced government": Richard Hofstadter, "The Founding Fathers: An Age of Realism," in R. H. Horowitz (ed.), *The Moral Foundations of the American Republic* (Cambridge: University Press of Oceania, 1986), p. 73.

88   "Government is not a machine, but a living thing": Wilson, *Constitutional Government*, p. 56.

88   " . . . the government would suffer the fate of the ammonites, trilobites, and mastodon.": For more on Wilson's general views of presidential power, see Scot J. Zentner, "Liberalism and Executive Power: Woodrow Wilson and the American Founders," *Polity* 26:4 (summer 1994): 579–99; Jeffrey Tulis, *The Rhetorical Presidency* (Princeton, NJ: Princeton University Press, 1988).

88   The federal government must evolve to survive: Wilson, *Constitutional Government*, p. 22.

88   Wilson encouraged presidents to view their office as "anything": Wilson, *Constitutional Government*, p. 8.

89   President a true "man of the people": Wilson as quoted in Mario DiNunzio, *Woodrow Wilson: Essential Writings and Speeches of the Scholar-President* (New York: New York University Press, 2006), p. 103.

89   Tyranny avoided only by "men of some wisdom and great honesty": Wilson, *Essential Writings and Speeches*, p. 327.

89   Support presidents with "particular qualities of mind and character": Wilson, *Constitutional Government*, p. 65.

89   President who "understands his own day and the needs of the country": Wilson, *Constitutional Government*, p. 65.

90   Failure of government a systematic failure, rather than a failure of men: Harvey Mansfield, *Taming the Prince: The Ambivalence of Modern Executive Power* (Baltimore, MD: Johns Hopkins University Press, 1989), pp. 286–87.

90   "Obsolescence of Republican virtue": Mansfield, *Taming the Prince*, p. 217.

Chapter 5. Misguided Entreaties

Page

93   "You have made this country one of the worst despotisms on earth": James M. McPherson, *Tried by War: Abraham Lincoln as Commander in Chief* (New York: Penguin Press, 2008), p. 171.

93   " . . . admit Congress to genuine, if only junior, partnership": Schlesinger, *Imperial Presidency*, p. 325.

94   " . . . force Congress to assume join responsibility": Jack Goldsmith, *The Terror Presidency: Law and Judgment Inside the Bush Administration* (New York: W. W. Norton, 2007).

94   "Personalities play a huge role in how presidential administrations actually function": Colin Campbell, *Managing the Presidency: Carter, Reagan, and the Search for Executive Harmony* (Pittsburgh: University of Pittsburgh Press, 1986), vol. 19, p. 264.

94   "Only a president can create a new mood of bipartisanship": "President George W. Bush," *New York Times* (editorial), 2 November 2004.

95   "We can only hope that . . . American voters . . . grant the awesome powers of the presidency to someone who has integrity, principle, and authority": "Looking at America," *New York Times* (editorial), 31 December 2007.

95   Unilateral exercise of power an affront to the Constitution: Bruce Ackerman and Oona Hathaway, "Obama's Illegal War," *Foreign Policy*, 1 June 2011.

95   Obama's intervention in Libya "illegal," "an affront to our constitution": Ewen MacAskill, "Libyan Bombing 'Unconstitutional,' Republicans Warn Obama," *The Guardian*, 22 March 2011; Felicia Sonmez, "Kucinich, Other House Members File Lawsuit against Obama on Libya Military Mission" *Washington Post*, 15 June 2011, http://www.washingtonpost.com/blogs/2chambers/post/kucinich-other-house-members-file-lawsuit-against-obama-on-libya-military-mission/2011/06/15/AGrzd6VH_blog.html

95   "Resolution goes too far": Jennifer Steinhauer, "House Rebukes Obama for Continuing Libyan Mission Without Its Consent," *New York Times*, 3 June 2011, A4; Pete Kasperowicz, "GOP to Members: Do not Support Troop Withdrawal from Libya," *The Hill*, 3 June 2011.

96   Freedom Pledge: American Freedom Agenda, *About Us*, 2007, http://www.americanfreedomagenda.org/About/default.html.

97   "Reminiscent of the kingly abuses that provoked the Declaration of Independence": Naomi Wolf, "Finally, Action! Ron Paul Introduces Bill to Defend Constitution!" *Huffington Post*. 18 October 2007, http://www.huffingtonpost.com/naomi-wolf/finally-action-ron-paul-i_b_69042.html.

97   American opinion on wiretapping, torture: Frank Newport, "Where Do Americans Stand on the Wiretapping Issue?" *Gallup*, 24 February 2006; Darren K. Carlson, "Public Believes U.S. Government Has Tortured Prisoners," *Gallup*, 29 November 2005.

97   America Freedom Agenda: Politico, "Richard A. Viguerie," *The Arena*, 2012, http://www.politico.com/arena/bio/richard_a_viguerie.html.

97   Conservative support for Freedom Pledge: Wolf, "Finally, Action!"

98   "Such was the case with the 2008 National War Powers Commission . . . .": Elements of this section were drawn from: William Howell, "A Restoration

of Balance? A Critical Examination of the Proposed War Powers Consultation Act," in Charles Dunn (ed.), *The Presidency in the 21ˢᵗ Century* (Lexington: University Press of Kentucky, 2011).

100   Ambiguities of the WPCA: Paul Findley and Don Fraser, "The Battle over War Powers: Limits Imposed by Congress on the President in 1973 Should Not Be Eased," *Los Angeles Times*, 22 September 2008, A17.

101   Partisan support of the president in Congress: William Howell and Jon Pevehouse, *While Dangers Gather: Congressional Checks on Presidential War Powers* (Princeton, NJ: Princeton University Press, 2007); David Clark, "Agreeing to Disagree: Domestic Institutional Congruence and U.S. Dispute Behavior," *Political Research Quarterly* 53:2 (2000); Douglas Kriner, *After the Rubicon: Domestic Constraints on the Presidential Use of Force* (Chicago: University of Chicago Press, 2011).

102   "The presidency can exercise no power which cannot be fairly and reasonably traced to some specific grant of power": a speech reproduced in William Howard Taft, *Limited Presidential Power* (New York: Columbia University, 1915–16).

102   Taft's address to Congress: Stanley D. Solvick, "William Howard Taft and the Payne-Aldrich Tariff," *Mississippi Valley Historical Review* 50:3 (1963): pp. 424–44.

103   Lincoln's suspension of habeas corpus: Ex *parte Merryman* 17 F. Cas. 144 (1861).

103   "If there is anything which is it is the duty of the whole people to never entrust to any hands but their own, that thing is the preservation and perpetuity of their own liberties": Allen D. Spiegel, *A. Lincoln, Esquire: A Shrewd, Sophisticated Lawyer in His Time* (Macon, GA: Mercer University Press, 2002).

103   Lincoln's support of the election process: Philip Gourevitch, in Harold Holzer and Joshua Wolf Shenk, *In Lincoln's Hand: His Original Manuscripts with Commentary by Distinguished Americans* (New York: Bantam, 2009), pp. 178–179.

105   On the expansion of presidential power during war, see, William Howell, Saul Jackman, and Jon Rogowski, *The Wartime President* (Chicago: University of Chicago Press, 2013); Nancy Staudt, *The Judicial Power of the Purse: How Courts Fund National Defense in Times of Crisis* (Chicago: University of Chicago Press, 2011); William Howell and Faisal Ahmed, "Voting for the President: The Supreme Court during War," *Journal of Law, Economics, and Organization*, forthcoming.

105   Crisis jurisprudence: *South Carolina v. United States*, 199 U.S. 437 (1905). For a review of this literature, see Howell, "A Restoration of Balance?"

105   "Validity of action under the war power must be judged wholly in the context of war": *Korematsu v. United States*, 323 U.S. 214 (1944).

Chapter 6. What Failure Looks Like

Page

106   " . . . bottomless gulf between what we say we want and what we do want": Joan Didion, "7000 Romaine, Los Angeles 38," in *Slouching Towards Bethlehem* (New York: Farrar, Straus and Giroux, 1968), p. 72.

107   Media coverage of Iran hostage crisis: Gaddis Smith, *Morality, Reason and Power: American Diplomacy in the Carter Years* (New York: Hill and Wang, 1987).

108   "The country associates assertiveness with leadership": Quoted in David Farber, *Taken Hostage: The Iran Hostage Crisis and America's First Encounter with Radical Islam* (Princeton, NJ: Princeton University Press, 2006).

109   Lack of precedence, understanding in Iran hostage crisis: Farber, *Taken Hostage*. Also David Harris, *The Crisis: The President, The Prophet, and the Shah—1979 and the Coming of Militant Islam* (Boston: Little, Brown, 2004). Harris notes that President Carter had to be told the difference between Shiite and Sunni Muslims.

109   "A problem so novel that appears entirely without precedent": David Patrick Houghton, *US Foreign Policy and the Iran Hostage Crisis* (Cambridge: Cambridge University Press, 2001), p. 28.

109   Walter Mondale quote: http://www.pbs.org/wgbh/americanexperience /features/general-article/carter-hostage-crisis/.

110   Carter's approval rating during the Iran hostage crisis: Houghton, *US Foreign Policy and the Iran Hostage Crisis*, p. 3.

110   Public approval of *America Held Hostage*: *Washington Post* editorial quoted in Jordan Michael Smith, "Contra Iran," *Columbia Journal Review*, 4 November 2009 ("America Held Hostage" was later renamed "Nightline" and became a highly popular news program that outlived the hostage crisis; indeed, it remains on the air today). On the flag burning, see Houghton, *US Foreign Policy and the Iran Hostage Crisis*, p. 2.

110   "It is time to speak with the power and the might of a first rate country instead of the wishy-washy language of diplomatic compromise": Daniel A. Darlinton, "Letter to the Editor," *Denver Post*, 4 November 1979.

111   Carter's approval rating: Houghton, *US Foreign Policy and the Iran Hostage Crisis*, p. 3.

111   Public opinion of Operation Eagle Claw: http://www.pbs.org/wgbh /americanexperience/features/general-article/carter-444-text/.

111   Carter believes Iran hostage crisis cost him a second term: Jimmy Carter, *White House Diary* (New York, NY: Farrar, Straus, and Giroux, 2010).

111   "In the three decades since . . . .": "Jimmy Carter's Legacy of Failure", Cinnamon Stilwell, http://www.sfgate.com/cgi-bin/article.cgi?f=/g/a/2006 /12/13/cstillwell.DTL.

112   Carter "wimpish, feckless": http://www.npr.org/2011/01/20/133086344/is-it-time-to-get-over-the-iran-hostage-crisis.

112   Carter's "weakness and indecision": Mead, http://www.foreignpolicy.com/articles/2010/01/04/the_carter_syndrome?page=0,0.

112   "President O'Carter": John Fund, "The Carter-Obama Comparisons Grow," *Wall Street Journal*, 22 September 2010.

112   "In the end, it undid him": Corporation for Public Broadcast, "General Article: The Iranian Hostage Crisis," *American Experience*, http://www.pbs.org/wgbh/americanexperience/features/general-article/carter-hostage-crisis/.

112   "One of the most disgusting moments of my presidency": "Bush calls Kanye West's rant disgusting," *MSNBC Today*, 3 November 2010, http://today.msnbc.msn.com/id/39988365/ns/today-entertainment/t/bush-calls-kanye-wests-rant-disgusting/#.

113   "Monumental failure of leadership": Matthew Cooper, "Dipping His Toe into Disaster," *Time*, 6 September 2005.

113   President's demeanor "hesitant and halting": quoted in Opinion Research Corporation, "A Year Later, Katrina Haunts Bush in Polling," *CNN*, 29 August 2006, http://articles.cnn.com/2006-08-29/politics/bush.poll_1_latest-poll-new-poll-opinion-research-corporation?_s=PM:POLITICS.

114   "The next day Bush finally returned to Washington . . . .": a full timeline of the events and actions during Katrina can be found at http://thinkprogress.org/report/katrina-timeline/.

114   "On August 30 . . . the *New York Times*": Joseph B. Treaster and Kate Zernike, "Hurricane Katrina Slams into Gulf Coast; Dozens are Dead," *New York Times*, 30 August 2005.

114   "We're not even dealing with dead bodies": Rupert Cornwell, "Engulfed: New Orleans Torn Apart by Katrina, America's 'Greatest Natural Disaster,'" *The Independent*, 31 August 2005.

114   Conditions in the Superdome: Scott Gold, "Trapped in an Arena of Suffering," *Los Angeles Times*, September 2005.

115   Bush's "cavalier attitude": Elisabeth Bumiller, "Democrats and Others Criticize White House's Response to Disaster," *New York Times*, 2 September 2005, http://www.nytimes.com/2005/09/02/politics/02bush.html

116   Bush "detached, disconnected, disengaged": http://www.huffingtonpost.com/arianna-huffington/the-flyover-presidency-of_b_6566.html.

116   "With time, the great city of New Orleans will be back on its feet": Office of the Press Secretary, "President Outlines Hurricane Katrina Relief Efforts," White House Press Release, 31 August 2005, http://georgewbush-whitehouse.archives.gov/news/releases/2005/08/20050831-3.html.

116   "Normal people at home understand it's not the president who's responsible for this": Bumiller, "Democrats and Others Criticize."

116   "The responsibility . . . rests with state officials": Adam Nagourney and Anne E Kornblut, "White House Enacts a Plan to Ease Political Damage," *New York Times*, 5 September 2005.

116   Federal response to Katrina: Amy Liu, Matt Fellowes, and Mia Mabanta, "Special Edition of the Katrina Index: A One-Year Review of Key Indicators of Recovery in Post-Storm New Orleans," *The Brookings Institute Metropolitan Policy Program*, August 2006, 1–16, http://www.brookings.edu /research/reports/2006/08/metropolitanpolicy-liu

117   "Searing and unfortunate image": Sheryl Gay Stolberg, "Year after Katrina, Bush Still Fights for 9/11 Image," *New York Times*, 28 August 2006.

117   "Right for the relief effort but wrong for president Bush's public standing": "Rove-elations: Former Bush Adviser Opens Up About Katrina, WMDs, Obama," *Fox News*, 5 March 2010, http://www.foxnews.com/politics /2010/03/05/rove-revelations-bush-adviser-opens-katrina-wmds-obama/.

117   Critics accuse Bush of staging a photo-op: http://thinkprogress.org/report /katrina-timeline/.

117   "I suppose that's the price we pay": Maureen Dowd, "United States of Shame," *New York Times*, 3 September 2005.

118   "What happened was the result of a long series of decisions": Kevin Drum, "Bush and Katrina," *Washington Monthly*, 6 September 2005.

119   "It was a perception altering event": Stolberg, "Year after Katrina."

119   Bush "detached and uncaring": Kate Anderson Brower and Catherine Dodge, "Bush Says New Orleans Flyover after Katrina a 'Huge Mistake,'" 5 November 2010, http://www.bloomberg.com/news/2010-11-05/bush -calls-new-orleans-flyover-in-wake-of-hurricane-katrina-huge-mistake -.html.

119   "Extraordinary measures" needed to fund government agencies: "As US Reaches Debt Limit, Geithner Implements Additional Extraordinary Measures to Allow Continued Funding of Government Obligations," *Treasury Department Blog*, 16 May 2011, http://www.treasury.gov/connect/blog /Pages/Geithner-Implements-Additional-Extraordinary-Measures-to -Allow-Continued-Funding-of-Government-Obligations.aspx.

120   "As it turned out, President Obama did not flex his muscle . . . .": As a number of recently published accounts document, Obama behind the scenes was wholeheartedly involved in these budget negotiations. See, for example, Bob Draper's *Do Not Ask What Good We Do* (New York: Free Press, 2012).

120   Obama's silence "depressing": Lincoln Mitchell, "The Debt Ceiling and Obama's Silence," *Huffington Post*, 1 August 2011, http://www.huffington post.com/lincoln-mitchell/the-debt-ceiling-and-obam_b_914882.html.

120   Bipartisanship over confrontation: Drew Westin, "What Happened to Obama?" *New York Times*, 7 August 2011, SR1.

120 "The ultimate failure of President Barrack Obama is that he is unable or unwilling to lead": John Mariotti, "A Failed Presidency—The American Problem," *Forbes Prosper Now blog,* 6 August 2011, http://www.forbes.com/sites /prospernow/2011/08/06/a-failed-presidency-the-american-problem/3/.

121 "clarified for the American people the likely fallout . . . .": A Gallup poll from May 2011 found 47 percent of Americans against a debt ceiling increase and a mere 19 percent in favor. In July, after the president went public with the need for an increase, those figures shifted to 42 percent against and 22 percent in favor. By August, though raising the debt ceiling remained unpopular, the numbers had shifted far closer to even (46 percent against to 39 percent in favor, though these figures now reflected opinion on the specific deal that was passed on August 1). http://www .gallup.com/poll/148454/debt-ceiling-increase-remains-unpopular -americans.aspx; http://www.gallup.com/poll/148802/americans-oppose -favor-debt-ceiling-agreement.aspx.

121 "Mr Obama needs to make clear that he will act unilaterally": Eric A. Posner and Adrian Vermeule, "Obama Should Raise the Debt Ceiling on His Own," *New York Times,* 22 July 2011, http://www.nytimes.com/2011/07/22 /opinion/22posner.html.

121 " . . . unilateral action will bring calm to the American people": Jennifer Epstein, "Obama Urged to Invoke 14th Amendment As Debt Ceiling Deadline Nears," *Politico,* 27 July 2011, http://www.politico.com/news /stories/0711/60038.html.

121 "The president should seriously look at whatever options he has": Epstein, "Obama Urged to Invoke 14th Amendment." Even Republicans did not seem entirely opposed to the idea of President Obama taking the reins in the debt crisis. Senate Majority Mitch McConnell actually recommended that Congress pass a bill granting Obama the ability to authorize spending increases should a deal on the debt ceiling not be reached by the August 2 deadline. Though it did not endorse unilateral action, implying as it did that the President needed congressional approval to act, the proposal did offer some insight into how willing both parties in Congress were for the president to take the lead. See Jackie Calmes, "Debt Talk Mired, Leader for G.O.P. Proposes Option," *New York Times,* 13 July 2011, A1.

121 Bill Clinton on the debt ceiling: Joe Conason, "Exclusive Bill Clinton Interview," *National Memo* 19 July 2011, http://www.nationalmemo.com/article/exclu-sive-former-president-bill-clinton-says-he-would-use-constitutional -option-raise-debt.

121 Obama did not "seriously look" at all his options: "To Escape Chaos, A Terrible Deal," *New York Times* (Editorial), 1 August 2011, A20.

121 Obama "ruled out options from the beginning": Paul Krugman, "The President Surrenders," *New York Times,* 1 August 2011, A21.

122   Debt ceiling redundant: Matthew Zeitlin, "The Debt Ceiling: Why Obama Should Just Ignore It," *New Republic*, June 24, 2011, http://www.tnr.com /article/politics/90659/debt-ceiling-obama-congress.

122   "Paying public debts . . . has priority over all other spending": Michael McConnell, "The Debt Ceiling is Certainly Not 'Unconstitutional,'" Advancing a Free Society (Hoover Institution) Blog, 4 July 2011, http://www.advancingafreesociety.org/2011/07/04/the-debt-ceiling -is-certainly-not-unconstitutional/.

122   " . . . not persuaded that that is a winning argument": Epstein, "Obama Urged to Invoke 14th Amendment."

123   " . . . the president's role as the ultimate guardian of the constitutional order": Posner and Vermeule, "Obama Should Raise the Debt Ceiling."

125   "The image of a gridlocked, dysfunctional Congress": Mark Landler, "Obama to Turn up Attacks on Congress in Campaign," *New York Times*, 31 December 2011.

125   Working with Congress no longer "a requirement": Josh Earnest, quoted in David Nakamura, "Obama's 2012 Political Strategy: Keep Attacking Unpopular Congress," *Washington Post*, 30 December 2011.

126   In the mid-to-upper twenties: Harold W. Stanley and Richard G. Niemi, Vital Statistics on the American Politics, 1999–2000 (Washington, DC: Congressional Quarterly Press, 2000), Table 6-2, pp. 244–45; C-SPAN 2009 Historians Leadership Survey, http://legacy.c-span.org/PresidentialSurvey /presidential-leadership-survey.aspx.

Chapter 7. Limits

Page

131   Garfield's response to his endorsement: Candice Millard, *Destiny of the Republic: A Tale of Madness, Medicine, and the Murder of a President* (New York: Doubleday, 2011), pp. 45–46.

132   Gore's acceptance speech: David Broder, "Take 2 Sleeping Pills Or Listen To Gore's Acceptance Speech," *Washington Post*, 22 August 2000.

132   George Bush on Al Gore: Frank Pellegrini, "Bush: Why Can't Gore Be More Like Clinton?" *Time*, 28 September 2000.

132   Press coverage of Gore vs. Bush: Maureen Dowd, "Liberties; Freudian Face-Off," *New York Times*, 16 June 1999.

132   "vaulting ambition": Michael Kranish and Scott Helman, *The Real Romney* (New York: Harper Collins, 2012), p. 3.

132   "eager to get the job": As quoted in Alex Leary, "Behind the Mitt Romney Paradox." *Tampa Bay Times*, 19 August 2012.

133   "inflame our political sensibilities . . . .": Jodi Cantor, "The Competitor in Chief: Obama Play to Win, in Politics and Everything Else," *New York Times*, September 2, 2012, p. A1.

134 Presidents cautious even during war: Howell and Pevehouse, *While Dangers Gather*.

136 Aftermath of 9/11, impact on Congress-president relations: William Howell, Saul Jackman, and Jon Rogowski, *The Wartime President* (Chicago: University of Chicago Press, 2013).

138 Bush accused of being a socialist: Deroy Murdock, "Comrade Bush's Car Bailout," *National Review*, 19 December 2008, online at http://www.nationalreview.com/articles/226574comrade-bushs-car-bailout-deroy-murdock.

138 "It's the president's job to make sure Congress doesn't have money to spend": GOP Primary presidential debate, Manchester NH, 26 January 2000.

138 "The surest way to bust this economy is to increase the role and the size of the federal government": General Election presidential debate, Boston MA, 3 October 2000.

138 "It seemed to me that elite central planners were determining the course of our nation": George W. Bush and Karen Hughes, *A Charge to Keep* (New York: William Morrow, 1999), pp. 172–73.

138 Bush "the most gratuitous big spender to occupy the White House since Jimmy Carter": Veronique de Rugy and Tad DeHaven, "'Conservative' Bush Spends More Than 'Liberal' Presidents Clinton, Carter," the Cato Institute, 31 July 2003, http://www.cato.org/publications/commentary/conservative-bush-spends-more-liberal-presidents-clinton-carter

138 Government spending in Clinton and Bush administrations: Veronique de Rugy, "Spending under President George W. Bush," Working Paper, March 2009; available online at http://mercatus.org/publication/spending-under-president-george-w-bush.

139 "The greater threat to economic prosperity is not too little government involvement in the market, it is too much government involvement in the market": "Bush Makes Case For Free-Market's Role in Crisis," *Associated Press*, 13 November 2008.

142 "Restricting somebody's right to challenge their imprisonment indefinitely is not going to make us safer": Barack Obama, "Floor Statement on the Habeas Corpus Amendment," 27 September 2006, http://obamaspeeches.com/091-floor-statement-on-the-habeas-corpus-amendment-obama-speech.htm.

142 Obama committed to "reestablishing our credibility as a nation committed to the rule of law": Kyle Trygstad, "Obama on SCOTUS Decision," *Real Clear Politics Blog*, 12 June 2008, http://realclearpolitics.blogs.time.com/2008/06/12/obama_on_scotus_decision/.

143 If Levin-McCain detention bill passes, "the terrorists have won": Chris McGreal, "Military Given Go-ahead to Detain US Terrorist Suspects without Trial," *The Guardian*, 14 December 2011.

143   White House demanded removal of exemption from military deten-
       tion for American citizens: http://motherjones.com/mojo/2011/12
       /why-obama-should-veto-ndaa-and-why-he-might-not.

143   "As commentator Glenn Greenwald wrote . . . .": White House clear that
       "they were going to veto the bill if it contained any limits on the Presi-
       dent's detention powers": Glenn Greenwald, "Obama to Sign Indefinite
       Detention Bill into Law," *Salon*, 15 December 2011, http://www.salon
       .com/2011/12/15/obama_to_sign_indefinite_detention_bill_into_law
       /singleton/.

Suggested Readings

If you are interested in reading more about any dimensions of our arguments, we encourage you to consult the following readings. The list, to be sure, is far from comprehensive. Below, we identify only those categories of scholarship that are most germane to the arguments developed in this book. Moreover, within these categories, many excellent studies on the presidency are omitted. The readings listed below, though, should at least whet your appetite.

CLASSIC STATEMENTS ON PRESIDENTIAL POWER

Edward Corwin. 1941. *The President: Office and Powers*. New York: New York University Press.

Richard Neustadt. 1960. *Presidential Power: The Politics of Leadership*. New York: John Wiley.

Clinton Rossiter. 1956. *The American Presidency*. New York: Harcourt, Brace.

Woodrow Wilson. 1911. *Constitutional Government in the United States*. New York: Columbia University Press.

CONSTITUTIONAL BEGINNINGS

Bruce Ackerman. 2005. *Failure of the Founding Fathers: Jefferson, Marshall, and the Rise of Presidential Democracy*. Cambridge, MA: Harvard University Press.

Jeremy Bailey. 2007. *Thomas Jefferson and Executive Power*. New York: Cambridge University Press.

Alexander Hamilton and James Madison. 2007 [1793–94]. *Pacificus-Helvidius Debates of 1793–1794*. Edited by Morton Frisch. Indianapolis, IN: Liberty Fund.

James Madison, Alexander Hamilton, and John Jay. 1987 [1788]. *The Federalist Papers*. New York: Penguin Books.

Jack Rakove. 1997. *Original Meanings: Politics and Ideas in the Making of the Constitution*. New York: Vintage Press.

Charles Thach. 1922. *The Creation of the Presidency, 1775–1789*. Baltimore, MD: Johns Hopkins Press.

Gordon Wood. 1998. *The Creation of the American Republic, 1776–1787*. Chapel Hill: University of North Carolina Press.

Historical Changes in Presidential Power

Peri Arnold. 2009. *Remaking the Presidency: Roosevelt, Taft, and Wilson: 1901–1916*. Lawrence: University Press of Kansas.

Forest McDonald. 1994. *The American Presidency: An Intellectual History*. Lawrence: University Press of Kansas. 1994.

Sidney Milkis and Michael Nelson. 2011. *The American Presidency: Origins and Development, 1776–2011*, 6th ed. Washington, DC: Congressional Quarterly Press.

James Pfiffner. 2009. *Power Play: The Bush Presidency and the Constitution*. Washington, DC: Brookings Institution Press.

Andrew Rudalevige. 2006. *The New Imperial Presidency: Renewing Presidential Power after Watergate*. Ann Arbor: University of Michigan Press.

Arthur Schlesinger. 1973. *The Imperial Presidency*. Boston: Houghton Mifflin.

Steven Skowronek. 1993. *The Politics Presidents Make: Leadership from John Adams to George Bush*. Cambridge, MA: Harvard University Press.

Jeffrey Tulis. 1987. *The Rhetorical Presidency*. Princeton, NJ: Princeton University Press.

The President's Unilateral and Legislative Powers

Matthew Beckmann. 2010. *Pushing the Agenda: Presidential Leadership in U.S. Lawmaking, 1953–2004*. New York: Cambridge University Press.

Jon Bond and Richard Fleisher. 1990. *The President in the Legislative Arena*. Chicago: University of Chicago Press.

Charles Cameron. 2001. *Veto Bargaining: The Politics of Negative Power*. New York: Cambridge University Press.

Phillip Cooper. 2002. *By Order of the President: The Use and Abuse of Executive Direct Action*. Lawrence: University Press of Kansas.

George Edwards. 1990. *At the Margins: Presidential Leadership of Congress*. New Haven, CT: Yale University Press.

William Howell. 2003. *Power without Persuasion: The Politics of Direct Presidential Action*. Princeton, NJ: Princeton University Press.

Charles Jones. 1994. *The Presidency in a Separated System*. Washington, DC: Brookings Institution Press.

David Lewis. 2003. *Presidents and the Politics of Agency Design*. Stanford, CA: Stanford University Press.

Paul Light. 2006. *The President's Agenda: Domestic Policy Choice from Kennedy to Clinton*. Baltimore, MD: Johns Hopkins University Press.

Kenneth Mayer. 2001. *With the Stroke of a Pen: Executive Orders and Presidential Power*. Princeton, NJ: Princeton University Press.

Andrew Rudalevige. 2002. *Managing the President's Program: Presidential Leadership and Legislative Policy Formation*. Princeton, NJ: Princeton University Press.

Legal and Philosophical Statements about the American Presidency

Steven Calabresi and Christopher Yoo. 2008. *The Unitary Executive: Presidential Power from Washington to Bush*. New Haven, CT: Yale University Press.

Louis Fisher. 1997. *Constitutional Conflicts between Congress and the President*. 4th ed. Lawrence: University Press of Kansas.

Jack Goldsmith. 2012. *Power and Constraint: The Accountable Presidency after 9/11*. New York: W. W. Norton.

Benjamin Kleinerman. 2009. *The Discretionary President: The Promise and Peril of Executive Power*. Lawrence: University Press of Kansas.

Harvey Mansfield. 1989. *Taming the Prince: The Ambivalence of Modern Executive Power*. New York: Free Press.

Eric Posner and Adrian Vermeule. 2011. *The Executive Unbound: After the Madison Republic*. New York: Oxford University Press.

Christopher Pyle and Richard Pious. 2010. *The Constitution under Siege: Presidential Power versus the Rule of Law*. Durham, NC: Carolina Academic Press.

Mark Rozell. 2002. *Executive Privilege: Presidential Power, Secrecy, and Accountability*. 2d ed. Lawrence: University Press of Kansas.

Peter Shane. 2009. *Madison's Nightmare: How Executive Power Threatens American Democracy*. Chicago: University of Chicago Press.

Gordon Silverstein. 1997. *Imbalance of Powers*. New York: Oxford University Press.

Public Expectations and Evaluations of U.S. Presidents

Richard Brody. 1991. *Assessing the President: The Media, Elite Opinion, and Public Support*. Stanford, CA: Stanford University Press.

Jeffrey Cohen. 2008. *The Presidency in the Era of 24-Hour News*. Princeton, NJ: Princeton University Press.

Thomas Cronin and Michael Genovese. 2004. *The Paradoxes of the American Presidency*. 2d ed. New York: Oxford University Press.

Marc Landy and Sidney Milkis. 2001. *Presidential Greatness*. Lawrence: University Press of Kansas.

Theodore Lowi. 1985. *The Personal President: Power Invested, Promise Unfulfilled*. Ithaca, NY: Cornell University Press.

B. Dan Wood. 2009. *The Myth of Presidential Representation*. New York: Cambridge University Press.

Presidents in Times of Crisis

Edward Corwin. 1947. *Total War and the Constitution*. New York: Alfred A. Knopf.

Louis Fisher. 1995. *Presidential War Power*. Lawrence: University Press of Kansas.

William Howell, Saul Jackman, and Jon Rogowski. 2013. *The Wartime President*. Chicago: University of Chicago Press.

William Howell and Jon Pevehouse. 2007. *While Dangers Gather: Congressional Checks on Presidential War Powers*. Princeton, NJ: Princeton University Press.

Harold Koh. 1990. *The National Security Constitution: Sharing Power after the Iran-Contra Affair*. New Haven, CT: Yale University Press.

Doug Kriner. 2010. *After the Rubicon: Congress, Presidents, and the Politics of Waging War*. Chicago: University of Chicago Press.

Clinton Rossiter. 1948. *Constitutional Dictatorship*. Princeton, NJ: Princeton University Press.

John Yoo. 2009. *Crisis and Command*. New York: Kaplan.

Mariah Zeisberg. 2013. *War Powers: The Politics of Constitutional Authority*. Princeton, NJ: Princeton University Press.

Index